LEOPOLD EIDLITZ

Brooklyn Academy of Music, interior perspective showing the theater decorated for a Sanitary Commission ball in 1864. Eidlitz's intense polychromy always used primary colors, never mixing them to obtain secondary hues. A. Brown & Co., lithographer. Museum of the City of New York, 29.100.2588.

Previous page: Eidlitz & Blesch, St. George's Episcopal Church, Stuyvesant Square, New York, 1846–49. Photograph by Jack Boucher, 1980. The first building that Eidlitz designed and one of the last to remain. HABS NY,31-NEYO,94-3.

Crystal Palace, New York, perspective drawing for Eidlitz's unbuilt competition entry, 1852. Avery Architectural and Fine Arts Library, Columbia University in the City of New York.

Iranistan, the P. T. Barnum House, Bridgeport, Connecticut, 1848. Sarony and Major, lithographers, published between 1852 and 1854. Prints and Photographs, Library of Congress. LC-USZC4-2470.

Broadway Tabernacle, perspective drawing, about 1858. The church, as built, was greatly simplified from this rendering. The flying buttresses and lower aisle roof were deleted, the tower was integrated into the body of the church, the openwork spire and rounded apse were both omitted, and the windows were redesigned to emphasize lighting from above the gallery level. Avery Architectural and Fine Arts Library, Columbia University in the City of New York.

Cloister, Broadway Tabernacle, about 1858. As built, the more decorative details, as shown in this drawing, were omitted. Avery Architectural and Fine Arts Library, Columbia University in the City of New York.

Reconstructed perspective view of the Assembly Chamber as it appeared in 1879. Watercolor by Peter Ferber for Mesick, Cohen, Waite Architects, Albany, New York. Andrea Lazarski, Project Researcher. John G. Waite Associates Architects Archive.

Reconstruction of the Assembly Chamber, New York State Capitol, Albany as it appeared in 1879. John G. Waite Associates Architects Archive.

Assembly Chamber as it appears today, New York State Capitol, Albany. © Andre Jenny/Alamy.

LEOPOLD EIDLITZ

Architecture and Idealism in the Gilded Age

KATHRYN E. HOLLIDAY

W. W. NORTON & COMPANY

New York · London

In memory of my grandfather and grandmother
Joseph Stevens Holliday and MaeBelle Plumley Holliday

FRONTISPIECE: Tweed Courthouse, rotunda as completed by Eidlitz and after restoration by John G. Waite Associates. Photograph by Robert Polidori.

For information about permission to reproduce selections from this book, write to Permissions, W. W. Norton & Company, Inc., 500 Fifth Avenue, New York, NY 10110

Manufacturing by Friesens
Book design by Kristina Kachele
Production Manager: Leeann Graham

Library of Congress Cataloging-in-Publication Data

Holliday, Kathryn E.
Leopold Eidlitz : architecture and idealism in the Gilded Age /
Kathryn E. Holliday. — 1st ed.
p. cm.
Includes bibliographical references and index.
ISBN 978-0-393-73239-9 (hardcover)
1. Eidlitz, Leopold, 1823—1908. 2. Architects—United
States—Biography. 3. Eidlitz, Leopold, 1823—1908—Catalogs. I. Title.

NA737.E3295H65 2008
720.92—dc22
          2007024224

ISBN 13: 978-0-393-73239-9

W. W. Norton & Company, Inc., 500 Fifth Avenue, New York, N.Y. 10110
www.wwnorton.com

W. W. Norton & Company Ltd., Castle House, 75/76 Wells Street,
London W1T 3QT

0 9 8 97 6 5 4 3 2 1

$$1$$

BECOMING AMERICAN

From the Moldau to the Hudson

IN 1887, AT THE AGE OF SIXTY-FOUR, AS HE WAS COMING TO THE END of his forty years of architectural practice, Leopold Eidlitz wrote a small book addressed to the workingmen of the United States. He called it *Big Wages and How to Earn Them*, and he filled it with practical, if somewhat paternalistic, advice about how to navigate the marketplace as a laborer, a building contractor, or even an architect. Though the epistle is outwardly an antiunion rejoinder, reading between the lines shows the deep-seated sincerity that informs its sentiments. The book's narrator (Eidlitz wrote the book under the pseudonym "A Foreman") introduces himself humbly:

> I am a laborer, and propose to say a word to my fellow-laborers on labor associations, on wages, and other kindred matters. When I say I am a laborer I do not mean that I carry a hod (although I must confess that from a child I have admired and envied the hod-carrier for his sturdiness and endurance), but simply that I am in the building business, in which I believe I have worked harder than any hod-carrier for the last forty years. I have worked harder, because the load I have carried has been exceptionally heavy. . . . I will write down my views as best I can, and if the worst comes to the worst, and I cannot convince any one, perhaps some one will answer what I have to say and convince me.[1]

Opposite: See page 35.

1.1 Old Town Square, Prague. This print was in Eidlitz's personal collection. Avery Architectural and Fine Arts Library, Columbia University in the City of New York.

This is an extraordinary passage, one in which a professional architect, and an extremely successful one at that, speaks of himself proudly as a laborer, not as an artist or even an engineer. Eidlitz's focus on work as the source of success rather than inspiration or genius is a recurring theme throughout the work. If coupled with a practical education and not with collectivized labor unions, hard work provided the potential for unlimited individual success. Knowledge and diligence combined gave any man the ability to provide well for himself and his family.

In this attitude, Eidlitz was consummately American, falling in place with the early democratic philosophy of the United States as espoused by Thomas Jefferson in his *Notes on the State of Virginia*.[2] The individualism of Thoreau's *Walden* or Emerson's "Self-Reliance" are antecedents as well, morphed forty years later into advice for individualists who live not in the New England countryside but in dense, urban cities. Louis Sullivan's later musings in such works as *Democracy: A Man-Search* continue the American tradition of celebrating the power of the individual to create his own destiny.[3] But Eidlitz's admiration of and insistence on the power of the individual has roots far more complex than suggested by this abbreviated American pedigree. Unlike Jefferson, Emerson, or Sullivan, Eidlitz was an immigrant. The fears and aspirations that caused him to leave his native Bohemia first for Austria and then for the United States motivated him throughout his entire life.[4]

PRAGUE IN THE 1820S AND 1830S

Eidlitz was born in Prague in the province of Bohemia in 1823 and spent the first sixteen years of his life there (fig. 1.1). Though he never wrote specifically about his early years, and in fact represented himself as an Austrian (not a Bohemian or Czech) in official paperwork, his youth in Prague was in fact crucial to the formation of his outlook.[5] It is tempting to search for the sources of these "reminiscences of the Moldau," as Prague's Vhava River was often called, in the unique forms of the city's Gothic architecture in Eidlitz's designs.[6] Indeed, in some of his designs, the high-peaked pinnacles of Prague's medieval architecture seem directly echoed (see figs. 3.11, 3.12, 4.4). But more important was the city's social and economic climate. During the early nineteenth century, Prague was not a great center of architectural activity, but it shared in the prosperity and security that the Biedermeier era brought to the lands of the Habsburg Empire. After defeating Napoleon at the Battle of Leipzig in 1813, ending twenty years of war, the Habsburg Empire was finally able to join fully in the advances that had begun to sweep through Europe with the rise of the Industrial Revolution. The 1820s and 1830s saw the rapid ascendancy of the bourgeoisie in Bohemia and in Austria, as new factories, banks, and civil engineering projects created both more income and more goods to

1.2 Old New Synagogue, Prague, ca. 1270. One of the central landmarks in the Jewish quarter of Prague in Eidlitz's youth. Harry Ransom Humanities Research Center, University of Texas at Austin.

purchase. Prague changed physically as well, with new bridges across the Vltava, new flood control projects, and new roads and railroads built to facilitate trade. Prague began its transformation from a medieval town into a modern city.[7]

For Eidlitz, this meant that his early years were spent, at least partially, in an environment of increasing potential for personal success. Technology and modernization were changing Prague for the better; one had only to look around the city to see its effects. But Eidlitz's ability to participate in this economic and social rejuvenation was inherently limited: he was Jewish.[8] Eidlitz's parents were Abraham and Judith Eidlitz; he had one brother, three years his junior, named Markus (who later changed his name to Marc in the U.S.). His father, at the time of his birth, was registered in the official roll books for Jewish families as a *Künstler*, or craftsman of unspecified

type. By the time Leopold left home for Vienna at the age of sixteen, his father was listed as a *Handelsmann*, or a small shopkeeper. The family was most likely not well off—the owner of a prosperous shop that did substantial business would have been registered as a *Kaufmann*, not a mere *Handelsmann*.[9] The family's address in the heart of the Prague Jewish ghetto also indicates a lack of resources, though they certainly were not destitute. The Eidlitz family was likely lower-middle-class and relatively secure, but far from pampered.

The social and economic conditions for Jews in Prague were at a crossroads during the years Eidlitz grew up there. Reforms instituted by the Habsburg rulers in the late eighteenth century had made restrictions on Jews less onerous: Joseph II's Edict of Tolerance, issued in 1781, assured religious freedom and allowed Jews to participate in a wider variety of commerce and trades.[10] Life in the Prague ghetto was still far from equitable, however, as limitations on property ownership and professional recognition remained intact (fig. 1.2). Jews continued to live in the officially delineated "Jewish Quarter," and Eidlitz, for example, had he remained in Prague, could have engaged in the building trades but could not have been recognized as a professional architect. The intent of the reforms was not to break down social differences, but instead to increase the empire's overall economic strength by getting as much productivity from each citizen as possible.

Ultimately, the reforms of Joseph II and Leopold II encouraged the assimilation of Jews into the Catholic mainstream. Young Jewish children, though allowed to attend services of their own faith, were often compelled to attend Catholic services in the small chapel located within the Jewish Quarter. Eidlitz's brother Marc was, in fact, destined to convert to Catholicism after his emigration to New York. There was frequent, if limited, contact between the Jewish community and the larger Prague population, primarily concerning financial and other business propositions. While by the 1820s Prague Jews seemed to live in harmony with their fellow Bohemians; the fact is, this harmony held only so long as Jews remained within the confines of their own economic and social hierarchies.

Though anti-Semitism was perhaps less pronounced in Prague than in nearby Germanic states like Saxony and Bavaria, the 1830s saw a gradual increase in tension that accompanied the outward liberalization and prosperity of the Jewish community. The last major updates to laws governing Jews had been enacted during Leopold II's reign, which ended in 1792.[11] Social and political conflicts in Bohemia between a nascent Czech nationalism and the German imperialism of the Habsburg Empire began increasingly to scapegoat Jews as a source of economic stress. While Jews had spent the last decades adopting the German language and customs in order to participate more fully in the life of the Empire, many Czech-speaking Bohemians began at the same time to reject German culture. The perceived financial success of the Germanic Jewish community increasingly drew criticism from Czech nationalists, and the tension erupted in anti-Semitic riots in Prague's Jewish quarter in 1844.[12] Eidlitz was safely in America by this time, but his parents and brother remained in Prague through these difficult years. After his father's death in 1847, Mark and their widowed mother also left for New York, just before the major exodus following the 1848 Revolution.[13]

Two elements of Eidlitz's youth in Prague are particularly important to his later development as an architect and a writer: his exposure to the burgeoning Jewish Reform movement and his education at the Prague Realschule. Beginning in the late eighteenth century in the wake of the Enlightenment and with the advent of the Emancipation reforms, Jews of the Reform movement began to reevaluate the practice of their faith. From the Enlightenment came a desire to view the world in scientific and rational terms; from Emancipation came a desire to assimilate, to fit into the cultural mainstream instead of maintaining a self-imposed exile. In Prague, as in most of Europe, this led to new ways of thinking about religion: the meaning of the Torah, the practice of certain rituals, even the use of the Hebrew language itself came into question. Typical of the new ways of thinking in the late eighteenth century were the writings of the Rabbi Zerah Eidlitz (possibly a great-grandfather of Leopold). Rabbi Eidlitz was both an expert on the Torah and an accomplished mathematician, and his scholarly work in mathematics showed an intense desire to reconcile the spiritual and the worldly.[14]

By the mid-1830s, Eidlitz could have attended synagogue at the first Prague Reform temple which was established in 1833.[15] Though we do not know which synagogue Eidlitz attended, the fundamental questioning of the tenets and practices of religious faith that the early Reform movement undertook undoubtedly informed Eidlitz's later outlook. The Reform movement had successfully broken away from age-old traditions, substituting German for Hebrew in services, eliminating gender-segregated seating, and in some cases introducing organ music as well. But more important than these external changes was a fundamental shift in thinking. At its roots, Reform Judaism acknowledged that the great changes in the world, from advances in science to shifts in social and political mores, had to be acknowledged in the practice of religion. This intellectual desire to reconcile the knowable, rational world and the spiritual world informs all of Eidlitz's writing and design: even the title of his great book *The Nature and Function of Art* echoes this dualistic view of the world as both subjective and rational.

Hand in hand with the Reform movement came the rise of secular education. In the Habsburg Empire, the emergence of *Realschulen* in the first decades of the nineteenth century was an essential component of modernization. These schools had a technical curriculum different than the traditional *Gymnasien* and responded to the new industrial spirit of the age by training future engineers, architects, and businessmen.[16] Participation in this secular educational system instead of the traditional synagogue-sponsored one became increasingly common for Prague Jews in the early nineteenth century. Embrace of the German language and educational system was the key to economic and professional advancement, and the Eidlitz family clearly had hopes and ambitions for a better life for their eldest son.

Leopold attended the new Prague Realschule, which began instruction in 1833, and graduated in 1838.[17] The two-year program had first been designed in 1820 by the eminent Franz Joseph von Gerstner, though its implementation was delayed. Remarkably, financial assistance was available to students who needed it, which may have made Eidlitz's attendance possible. Gerstner, a professor of mathematics at Prague University, had previously established the Technisches Institut zu Prag in 1806 by crafting a specialized and practical program with an emphasis on building sciences and polytechnics that existed independent of the older university. His Technisches Institut became the envy of the Austro-Hungarian Empire and served as a model for the eventual creation in 1815 of Vienna's Technische Hochschule. With the overarching goal of "rais[ing] the commerce of the Fatherland through scientific instruction," Gerstner's curriculum focused on creating both civil servants and engineers and managers for private industry. The program of Gerstner's Realschule also focused on mathematics, chemistry, and physics, producing engineers, scientists, and architects who could, if they chose, continue their studies at the Technisches Institut. Lectures ranged from topics in the natural sciences and geology to mathematics to drawing and foreign languages. At the Prague Realschule, Eidlitz would have learned about the latest advances in building materials and how to make technical drawings for machinery and for building. His exposure to architecture would have been as a building science—one that emphasized structure over style, technical considerations over aesthetic ones. His graduation certainly paved the way for his admission to the Technische Hochschule in Vienna.[18]

VIENNA

Eidlitz's move to Vienna from Prague at the age of sixteen is crucial to the further development of his intellect and career. Though he was hardly alone in his migration to Vienna—indeed, it was something of a trend for Jewish intellectuals to leave Prague for the Austrian capital—it was nonetheless a bold strike toward a new future.[19] Eidlitz could have stayed in Prague and continued his training at the technical university there; he could have begun work in his father's shop; he could have found work in Prague industry with his Realschule diploma in hand. But the lure of Vienna for a young man with aspirations would have been strong.

1.3 Vienna at the scale it would have appeared in Eidlitz's day, along Spittelberggasse.

Vienna's attitude toward Jews, for one thing, was in some ways more liberal than Prague's. Though subject to the same repressive bureaucratic regulation—he was required to obtain permission from the Prague authorities before leaving for Vienna; he then had to register with the authorities in Vienna as well—there were many Jews who had created immensely successful businesses.[20] The tension between Czech and German cultural influences was absent as well; in Vienna in the early nineteenth century, the dominant culture was German (only later in the century, after the 1848 Revolution, would the idea of an Austrian identity gather more steam).[21] And perhaps most significantly, Vienna was an important political and cultural capital city of Europe in ways that Prague had not been for hundreds of years. As the center of the Habsburg Empire, Vienna was more cosmopolitan and more connected to currents in western Europe. For Eidlitz, living and being educated in Vienna was a chance to become part of the mainstream of cultural and intellectual activity of the day.

The ascendancy of a moneyed middle class during the Biedermeier period in Vienna also helped create the idealistic and hopeful young architect who emigrated

1.4 Techsniche Hochschule, Karlsplatz, Vienna. J. S. v. Leytenbach, 1816. Neuwirth, *Die K. K. Technische Hochschule in Wien 1815–1915* (1915).

to the United States in search of opportunity. In post-Napoleonic Vienna, this new *Bürgertum* settled into a comfortable complacency, consuming the finest in textiles, clothing, and furniture and the music of Schubert and Beethoven (fig. 1.3). At the same time, there was an explosion of poverty in Vienna that contradicted the outward image of prosperity. The lower classes, increasingly attracted to the city by the promise of employment in its workshops, labored long hours for low pay and lived in wretched conditions. But the middle classes responded by romanticizing the tragedies of lower-class life: genre paintings became popular, depicting the virtuous working classes laboring happily at producing the goods and services consumed by the bourgeoisie. Eidlitz, who would have fit into this scheme somewhere in the middle, above the lowest classes because of his education but below the bourgeoisie because of his lack of wealth, held the burghers' romanticized vision of the world: with hard work and education one could escape the strictures of poverty.[22]

And so Eidlitz left Prague for Vienna in 1838 to continue his studies. In later years in America, Eidlitz told his friends and colleagues that he studied at the Technische Hochschule in order to become a land steward (much like an estate manager who would have been responsible for the upkeep and management of a large farm's buildings). He was careful not to suggest that his training was primarily architectural. But Eidlitz did not in fact enroll in the architecture or engineering programs of the Technische Hochschule; instead, he enrolled in its Kommerzielle Abteilung, or business school

(fig. 1.4). The business school was created to produce store and bank managers; its courses included topics like bookkeeping and "*Styl*," or, how to write business letters. While at the outset the business school was considered to be an important means of creating the new workforce for the industrial era, business education was never taken as seriously as the engineering and architectural programs by the administration, and in 1865 it was eventually eliminated as part of the institution's mission.[23]

Eidlitz represented his studies as being practically oriented, which they undoubtedly were. But "practical" in this case meant studying commerce and the exchange of money, not bricks and mortar, as his American colleagues came to believe. Furthermore, Eidlitz attended few classes and spent only half of the full year's term at the business school. He took no exams, receiving an evaluation in only one subject, the aforementioned *Styl*, in which he performed well. It was one of the hallmarks of the Viennese school that students could attend as few or as many classes as they wished, so Eidlitz's light schedule was not aberrant. Nonetheless, it is clear that he was not a devoted student of the business school. While this course of study was not inconsistent with a land steward's career path, Eidlitz's obfuscation created in his listeners the impression that he studied building maintenance, construction, and civil engineering in Vienna. Eidlitz did certainly have engineering and technical skills when he emigrated to the United States, but they did not come from the highly esteemed technical university in Vienna; instead, he acquired these skills at the little-known Prague Realschule.[24]

Though he was in the business school for only one term, Eidlitz surely attended the engineering and architecture lectures in the Technische Hochschule without being officially enrolled, thus absorbing its ethos if not its formal lessons. In the late 1830s, the major influence at the school was its founder Johann Joseph Prechtl. Although established with similar goals as the Prague technical institute, namely the promotion of a highly skilled workforce for the modern Austrian state, the Vienna version differed in its more open and more aesthetically oriented program. In Vienna, technical instruction remained thorough, with major areas of study focused on chemistry, mathematics, and mechanics. But the structure of the program was flexible, with little focus on granting diplomas, allowing the students to study as much or as little as they liked. And, perhaps most important for Eidlitz, the school offered lectures in art and architectural history and in architectural ornamentation. This was unusual for a technical institute; in fact, it created tension with the well-established Akademie der Bildenden Künste (Academy of Fine Arts), which regarded itself as the only proper venue for such lectures.[25]

As with the Viennese Adolf Loos's travels in America in the early 1890s, though, it is impossible to track Eidlitz in Vienna in the early 1840s. Beyond his attendance at lectures in 1838, it remains difficult to determine what Eidlitz did for the next three years in Vienna. Because his family was not well off, it is likely that they could not afford the fees for subsequent terms at the business school. His training at the Prague Realschule would have provided adequate training for him to work for a builder or architect, but his later silence on the subject implies, perhaps, that he was simply scraping by in a job he was not proud of. His early expertise in ironwork suggests work in a foundry; his later involvement in rapid transit in New York City hints at a possible role with the railway system, which was expanding quickly during the period; his later interest in photography and in banking suggest other possible professions in the business and financial worlds. But because Vienna's apprenticeship and police records for the late 1830s were destroyed in World War II, this period remains a missing piece of the puzzle.

Even without knowing the specifics of his movements, though, it is clear that the architectural culture and history of Vienna played a key role in forming Eidlitz's aesthetic vision. In the 1850s, he continued to subscribe to the *Allgemeine Bauzeitung*, Vienna's and Germany's primary architecture journal, and voiced a strong identification with the aesthetically nuanced technical pragmatism of the Technische Hochschule.[26] Eidlitz's years in Vienna (1838–43) predate the built examples of the Gothic Revival there, as typified by the construction of Heinrich Ferstel's Votivkirche beginning in 1854 and Friedrich von Schmidt's nearby Rathaus (1872–83). In the early 1840s, the neoclassical ideals of the Biedermeier era still held sway. But the intellectual currents that had led architects in other German cities to question the hegemony of the classical idiom were nonetheless in the air.

Eidlitz's move to Vienna also suggests another very important truth about his cultural identity: he identified with German culture and not Czech or Bohemian. Raised a Germanic Jew in Czech and Catholic Prague and educated in institutions created by the secularizing forces of the Habsburg Empire, Eidlitz by the time of his arrival in the United States would have been adept at juggling and reconciling opposing cultural forces: Czech and German, imperial and nationalistic, religious and secular, spiritual and rational, technical and artistic, commercial and intellectual. When Montgomery Schuyler wrote in Eidlitz's obituary that "reminiscences of the Moldau" filled his work, he meant it literally. But these echoes are less literal and more thematic than Schuyler averred. Eidlitz's early life informed his entire worldview, leading him to become a broad-minded and democratic architect who fiercely protected the principles that he believed were essential to any modern society: honesty, opportunity, and education.

AMERICA: BECOMING AN ARCHITECT

In 1843, at the age of twenty, Eidlitz departed Vienna for America, leaving his brother and parents behind in Prague. Again, the exact circumstances of his departure are unknown. He may have left in the company of a friend or distant relative with some expectation of finding connections when he arrived. In Vienna, interest

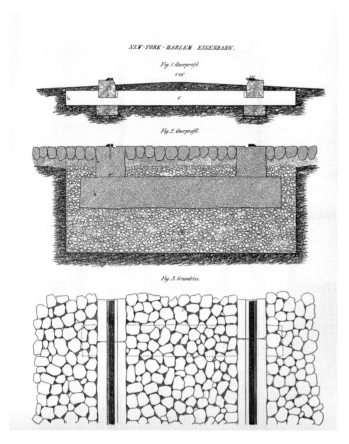

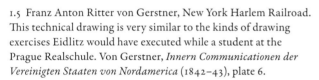

1.5 Franz Anton Ritter von Gerstner, New York Harlem Railroad. This technical drawing is very similar to the kinds of drawing exercises Eidlitz would have executed while a student at the Prague Realschule. Von Gerstner, *Innern Communicationen der Vereinigten Staaten von Nordamerica* (1842–43), plate 6.

1.6 "Insurrection in Vienna – The conflict at the cathedral," showing St. Stephen's during the 1848 revolutions. *Illustrated London News* (October 21, 1848).

in the United States was sparked by the publication in 1842 of a major survey of America and its railways by Franz Anton von Gerstner, son of the founder of the Prague Realschule. Von Gerstner's *Die innern Communicationen* chronicled his study of the railway industry as well as his observations about American life and commerce: "Can one deny the Americans the appellation of *the money making people*? Without doubt, they have earned this designation more than any other people."[27] Eidlitz may have embarked for New York after reading von Gerstner's book, inspired by its descriptions of technological prowess and economic opportunity (fig. 1.5).

Whatever the specifics of Eidlitz's embarkation, he arrived five years before the influx of German immigrants would begin in earnest after the failed revolutions of

1848 (fig. 1.6). In some ways, his early arrival provided a head start on establishing a career in America—there was less competition from fellow Germans for positions in the architecture and building trades. But the tide of English-trained architects in New York was definitely cresting at that time. English architects frustrated with the prospects for building a substantial career in New York City had already begun to fan out across the United States in search of greener pastures. The Irishman James Gallier, after practicing in New York for several years, left in 1834 for New Orleans; he would later savage the New York architecture scene of the 1830s for its lack of professionalism.[28] Others, like James Dakin, left when it became clear that the playing field in New York was too crowded; Dakin moved first to Mobile, then to New Orleans.[29]

But Eidlitz arrived in New York and stayed, and

1.7 Cyrus Lazelle Warner, Beth Elohim Synagogue, Charleston, South Carolina, 1839–43. HABS, SC,10-CHAR,41-2.

1.8 Portrait of Leopold Eidlitz and Harriet Amanda Warner, ca. 1868. The couple is seated informally on a porch of the family home. Eidlitz wears hiking boots and a bow leans against the side of the house. National Gallery of Canada, Ottawa. Gift of Dorothy Meigs Eidlitz, St. Andrews, New Brunswick, 1970.

within three years had begun to practice architecture under his own name. As with Eidlitz's youth, his early years in New York City are difficult to pin down. Many German-speaking architects, upon their arrival in the United States, chose either to find their clients within their own immigrant communities or to become partners with native English-speaking architects and remain behind-the-scenes as designers and technical advisers.[30] Eidlitz, at least during his first few years in America, followed this pattern, working for two architects: Cyrus Lazelle Warner and Richard Upjohn. Warner himself is a little-known figure, his best-known work being the Beth Elohim Temple in Charleston, South Carolina (1840–41), designed with the local firm Tappant Noble.[31] Upjohn, on the other hand, was the preeminent architect in America, and Eidlitz's acceptance into his office marked a major milestone in his career. Both men helped define Eidlitz's future as an American architect, albeit in very different ways.

Warner provided a personal rather than a professional means of establishing an American identity. It is unlikely that Eidlitz worked much for him. Warner's office was located at 122 Broadway (1842–47), just a few doors away from the offices of Richard Upjohn, where Eidlitz was likely most often employed.[32] The Charleston synagogue design is typical of Warner's work, exhibiting a fastidious attention to classical detail (fig. 1.7). The immaculate Greek Revival hexastyle Doric temple form was a conservative stylistic choice for Charleston and for the congregation. Eidlitz, even at this early stage of his career, was clearly uninterested in pursuing such a classical stylistic idiom. What is more important about Warner's commission for a synagogue, especially in terms of Eidlitz, was that it showed a liberality of character that most architects did not share in the nineteenth century. While not overtly anti-Semitic, most architects were nonetheless loyal to their own personal religious denominations when it came to accepting commissions. Richard Upjohn, a devout Anglican, for example, worked almost exclusively on Episcopalian churches. He steadfastly refused, in some cases, to design churches for congregations whose beliefs conflicted with his own.[33]

Even greater evidence of Warner's progressiveness comes from the fact that Eidlitz married his daughter, Harriet Amanda, in 1845. The couple went on to have seven children: Adolph (who died shortly after his birth

Marc Eidlitz

1.9 Portrait of Marc Eidlitz. *Marc Eidlitz and Son, 1904–1914*
(1914).

obituary for daughter Harriet who married Schuyler
Quackenbush in 1874 proclaimed her American heritage, noting she was "a descendent of John Adams." But
nowhere is there mention of her ability to trace her roots
on her father's side of the family to the humble Jewish
ghetto of Prague.[34]

Eidlitz's move to America was clearly an escape from
the restrictions and limitations imposed on him by his
Jewishness. While he never rejected involvement with
the Jewish community (he designed synagogues and
formed a partnership with the successful Jewish architect Henry Fernbach), he did not join a synagogue or
even publicly acknowledge his heritage. Instead, Eidlitz
represented himself as being simply German or Austrian,
and on official records in this country he Germanicized
his parents' names: Abraham and Judith Eidlitz became
the more acceptable Adolf and Julia Eidlitz.[35] Eidlitz's
daugher Mari Imogene was a Catholic and was married
with much pomp and circumstance at St. Ann's Church
in New York in 1887.[36] While intensely interested in
religious issues in the abstract, Eidlitz seems, after his
first few years in New York, to have shied away from
the practice of any particular personal faith. Later in his
career, it was unclear to his peers just what his religious
affiliation was. Montgomery Schuyler, a close friend, did
not believe he was Jewish, and scholars have previously
left his religious background an open question. What is
clear is that Eidlitz's marriage to Harriet Warner, ratified
by the Episcopal minister Stephen H. Tyng, provided an
opportunity to adopt a new social status, one that had
no questionable ramifications.

Even the arrival of his brother Marc Eidlitz and
their mother in New York in 1846 seems not to have
affected his allegiance to the Warner family (fig. 1.9).
While Leopold and Marc did work together—Marc
established one of the most successful building firms
in New York—the two branches of the family seem
to have remained cordial but distant. While Leopold
embraced the role of country gentleman, Marc lived on
the Upper East Side, on East 72nd Street, had stronger
ties to the German immigrant community, converted to
Catholicism, and eventually left the building business to
become president of the Germania Bank in 1888.[37] But

in 1847), Harriet (b. 1851), Elizabeth (b. 1851), Cyrus
(b. 1853), Julia (b. 1855), Leopold, Jr. (b. 1857), and Mari
Imogene (b. 1860). Warner was born in Wilbraham,
Massachusetts, and his wife, née Elizabeth Wadland
Adams, possessed American bloodlines: she could trace
her ancestry back to founding father John Adams (fig.
1.8). This kind of social validation was extremely important to the Eidlitz family through the years. The 1940

Leopold rejected his brother's path: instead of becoming a German Catholic with ties to the growing immigrant community in New York, he allied himself with the increasingly secular American gentry. The Warner and Eidlitz family's bucolic final resting place in Brooklyn's fashionable Green-Wood Cemetery is a fitting reminder of this transformation, intertwining the Adams bloodline with Eidlitz's permanently.

If through Warner Eidlitz found the means to declare his personal American identity, through Richard Upjohn he furthered the notion of his Germanness. Upjohn's detailed office records begin after Eidlitz's tenure, so the specifics of the working relationship remain unverified. But by all accounts, Eidlitz worked as a draftsman in Upjohn's office from 1843 to 1845, probably concurrently with his work in Warner's office. Though little evidence survives to tell us exactly how the two came to work together, it is telling that Upjohn in the 1840s developed an interest in German architecture. In 1844, for example, he began work on two commissions that show him, for the first time, designing in a German Romanesque style: the Church of the Pilgrims in Brooklyn and the Bowdoin College Chapel in Maine. Though scholars still debate the reasons and timing of Upjohn's sudden interest in German architecture, it is clear that Eidlitz's presence in his office was a major factor in directing it.[38] In the mid-1840s, before the exodus of Germans following the 1848 revolutions, there were not many German architects in the United States, and even fewer who had Eidlitz's passionate temperament and proficiency in English. Fresh from Vienna, where discussion about a truly modern architectural style filled the air, Eidlitz brought a new intellectual climate to Upjohn's office. Although the reform-minded principles of A. W. N. Pugin, the Ecclesiologists, and the English Gothic Revival were well in place there, Eidlitz's pragmatic training and exposure to the debates that ensued after the publication of Heinrich Hübsch's 1828 treatise *In welchem Style sollen wir bauen?* (In What Style Should We Build?) in the Viennese journal *Allgemeine Bauzeitung* showed that there were many other means of exploring the challenges of modern design.

Hübsch defined what he believed to be a new style appropriate to the challenges of the modern age: the Rundbogenstil, or round-arched style. The Rundbogenstil was based on Byzantine and Romanesque forms but had practicality as its watchword. Hübsch sought to create a plain, durable style suitable to the demands of secular buildings. Economical brick was the preferred material, used to create flat, regular façades with minimal ornament.[39] During Eidlitz's brief tenure in his office, Upjohn's work changed, reflecting his attraction to the Rundbogenstil. He did not completely abandon the archeological Gothic Revival that typifies his most famous design, Trinity Church in New York (see fig. 1.15). But his work took a new direction as typified in the Church of the Pilgrims, a commission Eidlitz was intimately involved with.

Eidlitz probably provided some of the working drawings for the initial design of the Church of the Pilgrims in the 1840s. A surviving perspective drawing shows the hallmarks of an Eidlitz drawing, with its frankly acknowledged urban setting and groups of fashionable parishioners strolling about in the foreground, quite unlike the usual Upjohn office productions with their focus on bucolic trees. Further suggestion of Eidlitz's involvement in these early phases of the church's design come from the fact that he very likely assisted Upjohn in the scheme to remodel the sanctuary's interior in 1854 and that decades later the congregation asked Eidlitz, and not Upjohn's son (who had inherited the family practice), to expand the church and to design a new and elaborate decorative scheme for the church's sanctuary (see fig. 2.26).[40]

Though Eidlitz certainly worked on the church for Upjohn in the 1840s, he was not its primary designer. The Rundbogenstil of the Church of the Pilgrims is decidedly an Upjohn design, with a blend of early Italian Renaissance details and an emphasis on a Renaissance-inspired round arch that is atypical of Eidlitz's own later design work (figs. 1.10, 1.11). The Church of the Pilgrims was a drastic departure from the Gothic Revival of Trinity Church. Gone is the archeological detail of finials and roundels, replaced by a simplicity and directness more typical of contemporary German design. Eidlitz, with his youthful expertise in German aesthetic debates

1.10 Richard Upjohn, Church of the Pilgrims, Brooklyn, 1844–46. *Congregational Quarterly* (1871).

1.11 Church of the Pilgrims with added parish house and tower by Eidlitz, 1868–70. *Congregational Quarterly* (1871).

and architectural history, was a catalyst for the change, facilitating and satisfying Upjohn's curiosity about an unfamiliar architectural culture.

Eidlitz also absorbed much from Upjohn about how to conduct an architectural business in America. Upjohn was consummately professional, and Eidlitz's building contracts in the early 1850s have a specificity and clarity that he must have learned while under Upjohn's tutelage.[41] Upjohn's facility in designing for Protestant congregations that desired varying expressions of their unique liturgies would have been instructive to Eidlitz as well. As a recent émigré from central Europe with experience of Jewish and Catholic religious spaces, Eidlitz could have found no better architectural office in which to learn about Protestant church design in America. More broadly, Upjohn was assuredly the initial source for Eidlitz's lifelong absorption of the principles of the English Gothic Revival. In Upjohn's office, Eidlitz's knowledge of German theory was counterbalanced by the English aesthetics of A. W. N. Pugin and John Ruskin. Although he never become a close adherent of Pugin's and Ruskin's principles, Eidlitz learned quickly that his familiarity with them was a key to winning

American clients, who admired their arguments about truth and honesty in building. Ministers and congregations knew Ruskin's arguments about honesty in structure and ornament, and it behooved an architect to absorb those arguments as well. Perhaps most importantly, though, winning the respect and confidence of America's best-known and most-revered architect in the 1840s gave Eidlitz confidence in his own abilities and spurred him to seek greater challenges.

THE FIRST COMMISSION: ST. GEORGE'S EPISCOPAL CHURCH, NEW YORK

After three years working in the shadows of Warner and Upjohn, Eidlitz began work on his first known commission, St. George's Episcopal Church, built 1846 to 1848, located on 16th Street and Stuyvesant Square in New York (fig. 1.12). In the 1840s, St. George's was a tremendously influential congregation and counted among its parishioners many of the wealthiest and most powerful citizens of New York, including Peter G. Stuyvesant, who in 1836 donated part of the farmland inherited from his great-great grandfather, Peter Stuyvesant (the last Dutch Director-General of New Netherland), to the city to form Stuyvesant Square. In 1846, he donated an adjoining lot for the building of the new church. Other notable parishioners would include future mayor Fernando Wood and financier J. P. Morgan. The Reverend Stephen H. Tyng became pastor in 1845 and quickly established the church at the vanguard of the Low Church Episcopal movement, one that focused on evangelism and mission work among New York's poor. Tyng was of a new generation of Episcopalians focused on reform. Suspicious of High Church emphasis on rituals, Tyng and other Low Church movement pastors emphasized the sermon and its message. The focus shifted to the interpretation of scripture and the education of parishioners rather than adherence to rote repetition of prayer-book recitations. As Tyng would later say, "Any man with Jesus in his heart can preach Jesus."[42] Scholar Kathleen Curran has noted that this attitude placed St. George's in direct opposition to Trinity Church, the oldest Episcopal Church in New York and figurehead of the High Church branch of the faith.[43]

Further emphasizing the divide was the fact that the two parishes were embroiled in a legal battle over control of land and property in St. George's parish.[44] The new St. George's was thus built specifically to provide a public symbol of the Low Church movement that embraced a more humble and restrained aesthetic while still evoking the majesty of God.

For this commission, Eidlitz formed a partnership with the Bavarian architect Charles Otto Blesch. As with his work with Warner and Upjohn, little specific evidence remains as to how they met and how they conducted their joint practice. The two designed at least five buildings together (four churches and a synagogue), and seemed to have worked together from 1846 to about 1851 when Blesch's name disappears from Eidlitz's building contracts. What evidence does remain suggests that Blesch was the more confident architect, with Eidlitz the communicator. Eidlitz, for example, negotiated building contracts and discussed programmatic needs with clients.[45] Blesch, a Munich Grand Prix winner who had studied with Friedrich von Gärtner, the primary architect of the Rundbogenstil, crafted buildings' exterior styles and composed the façades.[46]

Blesch & Eidlitz, despite their relative inexperience, won the St. George's commission by besting such experienced practitioners as Philadelphia's Thomas U. Walter. The committee's choice of the young Germans seems to have been based on two issues. First, the building committee greatly admired the simple, direct form of the design, which they described as being in the "Byzantine, or early Christian style of architecture."[47] Second, St. George's minister, Stephen Tyng, and Eidlitz had a profound intellectual affinity. Tyng's reform impulse, his desire to remake conservative religious practices in light of the new spirit of the age, resonated greatly with Eidlitz's own sense of personal and societal transformation. And finally, it no doubt helped Eidlitz's cause that he was already intimately acquainted with Tyng, who had performed the wedding ceremony for him and Harriet Warner just a year earlier.[48]

The resulting church towered over its East Side neighborhood. The initial cornerstone was laid June 23, 1846, and the first services began November 19, 1848,

1.12 Blesch & Eidlitz, St. George's Episcopal Church, New York, 1846–49. *AR* (September 1908).

though the church was not completed for another
year. It was consecrated on December 4, 1849. Built of
brown freestone, the church, still without its towers,
had cost $178,244.27.[49] The decision to complete the
towers came in 1855. Eidlitz substantially redesigned
what had initially been proposed as slate-roofed conical
steeples, replacing them with openwork stone spires (fig.
1.13). Upon their completion in 1856, the vestry of St.
George's, pleased with the work, gave Eidlitz the gift of
an additional $1,000 for his work.[50]

Designed only a few years after Upjohn's Gothic
Trinity Church, St. George's obviously lacked Trinity's
archeological fastidiousness. Gone were the painstak-
ingly constructed Gothic finials and roundels, replaced
by an emphasis on solid Romanesque construction
that at least gave the impression of economy. The rich
sculptural quality of Trinity is replaced by a more planar
and severe surface treatment, dramatically symbolizing
the difference between High Church opulence and Low
Church humility (figs. 1.14, 1.15). St. George's, at least
on its exterior, is full-fledged Rundbogenstil. Ornament
is reduced to the elaboration of joints where surfaces
meet: corbel tables where the roof line meets the wall,
geometric patterns along the borders of the round portal
arches, and bands along the wall buttresses marking the
transition from their thick bases to their thinner upper
reaches. The design of St. George's establishes three
important themes that recur in Eidlitz's work in the
coming decades: his tendency to divide the exterior and
interior of the building into two separate, though still
connected, design problems; his deep interest in ensuring that buildings overtly symbolized their uses; and his
desire to use the most advanced building technologies to
achieve these new programmatic ends.

Blesch was certainly responsible for the church's
Rundbogenstil exterior and for its symmetrical, balanced, and stable composition and proportions. The design of the original rectory in 1851–52 is a classic example
of Blesch's Rundbogenstil sensibility, the flat surfaces of
its barnlike volume articulated by simple but effectively
ornamental brickwork at the eaves and along the stringcourses.[51] His teacher von Gärtner's Ludwigskirche in
Munich may have provided a model for the church's

1.13 Spires of St. George's under construction, ca. 1856. Frederick
Langenheim, photographer. Robert N. Dennis Collection of
Stereoscopic Views, Miriam & Ira D. Wallach Division of Art,
Prints & Photographs, The New York Public Library, Astor,
Lenox, and Tilden Foundations.

front façade, as Curran has suggested, with its symmetrical spires, simple elaboration of cornice lines, and three-
portal entry (fig. 1.16). The Ludwigskirche, however,
was apseless, and the rear elevation at St. George's seems
descended from the German Romanesque basilicas at
Trier and Speyer. The modifications to the Ludwigskirche prototype, especially in the area of the apse, are
the result of Eidlitz's interpretation of Tyng's ideas about
liturgy and interior space. Eidlitz himself stated bluntly
that "the exterior was mainly his [Blesch's], the interior mainly mine," and this division of labor remained
consistent throughout the partnership.[52] While Blesch
relied on the exterior of the Ludwigskirche, Eidlitz most
certainly did not use the crisp Italian forms of its interior

1.14 St. George's windowless apse, probably just after the fire of 1865 and before the remodeling of 1866. American Scenery stereocard series.

1.15 Richard Upjohn, Trinity Church, New York, 1839–46. Photograph by the American Studio, N.Y., 1916.

as a point of departure. Instead, Eidlitz conceived of the interior of St. George's as a single, open volume, without subdivision or transept, and uncluttered by architectural detail (fig. 1.17). The inclusion of an apse and the omission of a transept in the church were two major departures from the Ludwigskirche model. Though precedent for this treatment can be found in traditional German *Hallenkirche*, or even in the meetinghouses of New England, Eidlitz's design advanced the conception of a simplified space for worship further. Reverend Tyng famously demanded that the pulpit of the church be furnished sparely with "not an altar, a table. A table, do you understand, that you must be able to see under and walk around," so that the focus of the congregation would remain on the minister and the sermon rather than the opulence of the surroundings.[53] Accordingly, the windowless apse served as a visual frame to the table, not

as a focus. (After a disastrous fire destroyed the church's interior in 1865, Eidlitz added windows to the upper level of the apse in the 1866 rebuilding.) No columns broke up the longitudinal focus of the nave; the roof was supported instead by a skeletal timber framework that served to emphasize the immense volume of the space beneath it. In New York, only the roof of St. John the Divine was higher.[54]

The most remarkable aspect of Eidlitz's design, though, came in the balcony seating. He created a cantilevered system that enabled the balconies to extend over the aisle seating without needing supporting columns. Cast-iron brackets tied into the masonry walls provided structural integrity. Again, as with Tyng's table, this allowed the parishioners' focus to remain clearly on the pulpit area, without visual interference from the structure of the building. It also reinforced the essential

1.16 Friedrich von Gärtner, Ludwigskirche, Munich, 1828–44, view along the Ludwigstrasse showing von Gärtner's Staatsbibliothek in the distance.
1.17 St. George's, interior perspective. *Putnam's Magazine* (1853).

unity of interior space by an implied weightlessness. As the roof floated over the enormous volume below, so the balconies floated over the heads of the congregation. This was a revolutionary development in church design that garnered much attention for Eidlitz. The public marveled at the miraculous floating balconies, made possible by the embrace of new building technology. Unlike his contemporaries such as James Renwick, who in the 1850s contemplated using iron as a substitute for stone in the tracery and vaulting of St. Patrick's Cathedral in New York, Eidlitz used iron to generate a subtly new conception of space.[55] His willingness to manipulate traditional structural principles produced a church that met the congregation's expectations but also pointed to new possibilities.

The conception of the church's exterior as an austere *Rundbogenstil,* and the conception of the church's interior as an uncluttered volume, point to crucial differences in Blesch's and Eidlitz's understanding of contemporary design in the 1840s. Both searched for means of creating structures that embraced the new exigencies of the industrial age. Blesch searched primarily through the simplification of historical round-arched forms, specifically using von Gärtner's academic *Rundbogenstil* as his model. Eidlitz, though, was more experimental. Like Blesch, he relied on the simplification of historical form, but in a freer way. The abstract idea of the *Hallenkirche* was more important than any particular model. The availability of cast-iron brackets as a structural support, most commonly used in bridges or as hidden structure in the 1840s, was justification enough for its novel use in a church's exposed balcony seating. Eidlitz had little use for specific historical precedents.

Scholars have found the seeming disconnect between

1.18 Bird's eye view of New York over Central Park, ca. 1859. Eidlitz's home would have been near the top left along the shoreline of Manhattan. B. J. Lossing, *History of New York City* (1884). Harry Ransom Humanities Research Center, University of Texas at Austin.

the approach to the exterior and that of the interior design of St. George's troubling, for it created a "hybrid church."[56] But this hybrid approach to design, evident in Eidlitz's first commission, was to become the most interesting and important aspect of his work. The polarity of his youth and education in Prague and Vienna, with its tension between practical and intellectual concerns, no doubt influenced this approach. His ability to be both academic and ahistorical, and to embrace both tradition and innovation with little regard for established practice, made him something of an anomaly in the world of American architecture. Eidlitz, at his best, was committed to a deeply intellectual process of analysis of building program that included both day-to-day use as well as a larger symbolism. For St. George's, Eidlitz listened closely to Tyng and delivered exactly what the client desired: a plain Low Church that still communicated the richness and inherent mystery of the Christian message.

His success in this commission was confirmation that his hybrid aesthetics could find a niche in America.

AMERICAN AND GERMAN
In late 1851, after spending some time living in New London, Connecticut, supervising the construction of a church there, Leopold and Harriet moved to the new suburban community of Bloomingdale, far up the west side of Manhattan, where the emerging middle class and a few truly upper-crust families were settling to escape the busy city to the south (figs. 1.18, 1.19, 1.20).[57] Their first daughter, Elizabeth, was one year old, and a new daughter, Harriet Frances, had been born in New London on April 12. The New York City of the 1840s and 1850s was in many ways the perfect setting for a hardworking optimist like Eidlitz, imbued with the romanticism of Biedermeier Prague and Vienna, to settle and raise a family. The sharp contrasts between wealth and

VIEW ON BLOOMINGDALE ROAD.

Broadway, New York.

Photographed by E. Anthony of New York

1859

poverty that Eidlitz had seen in Europe surrounded him in New York, but social and religious barriers, despite their profound impact on social circumstances, were more permeable in America. While many immigrants found themselves drawn into the nightmarish slums of lower Manhattan immortalized in Herbert Asbury's *Gangs of New York* (1928), Eidlitz, with his education, persistence, and, one imagines, a hearty helping of good luck, staked his claim to a prosperous American life.

Eidlitz's home overlooking the Hudson River, located at what today would be about 86th Street and Riverside Drive, was the perfect example of his Americanization (figs. 1.21, 1.22). On the one hand, the house was part of the American country cottage tradition, related to the pattern-book houses of A. J. Downing and Calvert Vaux. The "Swiss chalet" style cottage, with its gingerbread and with its siting to take advantage of the incredible views from Manhattan Island of the Hudson River, typified the ideals of the picturesque as espoused by Downing and Vaux in the 1840s and '50s (fig. 1.23). On the other hand, with knowledge of Eidlitz's continued study of trends in German architecture, one can easily see the influence of contemporary German house design as shown

1.19 View on the Bloomingdale Road. W. L. Stone, *History of New York City from the Discovery to the Present Day* (1872). Harry Ransom Humanities Research Center, University of Texas at Austin.

1.20 Broadway, New York, 1859. E. A. Anthony, photographer. Harry Ransom Humanities Research Center, University of Texas at Austin.

in the pages of periodicals like the *Allgemeine Bauzeitung* and by such figures as Georg Ungewitter. The house is remarkably similar to the country estates illustrated in the *Bauzeitung* and in the Potsdam-based *Architektonisches Album*; it is much smaller and more restrained, to be sure, but shares the massing and proportion of its German cousins.[58] Ungewitter, the author of numerous pattern books that circulated in the United States, was known to Eidlitz, who referred to him as "dear old Ungewitter."[59] Ungewitter's plans for traditional cottages were more dramatic than those of his American counterparts; instead of being quaint country houses, they often piled high into craggy, looming, anthropomorphic towers.[60]

Eidlitz's house fell somewhere in between. Though

1.21 Eidlitz residence, New York, 1851. *AR* (April 1896).

the surviving photographs of the house are grainy, the house appeared to have the compositional restraint of a Downing chalet, with its sturdy stone base surmounted by a board-and-batten second story, topped by a half-hipped roof with deep overhangs. But it also had the drama of an Ungewitter design, perched on the edge of a precipice, with the house seeming to expand as it moved upward. The details of the spindlework were elaborate but not overdone, enough to hint at the prosperity of the owner without excess.

Ultimately, the house was *both* American and German. It could have fit as well into Hietzing, the prosperous mid-nineteenth-century suburb of Vienna, as it did into the suburbs of New York. Its peculiar character

Fig. 46

reflected the synergy between the romantic movement in both cultures; it was a little bit Emerson and a little bit Goethe. Eidlitz well understood that in America he was finally free to partake of the middle-class life that was so tantalizingly near in Prague and Vienna, and his house, where he was to live for the duration of his career, gave him a tranquil domestic retreat from the professional stresses that were to come (fig. 1.24).

This dual identity informed the rest of Eidlitz's career. He began his life as a cultural hybrid: a Germanic Jew in Czech Prague, a poor Czech in opulent Vienna, a central European immigrant in New York. His training was varied as well: business and engineering on the one hand and history and art on the other. What makes Eidlitz so different from his contemporaries is his embrace of all these disparate influences. He saw no reason to choose one identity over another, one means of design, or one way of thinking. All methods were compatible, even desirable, when in the hands of an educated and hardworking individual.

1.22 The backyard of the Eidlitz residence in about 1865. Collection of the New-York Historical Society, neg#64830.

1.23 A. J. Downing, design for a "Swiss Cottage" as published in *The Architecture of Country Houses* (1850).

1.24 Eidlitz at home with his two daughters Elizabeth and Harriet, ca. 1868. National Gallery of Canada, Ottawa. Gift of Dorothy Meigs Eidlitz, St. Andrews, New Brunswick, 1970.

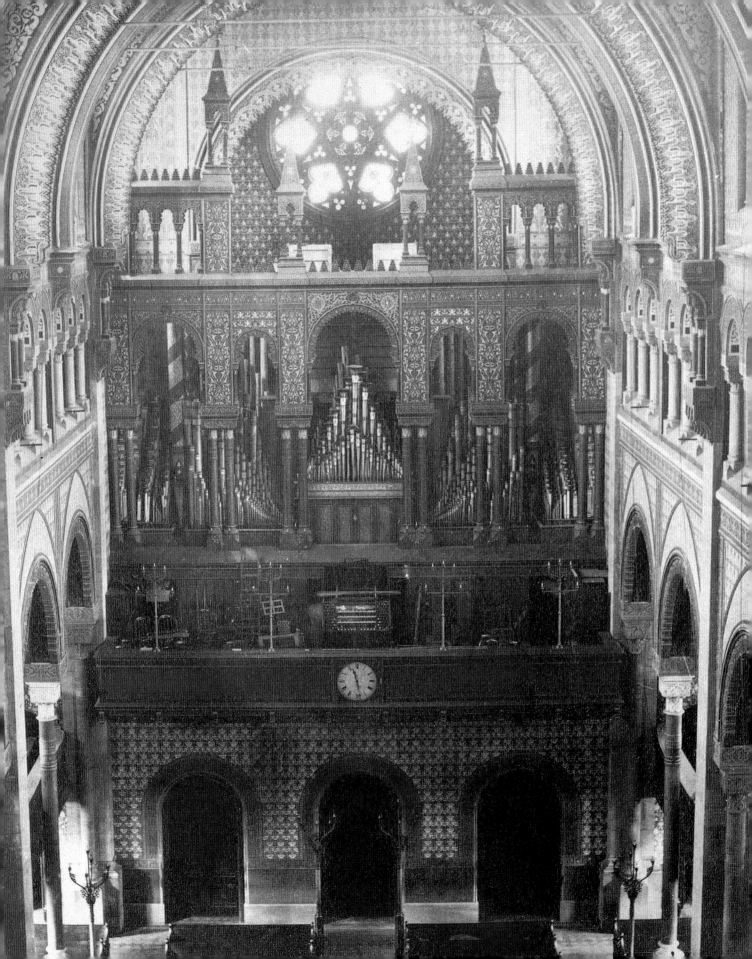

2

THE SCIENCE OF THE BEAUTIFUL

EVERY ASPIRING ARCHITECT HOPES FOR A COMMISSION LIKE ST.
George's to launch his career. Reviewed widely and positively in newspapers and
magazines, St. George's attracted attention to Eidlitz and proved his ability to
handle large commissions. After the departure of Blesch around 1851, Eidlitz rapidly
expanded his practice to include commercial and government buildings as well
as a handful of houses. Looking at their mix of Gothic, Romanesque, and Moorish inflections, his designs from this period appear to fit nicely into the traditional
conception of nineteenth-century American architecture as an eclectic series of
historical revivals. And without any record of Eidlitz's design process other than the
photographs and descriptions that survive, we might be left with this conclusion.
But Eidlitz began to write prolifically in the 1850s, and his essays paint a dramatically different picture of his practice than one might otherwise see.

Eidlitz began to pursue the path that transcendentalism offered in a serious
way in the late 1850s, decades after romantic notions of nature had begun to shape
the other American arts. In his pursuit of a modern aesthetic for architecture, he
pursued the Enlightenment quest begun in the eighteenth century, searching for answers about the meanings and functions of beauty and how it could influence and
reflect the evolution of a civilized society. Amid the great literature that emerged
from this intensely rational and scientific inquiry, the theme of nature as a guide to
artistic endeavor became the seed of English romanticism, German idealist philosophy, and then American transcendentalism.

Opposite: See page 79.

In the 1850s, Eidlitz, with his own roots in German aesthetic theory, became the conduit for transcendentalism to enter American architecture. With the publication of *Nature* in 1836, Ralph Waldo Emerson crafted its cohesive manifesto, arguing for the importance of the individual experience of nature as a path to personal spiritual enlightenment. Transcendentalism had its roots in the balance of three influences: German idealist philosophy, English romanticism, and American individualism. As Nathaniel Hawthorne aptly described it, transcendentalism was "German by birth" and the term "transcendentalist," as Emerson acknowledged, came from Immanuel Kant's use of the term to describe the importance of individual experience in the formation of understanding.[1] Transcendentalism was thus a peculiarly American interpretation of English and German aesthetics and philosophy that posited the primacy of nature and the landscape as the inspiration for not only enlightenment, but all creative endeavors. As Emerson wrote:

> The production of a work of art throws a light upon the mystery of humanity. A work of art is an abstract or epitome of the world. It is the result or expression of nature, in miniature. . . . The poet, the painter, the sculptor, the musician, the architect, seek each to concentrate this radiance of the world on one point, and each in his several work to satisfy the love of beauty which stimulates him to produce.[2]

In this statement, all the hallmarks of American transcendentalism are present: the emphasis on the individual vision, on the experience of nature, and on the importance of art as a man-made reflection of the beauty of the world.

Transcendentalism created a new class of American intellectual that was more secular, more individualistic, and more suspicious of convention. It acknowledged the revelations that science brought to the modern world and celebrated the mystery that remained. And for Eidlitz in particular, it made it possible to reject organized religion in favor of an agnostic and pragmatic intellectualism. But perhaps most important, transcendentalism

provided Eidlitz a foundation on which to build his organic idealism, using nature as a guide to creating a new, American aesthetic. Emerson's transcendentalism emerged from an American's digestion of German and English philosophy and aesthetics. And Eidlitz, never a true transcendentalist in the purely American sense, nonetheless paralleled Emerson's intellectual journey. This balancing act, of playing German ideas against more popularly accepted English and American ones, became Eidlitz's strategy for assimilating his more abstruse ideas to his New York audience.

In American painting and literature, the romantic idea of nature as guide, channeled through English poetry and landscape painting, had already had a pronounced impact in the first decades of the nineteenth century. Thomas Cole, Asher B. Durand, and other artists of the Hudson River School shared Emerson's emphasis on experience of the landscape as a revelatory experience. Their paintings showed America's wilderness not only as an aesthetic revelation, but one which could teach moral lessons. Thomas Cole's *The Oxbow*, exhibited in New York in 1836, epitomizes the painter's use of nature as a moral template, showing the battle between wilderness and civilization, between destruction and rebirth, ignorance and revelation. In literature, William Cullen Bryant's romantic poetry anticipated Emerson's transcendentalism. In his famous poem "Thanatopsis," Bryant, in a meditation on death and the passage of time, extolled the reader to "Go forth under the open sky, and list To Nature's teachings."[3] Asher B. Durand's 1850 painting of the same title contrasts the enormity and permanence of the landscape with the transience of man's existence.[4] By looking to the landscape, American philosophers, painters, and writers projected their desires for a new cultural expression of democracy. As a member of the Century Association, a private club for artists and writers established by Bryant, Durand, and Gulian C. Verplanck, Eidlitz came in contact with some of the most important cultural figures in America.

Eidlitz was deeply aware that Americans had increasingly begun to call for their institutions, arts, and letters to say something distinctive about their young country. Emerson himself declared, "There are new lands, new men, new thoughts. Let us demand our own works and laws and worship."[5] Thomas Cole saw America as a place with a limitless future: "... in looking over the yet uncultivated scene, the mind's eye may see far into futurity. Where the wolf roams, the plough shall glisten; on the gray crag shall rise temple and tower—mighty deeds shall be done in the now pathless wilderness; and poets yet unborn shall sanctify the soil."[6] And even more specific to Eidlitz's future, Horatio Greenough, an expatriate sculptor in the classical tradition, had in 1845 deplored the current state of American building, believing hopefully that "these United States are destined to form a new style of architecture."[7] The American intelligentsia clamored to be freed from the shackles of stylistic precedent and hungered for a native literature, art, and architecture.

One might argue that Andrew Jackson Downing's focus on bucolic country and suburban houses was in fact the first expression of American transcendentalism in architecture. And in a sense, this is true: Downing's aesthetic, which emphasized the need for Americans to reject city life and connect to the countryside to maintain their health and wisdom, is indeed a reflection of a growing middle-class notion of gentility that had its origins in Emerson and the Hudson River School. But Downing is more of a reflection of the growth of these middle-class ideals, a mirror held to its materialist concerns, than a serious contemplation of what transcendentalism might mean for architecture.[8]

In transcendentalism, Eidlitz found the perfect home for his hybrid identity, a place where his roots in German culture and philosophy could meet his American clients' incipient nationalism. Eidlitz's transcendentalism, however, differed markedly from the nature worship associated with Emerson, Thoreau, and the romantics of the Hudson River School. The balance between rationalism and romanticism shifted in Eidlitz toward the objective and the scientific. In other words, it was not the experience of nature that inspired the architect, but the model provided by nature: "[Architecture's] beauties can none of them be strictly copied from nature, for the simple reason that nature offers no precedent for them, but they must all be *reasoned out*

from acknowledged principles of beauty as they exist in nature, our only teacher."[9] As a result, Eidlitz was far more interested in rationalizing aesthetic issues in the mold of Kant and Georg Wilhelm Friedrich Hegel than in exploring more strictly romantic conceptions of the picturesque and sublime. While this distinction was probably lost on the vast majority of Eidlitz's American clients, it has broad implications for understanding his theory and design.

Eidlitz was the first architect to answer the call of American philosophers and painters, and he began to explore the idea of creating a new American style based in the objective study of nature. He wrote and lectured about the ideas he explored in his built architecture, defining sets of aesthetic and constructive principles for all architects to follow. Through careful analysis of buildings and their effects on the human body and emotions, Eidlitz believed he could create a "science of the beautiful" that would eliminate confusion about architectural effects and style.[10] This idealized organic science, based in the objective study of nature, would enable the creation of an architecture completely in harmony with the advancement of "human purposes and ideas," with the birth of modern democracy.[11] Eidlitz, pursuing a quest at once romantic and rational, became focused on the creation of an organic architecture that embodied the noblest ideals and emotions of mankind.

STYLE

One of the key aspects of Eidlitz's development of this theoretical stance was a dissection of the very notion of style itself. Eidlitz's experience of style in his work with Upjohn and Blesch was as a codified and essentially conservative force in design: buildings had to adhere to identifiable styles with identifiable characteristics. The *Rundbogenstil,* in particular, was an attempt to create a new style, one that had different characteristics than well-established styles, but a style nonetheless. Part of Eidlitz's attempt to create a modern American architecture was an abandonment of this notion of style, which was itself relatively new.

In the mid-nineteenth century, architects were nearly paralyzed by their self-conscious knowledge of the great

2.1 Blesch & Eidlitz, First Congregational Church of New London, New London, Connecticut, 1848–51. © Timothy Cook, photographer, 2007.

2.2 First Congregational Church of New London, view looking from the pulpit back towards the narthex showing the organ loft above the entry. © Timothy Cook, photographer, 2007.

buildings of the past. The field of art history, pioneered in eighteenth-century Germany by Johann Winckelmann, had begun the thorough documentation and interpretation of Greek art and architecture in his seminal *Geschichte der Kunst des Alterthums* (1764). Winckelmann's ecstatic appraisals of the beauty of Greek art and its reflection of a culture of political and intellectual freedom prompted an immediate focus by other schol-ars, largely German and including figures such as Karl Friedrich von Rumohr, on the artistic achievements of other cultures, from ancient Egypt to India. Buildings and paintings could be cataloged by their formal characteristics into styles, groups of objects whose similarities were more important than their differences. With a flood of historical writing on architecture available by the early nineteenth century, architects were faced with a new condition of practice: their choice of styles.

Architects on the one hand attempted to explicitly use the new art history as fodder for design. No longer was contemporary practice seen as part of a historical continuum—with the advent of art history as a discipline, architects clearly saw the past as separate from their own circumstance. The advent of nineteenth-

2.3 First congregational Church of New London, looking from the narthex toward the pulpit and the windowless apse. © Timothy Cook, photographer, 2007.

century revivals, ranging from the Gothic to Romanesque, Greek, Roman, Moorish, and Egyptian, was in part a reaction to this newly awkward sense of history as history. As a result, critics and architects alike began to craft elaborate positions promoting one style or another as the true idiom for the modern world. In England, John Ruskin and A.W.N. Pugin led the debates. Ruskin's *Seven Lamps of Architecture* (1849) and Pugin's *Contrasts* (1836) both argued, through different means, for the Gothic as the one true style of architecture that held promise for the modern world. Both were motivated

by an abhorrence of current architectural practice and a desire for a return to an era of medieval authenticity that predated the self-conscious pastiche of the present.[12] In France, the Neo-Grec, as practiced by Henri Labrouste, focused on the clarity and simplicity of Greek architecture as a source for a modern style that would capture the essence of French intellectual culture.[13] In Germany, Hübsch and Gottfried Semper both argued for the Rundbogenstil, while figures such as August Reichensperger argued just as passionately for the Gothic as the true style of the German fatherland. Georg Ungewitter promoted a Neugotik, a reinterpretation of the Gothic suited for all modern building types.[14] Complicating the matter was Hegel's proposition in his *Aesthetics* (1835) that every epoch of history would have its own emblematic style.[15] This emphasis on style as an indicator of *zeitgeist* made the reconciliation of history with the present even more fraught with self-conscious attempts at novelty.

It was in this minefield of stylistic convention and innovation that Eidlitz began his practice. As long as Eidlitz practiced with Blesch, the Americanized *Rundbogenstil* that had its sources in both Munich and Upjohn's office held sway. Flat façades, symmetrical compositions, and minimal ornament distinguished their work together at the Shaaray Tefila Synagogue (1846–48), the First Congregational Church in Norwalk, Connecticut (1849), and the First Church of Christ in New London, Connecticut (1849–54). The latter church in particular, built of a severe and unornamented gray granite, directly echoes the heavy planarity of the German Romanesque, while its central bell tower flanked by two stepped gables over the narthex is a direct inversion of St. George's and the Ludwigskirche, echoing both English and German vernacular forms (fig. 2.1). The New London building committee was intent on restoring pride of place in the wealthy whaling town to their church; the Second Congregational Church had recently completed a new, imposing, and extremely visible Gothic Revival structure atop a hill in a newer section of town, and the original congregation was feeling the sting of competition. As a result, their new church was also sited at the crest of a hill and looms authoritatively over the old

2.4 First Church of Christ, Pittsfield, Massachusetts, 1851–1853.

2.5 First Church of Christ, Pittsfield, view from the narthex looking towards pulpit. *Proceedings in Commemoration of the Organization of the First Church of Christ* (Pittsfield, 1889).

town, with its only exterior ornament provided by over-scaled corbel tables beneath the eaves. A groin-vaulted and granite-paved narthex beneath the tower provides a transitional space from the dramatic stone of the exterior to the startlingly informal wooden interior of the nave. A plain windowless apse, much like the original St. George's, is framed above by exposed wooden trusswork and along the sides by a wooden gallery, supported not by cast-iron brackets but by more conventional and less expensive wooden posts (figs. 2.2 and 2.3). The cohesive openness of the space, with subsidiary spaces subordinated to the unity of the whole, is also a holdover from

St. George's. The windows were originally of clear glass, allowing the light of day to illuminate the rather severe interior ornamented only by the cut patterns of trefoils found in the trusses and brackets.[16]

But when on his own, Eidlitz began to change his designs. While his interior treatments remained somewhat constant, his exterior compositions moved toward asymmetry and a general disharmony. The First Congregational Church in Pittsfield, Massachusetts, (1851–53), was ostensibly based on Blesch & Eidlitz's New London church. The Reverend John Todd and his building committee visited New London and, impressed, decided to hire Eidlitz, requesting a larger sanctuary and the inclusion of only one tower rather than three (figs. 2.4, 2.5, and 2.6). Unlike the New London church, with its severe Romanesque profile, the Pittsfield church positively bristles with gabled windows along its nave roof, echoed in the sharp peaks of the cross-gabled bell tower. The front elevation is based on an earlier symmetrical Blesch & Eidlitz design for the First Presbyterian Church of Brooklyn (Old School; completed 1851), but with the symmetry disrupted by the transformation of one of the side entry halls into a vertical tower.[17] Each of the portions of Pittsfield's tripartite façade is clearly and separately defined, with little proportional unity or symmetry to tie the pieces back together. The proportions of the front elevation are awkward, anchored at center by a steeply peaked gable end, flanked by the squat tower at right and the vestigial stair tower. The exterior walls are made more sculptural by the inclusion of buttresses, which were absent along the plain nave walls in New London. At New London, the building is contained, reserved, but at Pittsfield, the building begins to explode, as if its structure had been pulled apart to become a more dynamically sculptural object. With the departure of Blesch, Eidlitz entered the new transcendental phase of his career.

It cannot be overstated that without Eidlitz's essays it would be nearly impossible to read the importance of the organic ideal to the creation of his architecture. Without his essays, Eidlitz's churches would most likely be understood as awkward, ungainly, and perhaps somewhat unsuccessful examples of the Gothic Revival. But these buildings cannot and should not be read without using Eidlitz's theory as a guide. The intellectual and cultural climate that transcendentalism provided gave him a means to abandon the idea of style as style and to consider the building as an organism invested with physical and emotional functions, capable of evolving to meet the needs of society. Eidlitz's first essays appear in 1857 in the *Crayon*, a literary and art journal edited by John Durand, Asher's brother, and Eidlitz's sponsor for membership in the Century Association. "On Style," a lecture read to the American Institute of Architects and then published in the *Crayon*, proposed a new way for architects to look at history. Style was, according to Eidlitz, "the characteristic and peculiar mode of representing and expressing in the organism of a structure, the idea which has given rise to its erection, assisted at all times by a certain degree of progress in the science

2.6 The Reverend Dr. John Todd in the pulpit of the First Church of Christ, Pittsfield in about 1854. The whitewashed, windowless walls that frame the pulpit were originally ornamented only with tablets, as shown here, following the model established at St. George's.

of construction."[18] Though somewhat clumsily phrased, style was a rational equation, defined by the interplay between expression and construction, the subjective and the scientific. Style would vary, therefore, depending on culture, function, and construction. Contemporary architecture faced a particularly severe problem, since overdependence on styles of the past had arrested the "progress of architecture by forcing a rigid adherence to pre-conceived notions."[19] Architects now designed buildings based on historical models and consequently failed to express contemporary ideas.

The antidote to the problem of history was nature. If architects had forgotten how to create "monuments that will call up in the minds of men the virtues which man needs to make him a useful member of society," then they could look to nature for guidance.[20] But it was not the imitation of organic, natural forms that Eidlitz looked to, as the designers of Art Nouveau would do forty years later. Instead, it was the working method of nature that architects should adopt. In a passage that directly echoes Emerson's imagery, Eidlitz wrote:

How does [Nature] make men, lions, lambs, mountains, clouds, trees, etc. etc.? She constructs them each for their particular purpose, and makes that construction as beautiful as possible—every kind of beauty peculiar to itself. . . . So has the true architect endeavored from all time to construct his buildings *to the purpose*, with the greatest possible beauty—a beauty that should be expressive of the nature of his structure.[21]

A building's relationship to its purpose, which Eidlitz understood to mean both its mundane function and its social significance, should determine its form.

As a corollary to this functional point of view, Eidlitz defined architecture as "an idea in matter." A singularly ungainly phrase, the "idea in matter" is nonetheless crucial to Eidlitz's conception of an ideal and organic architecture. By abstracting the building to an idea, something ineffable and transcendent, one could begin to imagine its form. This acknowledgment of an inherent dualism in our perception of forms and beauty was indebted specifically to Hegel's aesthetics. Eidlitz's "idea in matter" is a paraphrase of his own translation of Hegel: "Hegel," he wrote, "defines *beauty absolute* as the shining of the idea through the sensuous medium."[22] Eidlitz took from Hegel the notion that art and architecture could communicate on various levels depending on the truth and purity of the idea expressed: "Only in the highest art are the Idea and the representation truly consonant with one another. . . ."[23] He thus attempted to pursue ideas rather than styles.

But Eidlitz did not advocate abandoning historical style altogether, simply changing the way it was used by architects. He complained that "architects study styles instead of architecture," meaning that they substituted an understanding of generalities for an understanding of specifics.[24] Instead, architects should absorb the "history of architecture as a whole"—not by dividing it into discrete stylistic chunks—and in the process learn the ability to discern its great individual monuments. These individual buildings, because they solved the problems of use and beauty in ways that still resonated with contemporary viewers, would form the basis of an architect's visual memory instead of a catalog of styles. Nature again provided a framework for design, in this case through the provision of an evolutionary scheme that determined which ideal forms were fit for modern buildings.

Here again, Eidlitz drew on German architecture theory, particularly Carl Bötticher, a student of Gottfried Semper's who believed that architects should combine their own practical knowledge, gained through work, with research into the history of architecture in order to create solutions for the present day. But this was not a justification for borrowing styles from the past; instead, it was a call for rational evaluation of history and style: ". . . we must not make use of tradition for its own sake; through scholarly research we must penetrate its spiritual and material qualities in order to arrive at an apprehension of the essential nature of tradition and an understanding of its forms."[25] Bötticher believed that through the study of history architects could see the greater evolution of buildings, guided by "nature." This rational, biological conception of nature agreed with Eidlitz's own, modulating the romantic, religious overtones that the transcendentalist invocation of nature generally implied.

The Brooklyn Academy of Music is an excellent example of how Eidlitz translated his ideas about the limitations of style and the potential of nature in design (Fig. 2.7). Built in 1860 at the behest of the Brooklyn Philharmonic Society, the theater, which was located at 176–94 Montague Street in the heart of prosperous Brooklyn Heights, confounded contemporary reviewers who variously labeled it as "Italian Gothic," "German Gothic," "technically Gothic," but also "decidedly Moorish."[26] The building was, in fact, not particularly Gothic at all. In some of its details, like the pointed arches of the windows, the corbel tables, and the bands of Nova Scotia stone that contrasted with the deep red brick, Eidlitz used elements of the Gothic form language. But

the building's overall massing, which made the separate interior spaces easily readable on the exterior of the building, led to an asymmetrical and decidedly unprecedented composition described at the time as being "dromedary-like."[27] The central portion of the façade, which anchored the overall composition, maintained a Rundbogenstil-derived flat, tripartite division. But the two flanking bays were not quite symmetrical; one had two doorways on the ground floor and the other had three. These flanking pavilions were seemingly randomly arranged, appearing not to be quite part of the same building. Instead, the structure appeared to be a collection of separate parts, as if the original had become too small and had several bays added over time in a functional adaptation to use. If the Academy looked Gothic, it resembled more a medieval streetscape with houses protruding and receding than a single cathedral or town hall.

This hodgepodge was reflective of Eidlitz's focus on

2.7 Brooklyn Academy of Music, Brooklyn, 1860–61. This view shows the green room and backstage at the left, and the entrance at the far right. *AR* (October 1908).

the effects of symmetry and asymmetry in massing. While strict symmetry, of Blesch's variety for example, could lead to a frozen beauty, asymmetry, he believed, led by contrast to *expression*. Though the formal definition of empathy theory by the German philosopher Robert Vischer was more than a decade away, Eidlitz, having read the aesthetic theories of Kant and Hegel, was clearly preoccupied with how art and architecture created direct emotional and physical responses in a viewer. An expressive architecture, for Eidlitz, was one that could capture the essence of man's existence: the ability to move, or "motion at will," distinguished animals from plants, and the ability to express "emotions of the mind" separated men from animals.[28] A building, therefore, to be reflective of the highest evolved values of

2.8 The drawing shows the delineations between the portions of the building more clearly than photographs. *Harper's Weekly* (February 2, 1861).

mankind, should embody those expressive emotions. By controlling asymmetry and creating dramatic contrasts in scale, color, and ornamental detail, Eidlitz believed a building could engender a visceral emotional response in the viewer, one that drove to the heart of architecture's purpose as a reflection of a "refined state of society."[29]

Goethe's mystical experience of Gothic architecture, recorded in 1772, informed Eidlitz's sense of architectural expression. Upon visiting Strasbourg Cathedral, a mix of Gothic and Romanesque, German and French influence, he expounded:

My soul was suffused with a feeling of immense grandeur which, because it consisted of thousands of harmonizing details, I was able to savor and enjoy, but by no means understand and explain. They say it is thus with the joys of heaven, and how often I returned to savor such joys on earth, to embrace the gigantic spirit expressed in the work of our brothers of yore. . . . How often the gentle light of dusk, as it fused the countless parts into unified masses, soothed my eyes weary from intense searching. . . . How fresh was its radiance in the misty shimmer of morning light, how happily I stretched out my arms toward it and looked at the vast harmonious masses animated by countless components. As in the works of eternal nature, down to the smallest fiber, all is form, all serves the whole.[30]

Eidlitz's goal as an architect was to create the rhapsodic reaction that Goethe recorded. While Goethe could not "understand and explain" his reaction, Eidlitz believed it was the architect's role to do just that: to understand how mass, space, and ornament affected people and to manipulate them through building.

2.9 "Grand ball, for the benefit of the Home for Destitute Children, at the Academy of Music, Brooklyn, Feb. 5th" *Frank Leslie's Illustrated Newspaper* (1880). LC-USZ62-75207.

2.10 J.C. Cady, Brooklyn Art Association, 1869–72. The Art Association was directly next door to the Academy of Music on Montague Street. *Harper's Weekly* (1872).

The Brooklyn Academy's asymmetry and unconventional massing thus takes on new meaning in light of Eidlitz's concern with "expressiveness." Each of the interior's physical divisions is clearly visible on its exterior: the theater inside ran parallel to the main street so that each of the major functional divisions appeared along the front façade (fig. 2.8). Minimal ornament and shifts in scale emphasized the divisions. The rightmost bay, for example, pushed forward with an exterior balcony that marked the foyer and main public space; the elongated central pavilion contained the theater space; to its left, the taller bay contained the stage and stage works; and beyond it a small recessed bay contained the green room, a cast and staff area. In the end, the building did somewhat resemble a dromedary, with a humped roofline that literally expressed the varying contours and scales of the varied theater functions. While Charles Garnier's Paris Opera House (1857–74) is often credited with being one of the first buildings to express interior functions on the exterior, Garnier was careful to maintain the essence of monumental symmetry in the building's grand façade. Eidlitz, by contrast, rejected any notion that a ceremonial entry façade should take precedence over any other portion of the building, focusing instead on "marked irregularity" that led to "peculiarity of expression."[31]

The interior, true to the model of practice Eidlitz established at St. George's, had a markedly different character (fig. 2.9, color plate 2, page 2). Large enough to hold 2,200 patrons, the theater had only twelve prosce-

2.11 New York Produce Exchange, New York, 1860–61. *AR* (October 1908).

2.12 George B. Post, New York Produce Exchange, New York, 1884. Photograph by August Loeffler, ca. 1899. LC-USZ62-83850.

nium boxes, devoting most of its interior to providing clear views so that "all can see the stage with ease and comfort." Described at the time as having a "barbaric splendor," the theater's ceiling was supported by exposed wooden trusswork painted in brilliant reds and yellows—though originally intended to be covered by canvas, Eidlitz apparently convinced the theater owners to allow the structure to remain exposed and polychromed for expressive effect. The balcony levels were supported by large wooden columns with decorative brackets, also painted in brilliant colors. Connecting the uppermost balcony level to the ceiling was a series of wooden arches that continued the line of the floor-level columns through to the level of the ceiling. This last feature was considered an "innovation" and "novelty," and the entire design had "an air of romantic warmth and life pervading this temple of music and the drama which will predispose the minds and imaginations of its fortunate inmates to the full enjoyment of the sweet sounds and fascinating personifications to be developed within its walls."[32] The theater's interior was one of Eidlitz's earliest investigations of color theory as a complement to the expressiveness of structure and mass: the more brilliant the color, the higher the emotional reaction to it.

The BAM, which burned in 1903, was one of Eidlitz's most successful designs. He was an investor in the theater, and it played host to myriad operas, balls, plays, and benefits throughout its long life. Its opening in 1861 was heralded as marking a new phase in the cultural life of Brooklyn. At the first concert (January 15, 1861), on the eve of the Civil War, the diverse program offered the best of European opera: selections from Weber's *Der Freischütz* to Mozart's *Don Giovanni* culminated with a performance of Giacomo Meyerbeer's *Schiller March*. Walt Whitman, a dedicated Brooklynite, described the building as "magnificent . . . beautiful outside and in."[33] J. C. Cady, when he began to design the Metropolitan Opera House, requested a behind-the-scenes tour of the BAM to study its widely admired plan and acoustics.[34] Upon its loss, the *New York Times* eulogized it, declaring, "We can think of no edifice in Manhattan the destruction of which would create in a greater degree the sense of the obliteration of a 'landmark.' . . . One might almost wish that its exterior might be exactly reproduced for its successor. . . ."[35] It was still understood as a Gothic building that in combination with Cady's Brooklyn Art Association Building, later built next door, and Peter B. Wight's Mercantile Library, built across the street, made up the "most picturesque and striking group of secular Gothic architecture to be seen in either borough or in fact in any American city."[36] But a brief comparison of the three buildings highlights the very problem with style that Eidlitz himself identified: these buildings are far more dissimilar than similar (fig. 2.10). The Academy, with its echoes of Rundbogenstil, lacks the ornamental splendor of either building and, in its fulfillment of Eidlitz's organic expressiveness, is far more unconventional in its massing. Its façade is flatter, less sculptural, allowing the building's volume to bulge and taper in a decidedly un-Gothic fashion.

The critic Montgomery Schuyler admired the BAM tremendously and was perhaps the only nineteenth-century viewer who grasped Eidlitz's intent. He aptly described it and Eidlitz's other buildings from this period as "works that were of no style and that yet had style."[37] Eidlitz's New York Produce Exchange, like the Academy, synthesized Rundbogenstil and Gothic sensibilities to emphasize functional and programmatic divisions within the building (fig. 2.11). With its three-bay organization and emphasis on the *piano nobile*, the

Exchange has a more ordered and perhaps less expressive character. But its greater area of blank wall combined with the great height of each of its three levels give the building a massiveness unlike any of Eidlitz's other secular designs. The extremely simple composition exposes the interior arrangement completely on the exterior, with the crossed-gable transept providing clerestory lighting to the great trading hall on the main floor. Decorative brickwork was again concentrated at key structural points: crenellated and turned brickwork marked the cornice and the divisions between the bays and floors. In the interior, a skeleton of exposed and brilliantly polychromed iron trusswork supported the roof, adding both structural clarity and a contrast to the austere, planar exterior.[38] A comparison with George B. Post's replacement for Eidlitz's outdated exchange, completed in 1884, reinforces the medieval, vernacular quality of the original (fig. 2.12). Post's tremendous Italian Romanesque palazzo is academic in character, a virtuoso reproduction of the past. Eidlitz's Exchange, with its direct simplicity, appears to be the work of a master mason.

Even when working within the confines of regular, symmetrical compositions, Eidlitz found means of manipulating proportion and massing to heighten expressiveness. The Continental Bank (1856–57) and the American Exchange Bank (1857–58), built during the first boom of bank-building in the emergent financial district on lower Broadway, both had flat, austere façades marked by an unusually large proportion of glazing (figs. 2.13, 2.14). Both were five stories tall and found some inspiration in the Rundbogenstil of Munich, with rusticated ground floors and series of very subtly pointed round-arched windows on the three floors above. Both banks had corner lots, allowing Eidlitz two façades to work with. As one reviewer of New York's bank buildings noted at the time, "Land is too valuable in the business parts of the City to admit of a building for business purposes being constructed so that all parts of it can be seen, or to afford an architect an opportunity of exhibiting his talent for design. The most that can be done is to give one or two façades of moderate extent; but all thoughts of the preservation of proportion must

2.13 American Exchange Bank, New York, 1857. Eidlitz had his office in this building for many years, from 1858–63, 1865–71, and 1875–90. *AR* (October 1908).

2.14 Continental Bank, Wall Street, New York, 1856–57. *AR* (October 1908).

be abandoned to the exigencies of a business location."[39] And it is the manipulation of proportion, particularly of windows, masonry joints, and cornices, that distinguishes Eidlitz's designs. While beginning with the Rundbogenstil, Eidlitz did not follow von Gärtner's example as closely as Blesch would have. Alexander Saeltzer's Astor Library in New York (1849–54), for example, was a much more faithful adaptation of von Gärtner's Munich Staatsbibliothek (1831–42) than either of Eidlitz's bank buildings, whose stone walls are too massive and whose

enormous, looming cornices are far too pronounced for the lighter Rundbogenstil (see fig. 3.16). The window surrounds, too, are detailed with tracery whose patterns are derived from rational geometric intersections based on the lines of segmental arches rather than conventional round arches and roundels. Even the pattern of the rusticated stone at the American Exchange Bank, so outwardly similar to von Gärtner's on the ground floor of the Staatsbibliothek, instead appeared to lack vertical joints, turning expected architectural conventions

2.15 Friedrich von Gärtner, Staatsbibliothek, Munich, 1827–43, center bays.

2.16 Calvert Vaux, Bank of New York, New York, 1856–58. This is a later photograph of the building, showing it after Vaux had added the top two floors to the original building. *King's Handbook of New York* (1892).

slightly askew (fig. 2.15). Eidlitz began with the simplifying rationale of the Rundbogenstil but infused it with both massiveness and creative detailing quite unlike it.

Compared with other New York banks of the time, like Calvert Vaux's exactly contemporary Italianate Bank of New York (1856–58), the sobriety and regular planarity of the façades become even more evident (fig. 2.16). Eidlitz's buildings have a heavy, straightforward, businesslike aspect, lacking the usual ornamental appendages like pediments and porticoes. A reviewer regretted that the pilasters framing the windows at the Continental Bank were not made of a more purely Italianate white marble, as it would have given the building "an airy appearance [like] the Leaning Tower of Pisa," surely one of the most startling comparisons in architectural criticism.[40] Vaux by contrast produced an "elegant" four-story brownstone with copious Renaissance details such as rusticated piers, projecting keystones, and plentiful carved rosettes.[41]

Both banks had large interior volumes on their main

floors and are often recognized as being among the first fireproof buildings in the city, constructed with layers of concrete, terracotta, and reinforcing cast-iron beams.[42] The entire first floor of the Continental Bank, measuring 50 feet wide by 60 feet deep, was occupied only by the banking hall, at 38 by 60 feet, and a side entry hall with the bank president and cashier's office at the rear of the hall. The ceiling was again polychromed, contrasting with the neutral walls and wooden floors in a way that one reviewer found unfortunate: "The dusky brown hue of the floor contrasts unfavorably with the richly painted ceiling; and the neutral tint of the walls, for the same reason, produces a cold and chilling effect." But it is these deliberate disruptions of convention and expectation, even if on a small scale as at these two banks, that typified Eidlitz's work. The science of architecture began with the idea of the building, analyzing its program, and finding ways of making structure and ornament dynamically expressive of that idea. Only through following this rational process could a modern architecture evolve.

In Eidlitz's antebellum secular architecture, the Rund-bogenstil ruled, but in his religious architecture it was the Gothic and the heavily ornamented Moorish that provided a stylistic template. For Eidlitz, the Gothic was the language of Christian architecture. Though when designing with Blesch, the Romanesque informed both St. George's and the New London church, as an independent practitioner, Eidlitz's numerous churches all contained variations on Gothic form combined with the "preaching box" popular with protestant congregations. He developed a theory of Christian architecture, published in 1858, that analyzed church history, style, and program that, as in his secular buildings, would allow an expression of the idea behind the building: the transcendence of God. Interestingly, Eidlitz never wrote specifically about synagogue architecture, perhaps out of a self-conscious, assimilative desire to distance himself from his own past or for the more pragmatic reason that far fewer synagogues were being built in the United States than churches.

Eidlitz's theory of Christian architecture placed him squarely in the middle of the various religious reform movements active in antebellum America. He responded to Protestant reformers' desire for plain "preaching boxes" and Jewish reformers' desire for more assimilated and "churchly" spaces. He addressed the stylistic precedents set by the previous generation of architects, like Upjohn, in which the Gothic was suited only for high church Anglicans and Episcopalians, while the more humble Romanesque sufficed for Presbyterians and Congregationalists. The result was an essay that emphasized commonalities rather than differences, and that focused on the underlying similarities of the experience of God in varying religious circumstances and spaces.

Eidlitz believed religious architecture was the highest form of design and presented the architect with the richest potential: ". . . religious ideas . . . are in architecture the most important and comprehensive."[43] In a religious edifice, regardless of denomination, the architect was confronted with the task embodying the highest ideals of mankind. In dissecting the program of the Christian church, Eidlitz again echoed German aesthetic theory. The Greek temple, conceived as a house for a god, was an architecture of the exterior, intended to impress and awe the people, who would never see its interior. The Christian church on the other hand, was an architecture of both exterior and interior, intended both to embody the mystery of God and to provide an interior space for prayer. The historical evolution of the Christian church, including the development of the nave, aisles, columns, arch, and pointed arch, was toward a perfected form that combined artistic and technical excellence. The programmatic goal of the church to "[feel] our own insignificance in the house of God," as Eidlitz put it, found its purest expression in the Gothic form with its combination of mathematically precise engineering and sublime evocation of light and shadow. The Gothic, he concluded, still provided the ultimate model for Christian architecture because of the centuries that had been dedicated to its perfection: "Through a space of twelve centuries, devoted men of deep religious feeling have in succession struggled to produce what we now see before us."[44]

This is yet another instance where Eidlitz appears to conform to mainstream architectural trends: Gothic churches sprang up everywhere in America beginning in the 1830s and '40s. There was Upjohn's Anglican Gothic and his more informal carpenter Gothic, transmitted through his books and mail-order plans. The New-York Ecclesiological Society propagated standards for the proper design of Episcopal churches through its journal the *New York Ecclesiologist*.[45] There was the Catholic Gothic of cathedrals from Texas and Louisiana to Baltimore, formal and opulent. And then there was evangelical Gothic, of the Low Church Episcopalians, Presbyterians, Congregationalists, and Baptists. Each denomination, or even more accurately, each congregation, had its own particular impetus in its adoption of the style, and these rationales were not necessarily compatible with each other.[46]

But Eidlitz crafted his pro-Gothic position in a distinct way. His appropriation of the Gothic would seem to have its sources in Ruskinian associationism: the historical connection between church and the evolution of the Gothic style is reason enough for its continued use. But Eidlitz specifically rejected Ruskin as a theorist because of his dependence on overly emotional and dogmatic religious sentiment.[47] His position has more in common with Friedrich von Schlegel's widely read essay on Gothic architecture that used a more carefully reasoned geographic and cultural analysis of the Gothic cathedral to assert its status as symbol of Christian, specifically Catholic, spirituality.[48] But as a nonobservant Jew, Eidlitz's approach to the design of Christian churches is particularly intriguing because of his broad and objectively intellectual approach to the contentious issue. It was not an Episcopalian, Presbyterian, or Catholic problem, but a *Christian* problem. Ruskin's and Upjohn's Anglicanism and Pugin's, Schlegel's, and Reichensperger's Catholicism made their analyses of style in religious architecture less *rational* to Eidlitz. His reasoning has much more in common with the cool rationalism of Viollet-le-Duc. Both, to borrow a phrase from Sir John Summerson, thought their way through "the romantic attraction of style to a philosophic point of view applicable to buildings at all times." But here again, a crucial difference separates them. Viollet's passionate argument for the structural rationalism of the Gothic stemmed in part from nationalism and a devotion to the cultural patrimony of France's cathedrals.[49] In America, Eidlitz had been freed from these religious and nationalistic strictures. His more detached perspective left him at liberty to contemplate religion and the nature of God as abstract and universal ideas. Unlike his brother Marc and other members of his family, he never converted to Catholicism and seems never to have joined a particular church. As an architect, his understanding of religion was agnostic, filled with a reverence for the church's overarching purpose if not at all for its particularities.

He was well aware that his clients saw the differences between religions as crucial to church design, noting sardonically in a later speech to the AIA that "the architect must be churchman, Presbyterian, Methodist and Baptist at the same time, to say nothing of the shades and variations of either of these sects which he is called upon to bring out in bold relief."[50] But Eidlitz, practic-

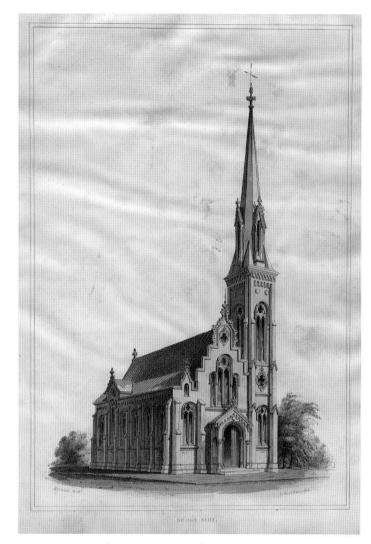

2.17 James Renwick, Jr., Design XVIII for a Congregational Church, perspective. As published in the Congregational Church's 1853 sample plan book: *A Book of Plans for Churches and Parsonages.*

ing as an American architect without allegiance to a personal faith, found himself freed from the religious restrictions and codifications of his youth and his homeland. "Religion," he wrote, "has always been the greatest and most fruitful motive for the construction of monuments. All religions centre upon the existence of a super Being, who regulates and governs the universe; yet, how various the conceptions of the Deity!"[51] The spiritual commonalities of the various denominations overrode their liturgical idiosyncrasies.

2.18 Second Congregational Church of Greenwich, Greenwich, Connecticut, 1856–58. Photograph ca. 1879.

Eidlitz designed churches for both urban and rural Presbyterians and Episcopalians, but he received his largest number of commissions from Congregationalists. With his mix of pragmatism and aestheticism, he was ideally suited to work with their no-nonsense ministers and building committees. In general, these clients, like Rev. Tyng at St. George's, were wary of the perceived excesses of the Catholic and Episcopalian churches and sought to create sanctuaries that could accommodate worshipers with minimal fanfare.[52] New England Congregationalists were descended from English and Scottish forbears who had suffered persecution for their beliefs at the hands of the Anglican clergy. They retained a deep suspicion of a clergy with too much authority and a church with too materialistic an outlook. Their churches were run by committees rather than clergy and practiced a Calvinist brand of discipline over members. They privileged the members of the church to make decisions often reserved, in other denominations, for the minister or priest and insisted on a community image of hard work and egalitarianism. By the mid nineteenth century, though Congregationalists had dominated New England's religious landscape, encroaching competition from Unitarians and even from Presbyterians, both congregations perceived to be less dogmatically severe, had begun to draw members away from the church.[53] Many congregations turned to new church buildings as a means of attracting and keeping their members.

In response to this new spate of church building, the newly organized national convention of the Congregational Church defined its principles in an 1853 book published to provide sample plans and instructions to congregations seeking to build new sanctuaries.[54] Their instructions, in keeping with the tenor of their faith, were eminently practical: choose a good site, use durable materials. On the issue of style, the church was equally practical, refusing to encourage their followers to choose between the two possibilities, the Greek and Gothic styles. "Let us have both," they intoned.[55] James Renwick, Jr., and Richard Upjohn, among others, provided sample plans and elevations ranging from simple wooden edifices with Gibbs-inspired steeples to more elaborate Romanesque concoctions; the Romanesque,

2.19 Second Congregational Church of Greenwich, aerial view, ca. 1954. The rounded apse-like area at the rear is a later addition that contains offices and meeting rooms, not an extension of the sanctuary.

many of the architects like Upjohn personally felt, was more appropriate to the Congregational faith than the High Church Gothic (fig. 2.17). Eidlitz later attributed the strangely crimped spire at the Church of the Pilgrims in Brooklyn to Upjohn's belief that "Presbyterians were not entitled to Architecture" (see fig. 1.10).[56]

Eidlitz designed five Congregational churches along the Gold Coast of Connecticut. Three of them, in Greenwich, Stratford, and New London, aptly illustrate Eidlitz's application of his principles of church design.

2.20 First Congregational Church, Stratford, Connecticut (1858–59). This view shows the church as it originally appeared before the tower and spire were remodeled to what was considered to be a more dignified Gibbs-like classicism.

Each church fits a different model: the New London church is German Romanesque; in Greenwich (1856–59), these German tendencies are balanced against an Upjohn-like vision of the English parish church, resulting in a more picturesque and rambling composition; and finally Stratford (1858–59) found Eidlitz working in a Carpenter Gothic, with simple wooden framing elaborating the structure of the building. None of these churches look particularly alike on the exterior beyond their adherence to a generally longitudinal plan with seating galleries and an bell tower on some scale. The constant, despite variations in proportions, materials, and ornamentation, is a focus on what Eidlitz called the "loftiness" of the structure, in which "the tendency of the structure must be continually upwards." As an

architect of religious buildings, Eidlitz viewed his role as giving a physical expression to the ideals of each congregation. In his approach to these church designs, Eidlitz vigorously pursued the idea that the notion of "God" was constant, expressed by "the infinite above," and that other aspects of the building were subordinate to this expansive notion of space.[57]

In Greenwich, the Second Congregational Church's building committee acknowledged that the church seemed to be losing its appeal to the community. Attendance and membership were down and a new church building, it was hoped, would draw straying church members back to the flock. To that end, the building committee decided on a stone church with a high tower that would express Greenwich's prosperity and success (figs. 2.18, 2.19). Though there was some dissent, with some church members feeling the resulting design was "too fine for a farming community," Eidlitz's design, supported by a detailed plaster model he had crafted, won the day and was accepted in 1856 with the provision that the building not cost more than a very substantial $32,500 (about $800,000 in today's dollars). To ensure adherence to this budget, Robert W. Mead, a church member, who was not a mason or builder, bid the contract himself, pledging not to charge the church more than the contracted amount, no matter how much it cost out of his own pocket. The resulting pride in the building was such that Mead's tombstone paraphrases Sir Christopher Wren's own inscription in St. Paul's Cathedral: SI MONUMENTUM CIRCUMSPICE (If you would see his monument, look about). Eidlitz also ultimately designed Mead's home in Greenwich, despite the fact that the total cost for the church eventually reached over $46,000.[58] An aerial view emphasizes the disconnection between the nave, bell tower, and stair tower, pulled even further apart than the Pittsfield church.

In Stratford, the congregation became weary of worshiping in a ramshackle building. But they also did not wish to spend an extravagant sum on a new building. Eidlitz proposed a wooden church for reasons of economy; he was never enthusiastic about the material as exterior cladding because of its lack of durability (fig. 2.20). The building committee, while pleased with Eidlitz's designs, negotiated with him about the details in order to control costs even further: both the length and width of the nave were reduced, the quality of finish on the interior of the spire was reduced, and the decorative scheme of the stained-glass windows in the sanctuary was simplified.[59] In the end, the church cost about $17,000, a sum that the congregation paid off easily without resorting to mortgages or loans.[60]

In each case, the exterior of the church was designed to reflect the ambitions of the congregation: the materials, the height of spires, the scale, were all chosen by the building committee. It was left to Eidlitz to create the public aspect from the chosen ingredients. The design of the interiors was in all cases done by Eidlitz in keeping with his theoretical programmatic division of the church into exterior and interior functions. Following the pattern begun at St. George's, the exterior style of the church did not determine the interior. Despite the variation in the grandeur of their exteriors, both the Greenwich and the Stratford churches had rustic interiors, much like those at both New London and Pittsfield, with exposed wooden beams, dark stains, and simple patterns in the woodwork (fig. 2.21). Wooden galleries with simple posts lined the naves, with ceilings supported by open trusswork. Each had a choir loft above the entry porch. There were important variations in plan, to be sure, but the feel and stylistic detailing of each church's interior is remarkably similar.

The interiors of the Connecticut churches were based on the traditional longitudinal sanctuary, included the seating galleries typical of low-church sanctuaries, and originally had simple stained-glass windows designed by Eidlitz. But the arrangement of vestigial transepts and the relationship of the pulpit to the congregation's space demonstrate Eidlitz's search for a new physical expression for the pragmatic tenets of the Congregationalists. Eidlitz took the egalitarian relationship between clergy and congregation as a starting point for designing the interior of each church and sought to create an interior space that was unified rather than hierarchical. The spaces are boxlike, with very little to suggest that the apse end of the church contains any special privilege.

The overall effect of each, despite variations in scale,

2.21 Second Congregational Church of Greenwich, interior view of nave.

is similar to that of St. George's: the volume of the space strikes the viewer first, and the building's exposed structure serves only to heighten the sense of an interior unity. At no point do the trusses, stencil work, brackets, or balconies distract from or encroach upon the sense of unified volume. As Brooks pointed out, by comparison to Upjohn's stylistically similar interiors, Eidlitz's have a greater sense of calm, with a greater emphasis placed on the space than on the ornament. These interior spaces show Eidlitz at his best: making small modifications to traditional design that refine its ability to express the "idea" behind the building. Eidlitz may have valued tradition, but he was by no means conservative in its interpretation. To be valid to the present, traditions needed to be updated, modified, and retooled to reflect modern conditions. In his Congregational churches, he broke the plane that had long separated priest and congregation by emphasizing volume.

Eidlitz, like his Congregationalist clients, was opposed to the use of unnecessary ornament. But this did not mean that Eidlitz, or the Congregationalists for that matter, was entirely opposed to it. Eidlitz, for his part, thought that the strictures against ornament in Protes-

2.22 Christ Church Cathedral, St. Louis, Missouri (1859–67), as built, showing front façade and bell tower as designed and built by Kivas Tully in 1911–12. HABS MO,96-SALU,89-1.

tant churches were too extreme. In 1859, Henry Ward Beecher, certainly the most famous Congregational minister, issued a call for a new building for Plymouth Church, his congregation in Brooklyn. With his immense popularity, the extremely plain church built on Orange Street in 1849 by Joseph Wells had become too small.[61] Eidltiz had apparently been asked to suggest a new design for the church before the public competi-

tion and had produced a "double-apsed clerestory such as some of the great Rhenish abbeys show," but Beecher had rejected it, stating, "What's the use? After me, you'll get nobody to fill it."[62] Eidlitz subsequently refused to participate in the competition, publicly excoriated Beecher's programmatic requirements, first to the AIA and then in the pages of the *Crayon*. Beecher, in keeping with his revolutionary stance on the individual

2.23 Christ Church Cathedral, perspective drawing by Eidlitz, ca. 1859. Avery Architectural and Fine Arts Library, Columbia University in the City of New York.

2.24 Christ Church Cathedral, nave looking toward the pulpit. Undated photograph by Emil Boehl. Missouri Historical Society, St. Louis.

relationship between God and supplicant, had asked for a sanctuary to seat 6,000 based on "secular" and not "church" architecture. Eidlitz questioned the wisdom of the preacher's desire for a secularized, ornament-free sanctuary and returned again to the idea of "expression."

It cannot be possible that a house of worship should be desired by any one without an adequate archi-

tectural expression. Besides, the high reputation of the pastor of Plymouth Church for love of Art and Nature, guarantees a desire on his part, at least, for an appropriate architecture, if not as an auxiliary to his teaching, at least as a necessity to his refined taste, which must spurn nakedness or impropriety of form in every object. . . . I maintain that the architecture so eminently successful in expressing the strong features

2.25 St. George's Episcopal Church, New York, with repainted interior, designed by Eidlitz and executed by Louis Cohn, 1866–67. Photograph by A. Moore, 1909. LC-USZ62-127578.

of *the church* contains sufficient elements and pliability to express every phase of the human mind.[63]

While severity and simplicity were well within Eidlitz's range, a completely unornamented box, such as Beecher sought, was not worthy of the church or of architecture. Beecher received over twenty entries, from the likes of Hunt and the immensely talented Jacob Wrey Mould, designer of many of Central Park's bridges, and though the competition was won by the relatively unknown Charles Duggin, the new building was never built. When the *Crayon* published an article by Eidlitz's friend John Durand excoriating the competition and architects' entries—with the exception of Mould's, which he admired—Eidlitz no doubt felt vindicated.[64]

The design for Christ Church Cathedral in St. Louis (1859–67), for an Episcopalian congregation, shows Eidlitz's mediation between these two extremes in church architecture. The building was not finished on the exterior according to Eidlitz's plans because of the interruptions in cash flow and labor caused by the Civil War (figs. 2.22, 2.23). The façade of the church in particular looks very little as Eidlitz designed it, as the narthex and bell tower were designed by Kivas Tully and added in 1911–12. Photographs of the church taken during construction indicated that Eidlitz substantially simplified the design in the 1860s; how he might have finished the façade is unknown. Eidlitz traveled to St. Louis to discuss the commission, which the building committee had deliberated at great length. The committee had invited plans from Richard Upjohn, C. N. Otis of Buffalo, and John Notman of Philadelphia, as well as Eidlitz. Otis, the least well known of the four, willingly sent in his drawings, but Notman refused to participate in the competition without payment, and Upjohn, after a campaign of letter writing, did the same. Eidlitz, acting on professional principle but manipulating its bounds, refused to participate without payment, but stated he would refund the money if he won; he traveled to St. Louis as part of his campaign to gain the commission. One imagines he was successful in his bid both because of his creative application of professional standards and because the rector was Montgomery Schuyler's second cousin and namesake, the Very Reverend Montgomery Schuyler.

As with many churches, the desire for both humility and finery created a potential for misunderstandings. The committee wished their architect to use both the "strictest economy" and the "most endurable materials" in order to create "something creditable to the Parish" that also was "comfortable and adapted to the present as well as the future."[65] Eidlitz presented them with his most modernized Gothic interior, stripped down to its most basic elements. At Christ Church, he finally had the chance to work on a large-scale interior in stone (Fig. 2.24). As a High Episcopal church, the strictures for plainness that Eidlitz had been working with were not as firmly held; here the watchword was instead economy. As in his other churches, Eidlitz provided a longitudinal nave with a transept that did not extend beyond the width of the aisles. At Christ Church, there was a true apse, with the communion table set inside and the pulpit set slightly forward and to the side. He eliminated the seating galleries in the nave in favor of true aisles, but in an unconventional twist, included them in the transepts, where the view of the minister was superb. Where in other churches Eidlitz had avoided heavy piers in the nave in order to keep the view unimpeded, at Christ Church the piers are massive. But

in keeping with his usual aesthetic, they were simple: they have no capital, no fluting or carving of any kind. They rose straight from the floor and into the pointed arches of the nave articulated only by a painted band of floriated ornament that emphasized the springing of the arches. The wooden roof above rose in a steeply angled pitch whose height was further exaggerated by the almost vertical trusses that supported them. The area under the peak of the roof was dark, unlit by the clerestory below it, and contrasted with the more brightly illuminated and light-colored stone below, creating the play of light and shadow that Eidlitz so poetically spoke about in 1858. The interior was utterly, monastically plain—unheard of for a major Gothic church in nineteenth-century America.[66] The combination of uncarved stone and simple wood was Eidlitz's solution to the need for both the highest-quality permanent materials and economy.

While we unfortunately know little about the decoration of most of Eidlitz's interiors from this era because they do not survive in pristine state, ornament was integral to Eidlitz's conception of an organic and expressive architecture, for ornament gave a building spiritual life and allowed it to speak to and teach its users. A building stripped to its bare functional and constructional minimum was not architecture at all. In the puritanical Connecticut churches, Eidlitz's opportunity for ornamental experimentation was minimal, but he took advantage when he could, exposing structural rafters and trusses and emphasizing the load-bearing posts and columns by adding greater detail. The spires, particularly the openwork stone spire at New London, used simple constructional geometry to emphasize their massiveness rather than their delicacy. He introduced color and pattern in the diamond-pane windows, which kept the view of the parishioners on the interior spiritual world and also relieved the severity of the plain stained wood of the interior walls, pews, and ceiling. But these ornamental elements did more than enliven otherwise dull spaces and surfaces. Eidlitz intended his combination of spatial innovation, structural honesty, and ornamental elaboration to be edifying and inspiring. While this sounds like an echo of Ruskin's devout medievalism, it was actually

2.26 Church of the Pilgrims, Brooklyn, with repainted interior, designed by Eidlitz and executed by Louis Cohn, 1871. *Congregational Quarterly* (1871).

seemed to undermine the original focus on the simple figure of a man preaching beside a table. The murals were executed in a manner very similar to that described at the Brooklyn Academy of Music and at the Produce Exchange, as highlights to the structure of the building that made the contours of construction, the transition from one surface to the next, more readable. Gilded bands of geometric ornament in a medieval Puginesque mode traced the line of the windows and chancel arch. Below these bands was a repeated pattern of overlapping circles with infill of floriated ornament in dark colors, and above the chancel arch repeating diamonds also infilled with flowering tendrils appeared in a lighter palette. Perhaps symbolizing Tyng's continued emphasis on biblical text, a continuous band of text ran along all four walls of the church, curving around the frames of the arches. Only portions are readable in surviving photographs, but a phrase from the book of Luke framed the chancel arch: GLORY TO GOD IN THE HIGHEST, ON EARTH PEACE, GOODWILL TO MEN; and another from John, I AM THE LIGHT OF THE WORLD, HE THAT FOLLOWETH ME SHALL NOT WALK IN DARKNESS, BUT SHALL HAVE THE LIGHT OF LIFE, encircled the second window on the northern wall. Eidlitz also worked with Cohn on his remodeling of the Church of the Pilgrims in Brooklyn, where the painting again gave new expression to the compartmentalized framework established by the Upjohn-designed system of wooden rafters and columns (fig. 2.26). The ceiling was painted a deep blue with golden stars, the walls with Renaissance-inspired roundels and arches in keeping with Upjohn's original Italianate design.[67] In these two interiors, the different approach to interior space and structure that separated Upjohn and Eidlitz is vividly clear.

While Eidlitz explicitly addressed his concerns and justifications for his Christian commissions, the motivations behind his synagogue designs are more obscure. While Eidlitz was on firm ground in using the Gothic as a form language for his churches, choosing an appropriate point of stylistic departure for the two synagogues he designed was a more complex issue. For both the Shaaray Tefila (1846–48, in partnership with Blesch) and the Temple Emanu-El (1866–68), Eidlitz used exotic,

part of Eidlitz's more complex and still-evolving rationale of organic idealism.

After a disastrous fire heavily damaged St. George's, Eidlitz's reconstruction in the late 1860s largely put the building back the way it was with one major exception: he hired Louis Cohn, a German painter with whom he would work repeatedly, to paint the upper walls of the church hall (fig. 2.25). The effect was dramatically different than the original preaching-box interior, drawing attention to the surfaces of the walls in a way that unusual styles: the so-called Byzantine for the former, and the Moorish for the latter. Scholars have pondered the reasons that reform congregations would choose such unusual and highly ornamental styles.[68] In the case of Eidlitz's two designs, the choice seems to have been made intentionally to set the congregations apart from other religious institutions in the city.

Blesch & Eidlitz's work on the Shaaray Tefila commission began in 1846, with the cornerstone laid in the midst of work on St. George's. Synagogue architecture in the United States was in its infancy, with examples like Charleston's (see fig. 1.7) erected in much the same Greek Revival style as some Christian churches. In 1840s New York, many Jewish congregations simply took over and remodeled churches as Christian congregations moved to larger or more desirable locations. Eidlitz, for example, in 1847 redesigned and refurnished the Methodist Chrystie Street Church for the Temple Emanu-El, a reform congregation still not wealthy or established enough to build its own home.

Eidlitz and Blesch chose a design derived from the "Byzantic" style for Shaaray Tefila, a German Orthodox congregation led by the eloquent and influential Rev. Samuel Isaacs (fig. 2.27). Born in Holland and raised in London, Isaacs came to the United States in 1839 to lead the B'nai Jeshurun Synagogue, an Orthodox congregation of primarily English Ashkenazim. Isaacs sought to enforce the observance of the Sabbath strictly and lost the support of many members. He and his supporters thus withdrew from B'nai Jeshurun and in about 1845 founded Shaaray Tefila "on pure orthodox principles."[69] From the pulpit there and in the pages of the *Jewish Messenger*, which he founded, Isaacs fought the growing tide of Reform Judaism that would begin in earnest in the 1850s with the influx of German Jews fleeing the 1848 revolutions. Interestingly, Shaaray Tefila appears to have been the only congregation that knew of Eidlitz's Judaism, as he was acknowledged as an "Israelite," surely a major factor in obtaining the commission.[70]

In an 1846 report on the imminent construction of the building, two reasons were given for the importance of the Byzantine style to the congregation: first, its association with the synagogues built by Portuguese Jews

2.27 Blesch & Eidlitz, Shaaray Tefila, New York, 1846–48. Lithograph, Jacques Judah Lyons Collection, American Jewish Historical Association.

during their persecution in the Middle Ages and, second, the very novelty of the style, which would set the synagogue apart from other existing religious edifices and publicly pronounce the success of Jews in America. Just what the term "Byzantic" means in the context of the design is puzzling. Byzantine, as used today, would refer to the round-arched, often domed architecture of the ongoing Roman empire centered on Constantinople, modern Istanbul. But as used in 1846, "Byzantine," as in the case of St. George's, could refer to the round-arched Romanesque or, in other cases, to the Moorish architecture of Spain as well. The architecture of Shaaray

Tefila was, in fact, a blend of Rundbogenstil with an early Christian basilica, and the building was apparently ornamented inside in a way that evoked the polychromy and dense ornament of the Moorish. Moorish and Saracenic forms were associated with the Sephardic Jews of Portugal and Spain—Byzantine forms, while equally exotic in New York, came from the East, not the West. Since the congregation was Ashkenazi, with origins in the Rhineland and eastern Europe, and not Sephardic (as was the first Jewish synagogue in New York, Shearith Israel), this confusion of Byzantine with Portuguese and Spanish form seems somewhat puzzling. When the congregation built a new synagogue by Henry Fernbach in 1868–69, it maintained again that the building had Byzantine origins, calling it "Byzantine Moresque."[71]

But the contradiction can perhaps be explained by the second reason for the buildings' style: it was its exoticism that was important. Nothing quite like the building's mixture of Byzantine, Rundbogenstil, and Moorish styles had been built in New York—and the design was intentionally dramatic, rooted in a desire for the building to reflect the ideas and actions inherent to its purpose. The commentator stated, "On looking at the front of the pile, the spectator will at once receive the impression that the building is intended for a place of worship, not of the poetical deities of the Greeks, nor the pompous trinity of the Christians, but of the mighty God of the Jews," a prefiguration of Eidlitz's later analysis of the "various conceptions of the deity."[72] The symmetrical façade did indeed portray an image of strength, with a large central bay, about 42 feet high, flanked by two smaller projecting aisles at about half that height, 24 feet. The lack of vertical towers deemphasized the tripartite organization of the façade, making it far more monolithic and evocative of that single "mighty God."

The composition is clearly related to Albert Rosengarten's Kassel synagogue (1836–39), published in the *Allgemeine Bauzeitung* in 1840. Rosengarten, a Jew, wrote a clear stylistic analysis of the synagogue form, arguing against the Gothic, classical, and Egyptian styles and embracing the Rundbogenstil and the early Christian basilica.[73] Blesch & Eidlitz's design clearly follows this model: at St. George's, Blesch composed a flat façade, its surfaces modeled only by the central circular window and projecting corbel brackets under the eaves of the projecting gable roof. Lacking heavenward-reaching towers, the center bay of the tripartite composition dominates, echoing the interior arrangement of early Christian basilicas. It also makes the synagogue a decidedly more earth-bound composition. The façade, at once grand and solemn, was well in keeping with the wishes of the congregation's rabbi, the Reverend Isaacs. At the ceremonial laying of the synagogue's cornerstone, he expressed his clear wishes for the new temple to express the prosperity and success of the congregation but also its humility: "The sole object of building a religious edifice should be for prayer to God, instruction to man, not for man-worship, for the clod of earth to deify himself, but a place for the earthworm to pour forth his heart's grief, to seek his God, and to spiritualize his own condition."[74]

No depictions of the interior of the synagogue have survived. We have only reviewers' impressions left to give a sense of Eidlitz's scheme, which was based in his own personal knowledge of the traditions of Judaism. As in St. George's, the contrast between exterior and interior was pronounced. The austerity of the temple's exterior disappeared, replaced with a richness of ornament and visible complexity of construction:

> The appearance of the Synagogue on the occasion was truly grand: the massy pillars supporting the groined oak ceiling, unsurpassed in this city, the wide-spreading arches, between which were seen the galleries filled with God's best gift to man, the real ornaments of creation, the mothers, daughters, and sisters of Judah, the splendid appearance of the ark, the doors of which of carved oak were covered with a most superb curtain, . . . the unique and truly elegant receptacle for the perpetual light, one of the most beautiful things in the whole Synagogue, . . . the elaborately carved oak pulpit and reading desk, and, in fact, the *tout ensemble* of the building presented a *coup d'oeil* on which the eye rested with gratification, and the mind reflected on with a fervent gratitude to the Giver of all good, that we had been permitted to partake of so truly blessed a consummation.[75]

The result was an interior space similar in layout to galleried Protestant churches, with aisle, nave, galleries, apse, and pulpit, but with each of the portions put to entirely different use. While the focus of the interior was clearly on the ark, Eidlitz eschewed the simple cantilevers of St. George's in favor of an elaborate system of carved wooden columns and rafters that met in a carved flower design. The simple roof rafters of St. George's transformed into a fully "groined ceiling." The elevated galleries functioned, as in all Orthodox synagogues, as segregated seating for women, and it is clear that the reviewer found the beauty of the galleries' construction an appropriate framework for the beauty of the women themselves. He went on to comment that light admitted through the clerestory windows and shining through the vaulting heightened the effect of mystery, creating contrast between the patterned light above and the solemnity of the dark below.

Another reviewer in the same journal, though, suggested that the unusual and elaborate woodwork, as well as the sheer volume of the interior space, might distract from its functionality:

> As it is, we may safely say, that it is by far the finest Synagogue in America, though this does not say that that it is the best adapted for the purpose for which it is designed. We should judge that ordinarily it will require much exertion in the minister to be distinctly heard all over the building, owing to the great height in the centre, and the declivity of the galleries, together with the many angles in the ceiling. In fact, the style of building is so new to us, and so little idea had we of the interior arrangements, that we have not as yet been able to make up our mind, whether to approve it for a Synagogue or not. But there can be no question that it is a beautiful structure, and highly creditable to the architect who designed it . . .[76]

Regardless of whether or not they liked the building, all reviewers agreed upon the "newness" of the design: its façade, ornament, and space. No one who described the building had seen anything quite like it before. It defied expectations and seemed to proclaim a new era

for synagogue architecture and for Jews in America: "the whole will be calculated to turn the mind to the sublime, and to spiritualize the feeling."[77] This kind of bold message and "newness" was clearly the kind of expressiveness that Eidlitz aimed for in his architecture.

The commission for Temple Emanu-El presented a slightly different conceptual problem. The Reform congregation, like the Congregationalists and Episcopalians Eidlitz worked with, was intent on having its building reflect its revisionist ideology. As the commission for St. George's had given a public face to the Low Church Episcopalian movement, the commission for Temple Emanu-El was for a landmark building, one that would represent the new face of the Reform movement in the face of Orthodoxy and Christianity. Temple Emanu-El was the first Reform congregation in New York, established in 1847, and was by the 1860s the largest and most prosperous in the city. Though the congregation had started small, under the leadership of Dr. Samuel Adler, a prominent German leader of the Reform movement, with the influx of Germanic immigrants, it grew quickly during the 1850s. Central to the Reform movement was the desire to modernize their mode of worship: services were conducted in German at Temple Emanu-El instead of in Hebrew (they were in English at the Orthodox Shaaray Tefila), and myriad other changes were made to the liturgy. Observation of the Sabbath was far more relaxed, the main point of contention between Isaacs and his Shaaray Tefila adherents and relative newcomers like Adler.[78]

In terms of architecture, Reform synagogues required a new conception of space, one that resembled the longitudinal arrangements of Christian, and more particularly Protestant, churches. While in traditional synagogues the bimah had been placed centrally, surrounded by individual seats so men could come and go, and pray and study individually, the Reform temple placed the bimah at the eastern end of a nave near the pulpit and ark, and arranged pews in rows for a group- and sermon-oriented service. The women's seating galleries, traditionally screened, became more open to the nave, allowing women to see the services below. And in some Reform temples, like the Temple Emanu-El, women were allowed to mingle with the men, sharing pews. In this larger context, it is clear that Eidlitz used his experience designing these kinds of buildings—longitudinal boxes with seating galleries—in his spatial conception of the Temple Emanu-El. Again, Eidlitz viewed the commonalities of religious experience as more important than their differences, and the opportunity to demonstrate this, by designing a synagogue using the same fundamental spatial and structural template as a Christian church, was a powerful demonstration of this principle.

When the members of Temple Emanu-El decided to move to a new synagogue in the early 1860s, they invited designs from several prestigious firms, hoping both to elicit the best possible plans and to earn the respect of New York's religious communities. With a site in a prosperous neighborhood at Fifth Avenue and Forty-Third Street (today half a block from the New York Public Library), the congregation clearly intended to make an impressive architectural statement (fig. 2.28). Eidlitz formed a new partnership to craft his entry: Eidlitz & Fernbach. Henry Fernbach (1829–83) was Jewish and had emigrated in the mid-1850s from Berlin, where he had studied at the Bauakademie. Where Eidlitz's earlier partnership with Blesch had been with a more experienced architect, this one was with a less experienced one. Eidlitz and Fernbach worked together only on this design, so it is difficult to determine what exactly motivated Eidlitz to collaborate. Eidlitz perhaps understood that as a lapsed Jew, having a partner who actively worshiped could stand the firm in good stead. Or, he appreciated that Fernbach's more recent time in Berlin made him conversant in the latest developments in German synagogue design and thus an even more valuable asset in the competition.[79] Eidlitz was not, as has been mentioned, a member of Temple Emanu-El.[80] Whatever the reasons for the partnership, it was a successful one, for Eidlitz & Fernbach, in winning the commission, bested some of the finest architects in New York, including Richard Michell Upjohn (Richard's son), Renwick & Sands, Alexander Saeltzer, and the relatively unknown Julius Munckwitz.[81] None of the other invited designers had experience with synagogues; the building committee had instead considered them because of their

potential to add to the prestige and legitimacy of the design in the eyes of the public. Eidlitz's reputation as a designer of prominent Christian churches, particularly St. George's and the Broadway Tabernacle (see chap. 3), was thus an equal boost in the competition. His brother, Marc Eidlitz, now converted to Catholicism, was the contractor. The cornerstone was laid on October 30, 1866, for a building that was to cost a reported $600,000.

Eidlitz & Fernbach's design for Temple Emanu-El used Gothic structure and plan combined with ornamental schemes from Moorish and so-called "Saracenic" sources (fig. 2.28). It was a masterpiece of Eidlitz's career, an exercise in every way of his ideas about organic expression. The exterior of the building had a Gothic cast with a twin-towered, rose-windowed westwork on its front façade. But in its details—in the polychromed pointed arches topping the nave windows; in the awkwardly proportioned minaretlike towers, 170 feet high, covered in arabesque relief carving—it was Moorish. In section, it resembled early Christian churches, with a central nave rising 72 feet, well above the level of the galleried aisles, to provide for ample clerestory lighting. In plan, the synagogue was Gothic, with a traditional longitudinal plan complete with full transept. The cross-shaped plan reflected the Reform movement's concern with modernizing religious practice. It was immense: the ground floor held 1,800 congregants, with the minimal balconies holding an additional 500. The forbidding, monolithic exterior belied the interior, where the building dissolved into a fantasy of ornate Saracenic and Moorish carved detail, rapturous color, and reflected light. It was a study in contrasts between heavy and light, darkness and luminosity, unadorned planarity and detailed ornament. Dramatic and unconventional shifts in color, texture, and scale produced exactly the kind of aggressively engaging architecture to which Eidlitz aspired.

As with Shaaray Tefila's earlier exoticism, justified by a specious reference to Sephardic precedent, scholars still debate the precise reasoning behind the use of Moorish ornament in both Orthodox and Reform synagogues. Beginning with the first "Moorish" synagogue, designed

2.28 Eidlitz & Fernbach, Temple Emanu-El, Fifth Avenue and 43rd Street, 1866–68. Photograph taken summer, ca. 1885.
Collection of the New-York Historical Society, neg#69103.

2.29 Eduard Knoblauh, Oranienburgstrasse Temple, Berlin, 1859–65. *Illustrated London News* (September 1866).

2.30 Dedication of the Temple Emanu-El, 1868. *Frank Leslie's Illustrated Newspaper* (October 3, 1868). LC-USZ62-75926.

by Blesch's mentor Friedrich von Gärtner at Ingenheim (1830–32), many Reform congregations in Europe utilized these exotic forms in their synagogues in an effort to embrace a romanticized vision of themselves as Semitic or Oriental in origin. While this may seem contradictory in today's terms, the mid-nineteenth century embrace of Jewish ethnic identity created a sense of community pride in the Gilded Age. The Moorish forms were clearly unusual in European and American cities, and gave the buildings a character distinct from other re-

ligious edifices. Visual difference was desirable to many congregations in a period when the legal conditions for Western and Central European Jews was improving, and they quickly began to build exotic temples: Semper's Dresden synagogue (1838–40), often considered the progenitor of the trend, was followed in Vienna by Ludwig von Förster's Leopoldstadt Synagogue (1853–58) and in Prague by the "Spanish" Synagogue (1867–68). For the United States, the most influential synagogue was Berlin's Oranienburgerstrasse Temple, designed by Eduard Knoblauch and built 1859–65 (fig. 2.29). The Berlin synagogue was universally acclaimed and spurred congregations in America to follow its general aesthetic, with the Isaac M. Wise Temple in Cincinnati leading the way in 1865, followed quickly by Temple Emanu-El (fig. 2.30).

Some have suggested that Fernbach was the author of the Moorish details of the building because his time in Berlin would have made him more familiar with the new Moorish-style synagogues. Because of a lack of knowledge that Eidlitz was Jewish, it has also been suggested that because Fernbach was Jewish, he would have been more comfortable designing a synagogue.[82] But Berlin's Oranienburgerstrasse Temple was built after Fernbach left for the United States, and Eidlitz would thus have been as familiar with it as Fernbach was. Furthermore, Eidlitz, being Jewish and extremely well read, would have been quite aware of current trends in European and German design and knowledgeable about Moorish design in general. Through Blesch and their work on Shaaray Tefila, Eidlitz became aware of the shift toward exoticism in synagogue design very early, and more than likely was familiar with von Gärtner's Moorish Ingenheim design. The *Allgemeine Bauzeitung*, for example, carried occasional color plates depicting the ornament of the Near East; Eidlitz also admired the work of Owen Jones, whose illustrated folios of the Alhambra had appeared between 1841 and 1845. Having designed and built P. T. Barnum's mansion Iranistan in 1848, Eidlitz had long been conversant in the creation of orientalized ornament. Upon the building's completion, Eidlitz received all credit for the design in published sources, though the temple seems to have maintained a closer relationship with Fernbach, whom they later asked to design a small pastoral residence (unbuilt) in 1877.[83]

Eidlitz, who was far more established in New York architecture, was surely the major designer of the building and its ornamental scheme. Fernbach was a member of the AIA and had numerous occasions to correct those who ascribed the building to Eidlitz exclusively, but he seems not to have taken the opportunity.[84] After Temple Emanu-El, Fernbach went on to design other New York synagogues independently, including the similarly ornate but much smaller Central Synagogue of 1872 (fig. 2.31). Comparison of the Central Synagogue with Temple Emanu-El indicates that Eidlitz gave the temple its overall composition based on the Christian models he had been working with for twenty years. He gave the building a greater mass and solidity than a solo Fernbach

2.31 Henry Fernbach, Central Synagogue, New York, 1872. *Harper's Weekly* (1872).

design might normally obtain; Fernbach's interior for the Central Synagogue also lacked the vivid imagination of Eidlitz's Temple.[85]

The exterior of Temple Emanu-El was composed of heavy ashlar masonry composed of variously colored sandstones from quarries in New Brunswick, New Jersey and Cleveland, Ohio. The planar walls were pierced only by high windows, lending the building a fortresslike air. The building's exterior statement is one of strength, fully in keeping with the Reform congregation's desire to announce its presence and prosperity to New York. The demolition of the temple building in 1927 is a great architectural tragedy, for its interior was, by all accounts, a tour-de-force of color and ornament (fig. 2.32). The

2.32 Temple Emanu-El, interior looking toward the Ark. *AR* (September 1908).

New York Evening Post raved over the design in 1868: "Attractive as the exterior is, the interior far surpasses it. On entering the building we seem transported to another sphere. Here we enter on the realm of color; forms seem to have vanished or to resolve themselves into radiant splendor." On the interior, Eidlitz aimed for the transcendent spirituality of Goethe; the blue, vermilion, and gold shimmering in the light of oil lamps created an ethereality that contradicted the massiveness of the temple's exterior. Only primary colors were used—in keeping with Eidlitz's tenets, no mixed hues appeared. Panels in the ceiling were painted a dark blue and embellished with golden stars, and the arches and walls were painted with yellow, blue, red, black, and white. The *Evening Post*'s reviewer had evidently spoken with Eidlitz before writing his article, for he rhapsodized over the color scheme: "Color as here employed, conforms to natural law, and is therefore a truth in itself. None of its combinations suggests the intellectual perversity associated with the Renaissance symbols so conventionally applied to public and private edifices everywhere."[86]

As with Eidlitz's Gothic designs, there is nothing archeologically correct about his Moorish designs. Photographs of the interior show bands of complex painted geometric patterns interspersed with carved, sculptural variations on the theme. The underside of the arches that framed the seating galleries, for example, were animated with cusped forms created by the intersection of interlocking arches (Fig. 2.33). Based on the visual theme established by the famous interlocking lobes of the arches at the Great Mosque at Cordoba and at the Alhambra, Eidlitz's interpretation was different in character. The interlocking arches were based on segments of circles and thus established a very shallow, rolling visual rhythm. The paired arches of the Tablets of Law that adorned the wall above the ark established another visual motif echoed in the jagged, cusped edges of the arches that spanned the nave. Contrasting with this three-dimensional geometric ornament were painted bands of floriated ornament, flowering vines covering the flat surfaces between the structural elements of the building. Rachel Wischnitzer suggested that Eidlitz's designs for the rose windows of the transepts and main façade derived some of their forms from a recombination of the Shield of David, as he would have seen it in the Altneuschul (Old-New Synagogue) in Prague, and the rose windows in the Cathedral of Burgos in Spain.[87] The arches that spanned the nave alternated in form, one a traditional round-headed arch covered in painted floriated ornament, the other a carved round arch with its bottom edge defined by a reinterpretation of the jagged geometry of muqarnas (fig. 2.34). This kind of formal experimentation is often dismissed as mere eclecticism:

borrowings from disparate sources recombined into a bizarre pastiche. But Eidlitz's experimentation was not mere visual playfulness; it had serious formal implications in evoking the transcendence of the "single mighty God."

The interior space provided Eidlitz an opportunity to mix the prototypes he had been using for the past twenty years to design Christian churches. The temple had a longitudinal nave with a transept that did not extend past the width of the aisles; it also had seating galleries that lined the entire nave below the clerestory. The arrangement of the galleries was, as at St. George's, somewhat innovative, as they were not in this case attached to the exterior walls along their length, but attached only at the corners within each bay unit: to the massive piers on the nave side, and to piers projecting from the exterior walls. This allowed light from the large nave windows, which the galleries somewhat blocked, to enter the building more freely. While most Reform temples were doing away with seating galleries, which had traditionally been set aside as seating for women, at Temple Emanu-El the somewhat peculiar galleries were intended to serve as overflow seating. The temple became so popular, however, that the galleries were nearly always filled, leading to complaints about their impeded views of the ark.

Some criticized the inclusion of a transept in a synagogue; Montgomery Schuyler, in particular, felt it inappropriate to use a Christian form in a Jewish religious space and assumed that the architect must not himself have been Jewish to use such a device. On the other hand, since one of the goals of the Reform movement was to become more mainstream, the use of a recognizable Christian form would have been quite appropriate. On a purely formal level, Eidlitz was clearly interested in the transcendent effects of lighting in this building and the transept allowed extra light to pour in front of the ark and the reader's pulpit. When combined with the hidden windows behind the ark that mysteriously lit the far end of the nave and with the gilded walls, the effect must have been brilliant. And, on the practical side, Reform temples placed the pulpit and reader's desk forward of the ark, and the inclusion of a transept

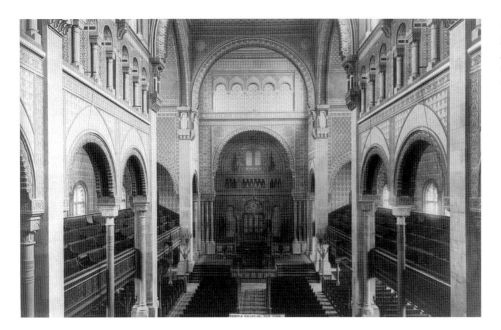

provided a needed ceremonial space.[88] Interestingly, though, when the congregation abandoned the Eidlitz & Fernbach building for a new one on the Upper East Side completed in 1929 by Kohn, Butler, and Stein, they specifically chose a rectangular plan without a transept, finding it more appropriate than the cruciform plan it replaced.[89] When the Eidlitz synagogue was sold and demolished, the congregation also apparently destroyed any records relating to the by-then-beleaguered building.

Temple Emanu-El was immensely successful and became Eidlitz's best-known building in New York. Its opulent interior was a source of fascination to the community at large. Its opening was reported on and illustrated in *Harper's Weekly* and *Scientific American*. The famous diarist George Templeton Strong, an Episcopalian and a parishioner at Trinity Church, made a visit to view the famed interior. William Ware considered it Eidlitz's best work. It was the only building by Eidlitz included in A. J. Bloor's history of New York architecture that he presented to the AIA in 1876.[90] It is ironic that Eidlitz, with his professional focus on Christian churches and his own desire to leave his Jewishness in the past, became most identified with a synagogue.

For while Eidlitz himself privileged religious architecture above all other forms, he clearly struggled against its

conventions. Rather than adhere strictly to the proscriptions of sectarian dogma, he took every opportunity to make small changes in scale, in plan, and, most of all, in conceiving of interior space in order to make the buildings more meaningful. Though today the differences between an Eidlitz-designed church and a more traditional one by Renwick, Withers, or Upjohn may seem slight, the implications of the different approaches led architects in vastly different directions: one that sought to justify the use of traditional forms, as in Trinity Church, and the other that sought to revise them, as in Christ Church Cathedral and Temple Emanu-El.

Eidlitz's focus on the idea of building as the generator of its form, his desire to let organic models of evolution drive architecture, clearly played out in very different ways in different buildings. The exterior trappings of a building, while crucial to its success as an expressive aesthetic object, were subservient to that initial idea. The use of historical styles, which had associative power in his clients and subjects, was an integral part of his search for a new approach to design that could present the striving of American institutions to define their modern world. His presentation of these ideas in essays that are at times highly rational (as in his objective definition of the qualities of the Christian deity) and at others highly romantic (as in his poetic description of the transportative effects of a Gothic church on a worshiper) only amplifies the complexity of his vision. Rather than simply laying out his rules of design by building, Eidlitz attempted to appeal emotionally to his listeners, to *persuade* them of his position. Whether or not this was the best approach to take is debatable, but it does tell us one more important thing about Eidlitz: he passionately believed in architecture and its ability to express the nobility and idealism of mankind. The direct and plainspoken approach of his contemporaries A. J. Downing or Calvert Vaux held little appeal for him. This is perhaps where the similarity to German romanticism and American transcendentalism is greatest: in Eidlitz's style of presentation. Poetic and laden with visual imagery, Eidlitz's language was as idealistic as his building.

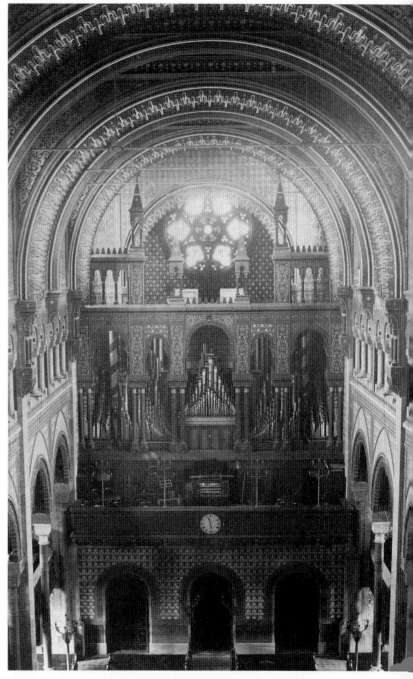

2.34 Temple Emanu-El, interior looking toward entrance and rose window.

3

"BY NO MEANS A REPRESENTATIVE MAN"
Allies and Enemies

THE FORMATION OF THE AMERICAN INSTITUTE OF ARCHITECTS IN
1857 marked a new phase in Eidlitz's career and in the history of American architecture. Prior to this time, despite an earlier, unsuccessful attempt to form a professional group in 1837, American architects had struggled for public recognition of
their unique and specialized design abilities. By forming a professional group, as
many other vocations had done in the early nineteenth century, architects hoped
to distinguish themselves from builders, engineers, and others who were involved
in the creation, but not the artistic design, of buildings. The thirteen New York architects who joined together to form the group, including Eidlitz, Richard Upjohn,
Richard Morris Hunt, and Jacob Wrey Mould, sought a new legitimacy in the eyes
of the public. They focused on tangible things like standard fees and ownership of
their designs and drawings, as well as intangibles like a greater degree of professional
recognition. They wished to be considered as artists instead of tradesmen, as gentlemen instead of mechanics and laborers. Architects that previously had exchanged
ideas through reading or personal associations (like Eidlitz's with Upjohn) now had
new sources and new audiences.[1]

But even as the members sought a general sense of professional legitimacy, they
also sought validation in each other's eyes. The AIA provided a forum for the promotion of the interests of architects as a group. However, the members were immediately competitive with each other. Coming together once or twice a month made
them increasingly aware that they sought the same commissions and participated in

Opposite: See page 92.

the same competitions. Discussions were often heated as the architects attempted to claim their areas of expertise. Detlef Lienau, an architect who was German by birth but French by taste, remarked at the second annual AIA convention that "the diversity of associations, and the consequent diversity of education of the different members of this body, have not only become apparent by the variety of the styles represented in the works produced by the different artists, but also in the expression of different opinions and ideas in the discussion of matters pertaining to Art at our regular meetings . . . our discussions have often been excited, because earnest and sincere."[2] Though Lienau remained optimistic that their common interests would surmount their differences, the meetings of the 1850s and early 1860s achieved few of the AIA's tangible goals, as conflict among members trumped unity.[3]

The period has often been defined by an internecine "battle of styles," a point of view promoted by the reminiscences of those on the "winning" Beaux-Arts team. George B. Post, for example, a student in the Hunt atelier in 1858, later wrote of his time in Hunt's office:

> Examples of good work were so rare that our ideals of perfection were incoherent and doubtful, and were swayed now in one direction and now in another by the literary warfare then prevailing between Gothic and Classic camps. Mediaevalism was sustaining itself by the religious ardor of Pugin and the brilliant rhetoric and poetic imagery of Ruskin. Sentiment was keenly aroused, but discipline was silent. But through the atmosphere, thick with prejudice and controversy, there was an intellectual movement in the midst of it exceedingly attractive to young men of education and artistic instincts.[4]

The "intellectual movement" that Post refers to is the importation of French architectural thinking as embodied first by the Neo-Grec approach to style, but ultimately by the monumental classical grandeur of the École des Beaux-Arts. Eidlitz, a prime figure in the "literary warfare" in America, fought the importation of its ideals at every turn.

The mid-century discussions and disagreements are crucial to a complete understanding of what American architecture would become in the 1880s and 1890s. The lines between organic and Beaux-Arts design principles, between polytechnical and Beaux-Arts educational systems, and between populist and elitist views of the architectural profession were all drawn in the 1850s and '60s. The formation of Richard Morris Hunt's atelier of young and talented architects during 1857, the AIA's first year, was a direct challenge to the potential efficacy of the organization. On the one hand, mature professionals intended to meet, exchange ideas, and promote the future of the profession as a group. And on the other, one member had organized a private school that, by passing on one individual's ideas to the next generation, undercut the larger group's ability to define the future of the American profession.[5] Eidlitz again and again delineated his position on the side of an organic and rational architecture, pitting himself against Richard Morris Hunt and his disciples. Though the list of allies for each pole was fluid during the early years, by 1870 control of the AIA and its theoretical and practical positions was solidly in the hands of the Hunt atelier.

THE "CAST IRON" DEBATE

Internal tensions within the AIA are aptly illustrated by an exchange of ideas that took place at two meetings in 1858. On December 7, the 26-year-old Henry Van Brunt, newly arrived in New York City from Boston and recently installed in Hunt's atelier, presented a paper entitled "Cast Iron and Architecture." Van Brunt, who had graduated from Harvard College in 1854, was, by comparison with other members of the AIA, young and inexperienced. His paper, though thoughtful and filled with youthful optimism, also contained a critique of the previous generation's use of cast iron that must have rankled. It contained two major ideas: that cast iron had been poorly understood and used by architects and that the future of architecture lay in fully embracing *all* the uses of this new material as the true expression of the "iron age." Van Brunt suggested that architects had woefully neglected the potential of this new material:

"[Iron] has been again and again offered to the fine arts. But architecture, sitting haughtily on her acropolis, has indignantly refused to receive it, or receiving it, has done so stealthily and unworthily, enslaving it to basest uses and denying honor and grace to its toil."[6] In other words, the use of cast iron had been unjustly confined to hidden structural purposes.

But far from promoting what would be a protomodernist approach to cast iron, in which structural use would be exposed to view and celebrated, Van Brunt was interested in bringing cast iron onto the façade as a decorative material. Undisturbed by the casting of historical forms, like Corinthian columns, in iron—as other nineteenth-century critics and architects were—van Brunt suggested that this malleability and mimesis were the true potential of iron as a material. To embrace iron, the designer should make the forms as elaborate as he wished, painted in as many colors as he saw fit. In conclusion, he declared, in a phrase that prefigures the tenets of the postmodernism of the 1960s and 1970s, ". . . let the cast iron decoration of our own age not only confess but boast its superficiality."[7] The surprise and novelty of the use of cast-iron decoration was seen as a desirable end unto itself and one that would reconnect architecture with the public: "For what charm so potent, to break through the weariness of life, as novelty?"[8]

His position was an obvious critique of the pious sermons of Ruskin on the subject of the immorality of "dishonest" cast-iron decoration in *The Seven Lamps of Architecture*, and a direct contradiction of the search for an architecture that found its roots in nature, as expressed by Emerson, Greenough, and Eidlitz. Instead, van Brunt contended that: "the *farther* man gets from nature in his creations, without denying the instructive beauty of her forms, the more boldly he asserts his intellectual freedom and the creative powers of his mind [emphasis added]."[9] His statement was thus an attempt to break with the intellectual trends that had been suggested for architecture in the 1840s and '50s and to strike out a new course for American architecture in the 1860s. This course would be charted by *architects*, and not by the critics, philosophers, and artists to whom he was responding.

Van Brunt's paper, despite its lucidity, did not sit well with Eidlitz. By the AIA's next meeting on December 21, he had prepared a lengthy and thoughtful rebuttal to van Brunt. While on the surface it may have seemed that Eidlitz was merely annoyed that a young, inexperienced architect made bold to express his rather lofty ideals, there were actually serious and substantive differences between Van Brunt's and Eidlitz's views on cast iron and, even more broadly, the purpose of architecture. Because of Eidlitz's abrasive and paternalistic tone, the substance of his response was largely lost on the AIA audience. But later scholars also seem to have missed the subtleties of his argument. As a result, Eidlitz has been portrayed as a Luddite who rejected the potential of the new industrial materials of the age, placing him squarely as an American exponent of the backward-looking Ruskin and of the Arts and Crafts ideas of William Morris.[10]

The reality, though, is far more complex. Eidlitz did not reject the use of cast iron. Instead, he assailed Van Brunt's suggestions for its potential. His position countered van Brunt's on both pragmatic and aesthetic grounds. Far from believing that architects had rejected or neglected cast iron, Eidlitz declared that any material that routinely composed 30 percent of a building's budget, as it did in current practice, was indeed heartily embraced. Eidlitz had been putting cast iron to novel and visible structural uses since the mid-1840s, as in St. George's cantilevered galleries and the exposed ceiling trusses of the Produce Exchange and the Springfield City Hall in Massachusetts. His competition entry for New York's Crystal Palace of 1852 proposed a skeletal system of interlocking cast-iron columns and trusses that culminated in a "suspension roof" that would use tension cables to create a broad interior space without vaulting (color plate 3, page 3).[11] Eidlitz, in an early demonstration of his versatility and entrepreneurial spirit, filed a patent for a bank-safe design in which a frame of chilled iron surrounded a core of bent sheets of boiler iron with wrought-iron ribs that was then filled with molten iron. The result was a safe "impenetrable by the hardest drill" (fig. 3.1).[12] With this multifaceted experience of the material, Eidlitz clearly would not tolerate questioning of his understanding of it.

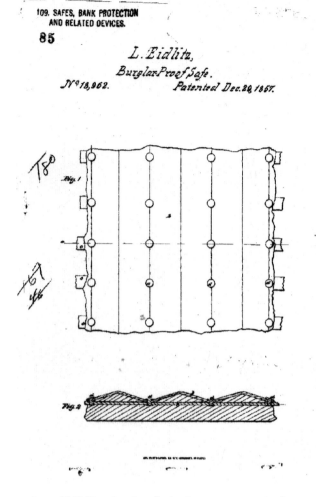

L. Eidlitz,
Burglar Proof Safe.
Nº 18,962.   Patented Dec. 29, 1857.

3.1 Leopold Eidlitz, drawings for bank patent no. 18,962, for a
burglar-proof safe (1857).

For Eidlitz, iron was a structural material appropriate for the skeleton of a building but not for its skin:
"iron *never* can and *never will* be a suitable material for
forming the main walls of architectural monuments."[13]
Eidlitz's reasoning was based in part on pragmatic material concerns. As it was made in the 1860s, iron was not
always strong, durable, and, most important, fireproof
enough to clad a building. Though the fireproofed iron
storefronts of James Bogardus and the Badger company
had already begun to proliferate in New York, Eidlitz
was correct, to a degree, in his statements about iron as
it existed in 1858. George Carstensen and Charles Gilde-

meister's Crystal Palace, built in 1853 after they won the
initial competition, burned in a short fifteen minutes in
1858 (fig. 3.2). Eidlitz's own Continental Bank, widely
acknowledged as the first fireproof building in New
York at the time, used a combination of masonry and
concrete to fireproof the structure, which was reinforced
with insulated iron beams.[14] It was not until the 1870s
that American architects became more generally aware
of the physical properties of their building materials and
that the principles of fireproofing, as Eidlitz and others
had begun to practice them, became further developed
and more widely accepted.[15]

Eidlitz also objected strenuously to Van Brunt's suggestion that iron made the perfect material for façades
on aesthetic grounds. The disagreement centered on
defining the essence of the material: how was one to use
iron "honestly"? Eidlitz firmly believed that just because
iron *could* be molded into any form did not mean that it
should be used to drape storefronts in Corinthian columns. Following Van Brunt's logic, he asserted, meant
that iron would be used "for show more than any other
purpose."[16] Eidlitz reiterated that the true "honesty" of
iron was in its use as a structural material. The actual
structure of a building, whether composed of stone
or iron, was the best ornament Eidlitz could conceive
of: "If a bold stone arch is wanted for the security and
strength of construction, that bold arch is the most
beautiful object I can possibly imagine in such a place."[17]
Van Brunt's "iron age" and its free use of cast-iron ornamentation would be the death of architecture, allowing
the structure of the building to be draped in "flimsy and
trifling ornament, bought at a shop, and hung up with
tenpenny nails."[18]

In addition to these substantive issues, Eidlitz also
portrayed Van Brunt as an upstart neophyte who, because of his own lack of practical experience, had grossly
underestimated the sophistication of his elders: "The
logic [of Van Brunt's paper], where sound, is fortified
with a multiplicity of positions, from which favorable
views may be had of the author's conquered territory,
which, with the unerring skill of the landscape-gardener,
is magnified into interminable parks, endless avenues,
distant fields, broad sheets of water, yes, even moun-

tains in the background—all on a three-acre lot of most unpromising natural advantages."[19] Eidlitz's tone in painting this extraordinarily picturesque insult was condescending and acerbic, to say the least, and it undercut the seriousness of his rebuttal. In this, as in other AIA debates, Eidlitz made it exceptionally difficult for other architects with more delicate social sensibilities to agree with him against Van Brunt.

After Eidlitz's presentation, Hunt immediately jumped to Van Brunt's defense. Hunt, who himself had only practiced in the U.S. for two years, declared that the rise of the decorative use of cast iron could not be avoided and made a thinly veiled jab at Eidlitz, suggesting that architects who were too bookish and intellectual were the only ones who could possibly object to it: "If educated architects with us will not undertake to keep pace with the spirit and requirements of the age, they must expect to be, in a great measure, supplanted by those who, not so fettered by books and authorities, exert themselves only to satisfy these requirements in the most direct, simple, and economical way."[20] He sought, instead, to justify the use of cast-iron façades by agreeing with Van Brunt that clients wanted them,

therefore, architects must find a way to provide them. James Bogardus's cast-iron storefronts, such as the 1849 Laing Building in New York, were the obvious example of current practice; Hunt's later design for a store for his brother-in-law, Alexander Van Rensselaer (1871–72), among others, showed his full and continued support for the utility of cast iron as a façade material (fig. 3.3).[21] Nowhere did Hunt's response actually deal with the substantive issues Eidlitz raised; he simply thought them irrelevant to the exigencies of current practice.

This pattern of communication between Eidlitz and his fellow AIA members was repeated often. In discussions, Eidlitz's tone was often condescending; further, his topics were abstract and intellectual in nature. Eidlitz's series "The T-Squares," for example, published anonymously in the *Crayon*, satirized the building industry and skewered everyone involved in architecture, from patronizing clients to ignorant builders. Unfolding a story told by an old wooden T-square to a newfangled steel T-square, the series emulated the romantic fiction of Goethe and Washington Irving in an attempt to be both humorous and instructive about the failings of architecture in America. In the end, though, Eidlitz's scathing pen simply painted a bleak picture, using humor too pointed in its criticism to be very funny.[22]

Eidlitz was tenacious and argumentative, unwilling to let a point go, which is probably why his essays were ignored. Instead, his assertive manner was remembered. Frederick Law Olmsted, for example, when suggesting architects to write about Central Park for the *Atlantic Monthly* summed up their literary voices concisely: "Van Brunt, Richard Hunt and Eidlitz [know the Park] better than any other of our architects. They have each had a residence in Paris [*sic*], I believe, and each writes well on professional subjects. . . . The architects would each write critically & conscientiously. Van Brunt religiously, Eidlitz spicily."[23] William Ware, a student of Hunt's who went on to establish the architecture programs at MIT and Columbia, later dismissed Eidlitz as merely a "conspicuous German."[24] Charles Babcock, who established the architecture school at Cornell and had been a fellow employee in Upjohn's office, when asked to assess Eidlitz's career, replied by evoking Emerson's profiles of great nineteenth-century figures "Lectures on Representative Men," but stating to the contrary that Eidlitz "was by no means a representative man."[25]

As a result, Eidlitz's "spicy" contributions to the intellectual life of American architecture have been almost completely overlooked. The success of other AIA members like Hunt, Van Brunt, and Ware in promoting their own ideas about classical architecture and the Beaux-Arts, and the failure of Eidlitz to find a large audience for his own sensibility, has obscured the substantive debates that engaged architects of the period. The conflict between Eidlitz's vision for architecture and the classical Beaux-Arts school was most pronounced in the AIA's early debates on architectural education.

EIDLITZ, THE AIA, AND EDUCATION

In 1897, Eidlitz stated, with typical bombastic certainty: "The system of the École des Beaux-Arts, which is imitated in many schools outside of France, is utterly subversive of possible logical architecture."[26] By that time, Eidlitz was not alone in his suspicion of the French educational system; in the wake of the 1893 Chicago World's Fair, Louis Sullivan had famously bemoaned the corrupting influence of the Beaux-Arts. But by this late date, the system had taken hold in America, and architects trained at schools such as Columbia, the University of Pennsylvania, and MIT owed to it their expertise in planning, draftsmanship, and the language of classicism.

While Sullivan's was a new voice in the critique of the Beaux-Arts, Eidlitz's criticisms were by the 1890s a familiar refrain to American architects. Decades earlier, in the 1860s, when the Beaux-Arts model of education gained its strength in New York and Boston thanks to the expertise of Hunt and his student William Ware, Eidlitz was a vocal opponent. But far from being merely a critic, he also offered a positive alternative. Eidlitz's interest in using the AIA to promote education came as early as 1860, when he first suggested forming a committee to investigate the formation of a college to educate architects.[27] Later, as the chair of the AIA Committee on Education (of which Ware and Thomas U. Walter of Philadelphia were also members), Eidlitz authored a report detailing how the AIA could promote the profession by establishing a new, national school for architects based on the polytechnic system; AIA members referred to this national school as the "Grand Central School of Architecture."[28] He presented the report in 1867 as a direct challenge to Ware's newly instituted architecture program at MIT, which began in the same year; Ware established a similar architecture program at Columbia University in 1881. Eidlitz's report was roundly rejected and his suggestions dismissed, like his views on cast iron, as irrelevant to current practice. Though discussion of the plan continued through 1868, in December, Eidlitz dramatically quit the AIA, leaving the school without a sponsor. Though the exact cause of his departure remains unknown, the breach was definitely unamicable and permanent.[29]

Eidlitz based the proposed curriculum on the German polytechnic models he was familiar with from his own training in Prague and Vienna, and emphasized the necessity of a harmonious balance between technical expertise and aesthetic creativity. The school would train not only architects, but also engineers, draftsman, businesspeople—everyone involved in the design and construction process. It would, of course, be located in New York, and talented individuals from around the country would train at the AIA's school side by side with underprivileged New Yorkers on scholarship. The AIA, and not a governmental agency, would run the school, ensuring that its curriculum always reflected the most current thinking in design and professional ethics. It was an idealistic and ambitious plan that was met with bemusement by his fellows at the AIA, who found it impossible to consider any model for education except the French or possibly the English apprenticeship model; existing polytechnical schools in the United States, especially in Philadelphia, were never acknowledged by the AIA as potential models.[30]

In some ways, Eidlitz's plan appears to be similar to Ware's MIT program. Both insisted on training individuals in both science and art, though the balance between the two fields was certainly different; both bemoaned the current state of architectural education and the profession in general. Neither considered the issue of style tantamount to the creation of an architectural school. But underlying Eidlitz's plan were three important assumptions that distinguish it from the system that eventually developed in America: that the education of architects should be accomplished in an independent setting that emphasized *all* aspects of architecture, including engineering, business, and art; that practicing architects should be deeply involved in the day-to-day instruction of the next generation of professionals;

and that access to education should be available to all, regardless of social class or economic means.

First, the creation of a separate school for architects, not one that was part of the American university system, was essential to the plan. Eidlitz believed a new start, a brand-new school that allowed architects to control a curriculum independent of long-standing traditions, was the way to cast off the mistakes of the past. As a student at the new schools of technology and architecture in Prague and Vienna in the 1810s, Eidlitz was sensitized to the potential for new institutions to promote new ways of thinking. In the Habsburg Empire, the emergence of polytechnic schools in the first decades of the nineteenth century was an essential component in modernizing the states in central Europe. These schools were separate from the well-established universities and responded to the new industrial spirit of the age by training engineers, architects, and businessmen and not primarily military engineers, as the French polytechnic schools did.[31] Eidlitz's school was to be imbued with similar modernizing ideals, albeit with the absence of state sponsorship. The independence, narrow focus, and flexibility of the school would keep it from being submerged within the bureaucracy of a university and allow it to respond quickly to developments in contemporary technology and aesthetics.

On the other hand, Ware, as a Harvard graduate and the son of a Harvard professor, was a product of the American university system and saw its potential to accommodate new programs of study without having to start completely from scratch—a difficult prospect in the post–Civil War years. Ware was also dedicated to the notion of the architect as a cultured, educated man, writing that "the most important qualities in an architect are good sense and good taste, and it is a general, not a technical education, that one must look to, to furnish them."[32] Eidlitz's attitude is idealistic and revolutionary, while Ware's is certainly more realistic but also more intellectually and socially conservative.

Equally important was the involvement of practicing architects in running the school. The members of the AIA's Committee on Education were to be its presidents and deans; AIA members at large were to be among the instructors. In time, Eidlitz suggested that the equivalent persons in the engineering professional organization could be invited to join in the administration of the school. Eidlitz probably had in mind the Polytechnic Association of the American Institute, a professional association of engineers that met at the Cooper Union. At MIT, the chief professor of design, Eugène Letang, came to the United States from France in 1871, meaning that, while he was an expert in the teaching of architecture, he had little understanding of the conditions of practice in America. For Eidlitz, this situation was appalling: it was a working knowledge of practice that would create a good teacher and thus good students. It was, indeed, the duty of American architects to teach the next generation so that society at large could benefit from the improvement of the architecture that they saw in their cities every day.

Eidlitz's larger goal, to benefit society, is most obviously absent from the Beaux-Arts system as implemented in the United States. By locating the education of architects within the university system, the elitism of the profession in the coming decades was ensured. Eidlitz, himself the son of a poor shopkeeper in the Jewish ghetto in Prague, was able to improve himself and his lot in life by attending the Realschule in Prague without paying tuition. Pervading all his writing about art and architecture was an unwavering belief that education was the key to the betterment of all men and women. The AIA's school for architecture was to be open to all the people of the United States and even Cuba and Mexico; and in particular the trades program was to serve the people of New York, educating all who desired to learn a trade within the architectural arts, not just those who could afford it.

This underlying social agenda most dramatically separates the two schemes for architectural education. Eidlitz envisioned the architect as an educated man; Ware envisioned the architect as an educated *gentleman*. In this respect, the Cooper Union, established 1859, was far more similar to Eidlitz's vision of the proper setting for a modern school of architecture than MIT or Columbia. Sponsored by the immensely wealthy philanthropist Peter Cooper for the benefit of the people of New York,

the Cooper Union offered a range of practical classes, from art to accounting.[33] In fact, it is likely that Eidlitz envisioned a partnership between the AIA and Peter Cooper in creating the new polytechnic school.[34] Ware's eventual admission of architecture office helpers and draftsmen to his Columbia architecture program in 1891 was controversial, with some fearing it would dilute the quality of the program.[35] By contrast, these are among the very people whom Eidlitz hoped to serve from the beginning.

Eidlitz's plan was doomed to fail in large part because of his overly idealistic and uncompromising nature. To suggest that the AIA create and sponsor a new school of architecture in the 1860s, when it could not even manage to create a library for use by its members, was obviously wishful thinking. But the immediate rejection of his ideas by the majority of his fellow members of the AIA is symptomatic not just of the impossibility of the plan, but of a fundamental disagreement about how to position architects in the modern world. In the report of the Committee on Education from 1869 (the committee did nothing in the year following Eidlitz's departure), the conclusion is that the AIA should be a passive presence vis-à-vis education, stating that the "objects . . . of this committee are undefined."[36] Instead, the development of education should be left for each individual city or region to develop on its own, in harmony with its particular conditions. This is, of course, what eventually transpired. Eidlitz's plan was too grandiose to be practicable, and though there were others who objected to the adoption of the French Beaux-Arts system, their objections were weak. Russell Sturgis, then a young architect who had trained with Eidlitz before studying at the Technische Hochschule and Akademie der Bildenden Künste in Munich, commented that: "A few of us would dissent from a too hearty endorsement of the Paris system, while, at the same time, we may not have a better one to offer."[37] It would be years later that Nathan Ricker established his German-inspired program at the public University of Illinois, responding to regional conditions in Chicago and Illinois that allowed interest in a polytechnic and theoretical education to flourish.[38] Herbert Langford Warren's architecture program at

Harvard, also established later, in 1896, sought to counter the academicism of Beaux-Arts programs by returning a practical sense of construction and American social conditions to his curriculum.[39]

By contrast, in New York, architects like Hunt and Ware wanted the next generation of architects to be made in their own image: patrician Americans finally coming into their own as architects, throwing off the influence of previous generations of immigrant architects like Eidlitz. Hunt's atelier, followed by Ware's programs at MIT and later at Columbia, created cultured, liberally educated men sensitive to the great architectural traditions of Europe but proud of their own flourishing country, able to mingle with the emerging social elite of New York. Their educations were largely unsullied by the mundane realities of bookkeeping or by the presence of the lower classes.

Eidlitz's departure from the ranks of the AIA in 1869 is symbolic of a greater rift between him and the direction American architecture would take in the 1870s. This basic disagreement about the very purpose of architecture, not just its style, is fundamental to the practice of architecture in the mid nineteenth century. The formation of the AIA gave the profession a focus on art more than science, on design rather than theory, and on pretension more than populism. Seeing that the group did not provide the kinds of allies he sought in his quest for an organic and democratic architecture, Eidlitz looked for them elsewhere, among public-minded businessmen, churchmen, engineers, and politicians.

FELLOW REFORMERS
It is perhaps no surprise that Eidlitz, a reformer in architectural aesthetics and professional standards, brought his reform spirit to bear on the wider world as well. An antislavery Democrat and an active participant in citizens' groups for better government in New York, Eidlitz became involved in politics during a period when corruption, poverty, and violence were endemic to city life. His belief in architecture as a transformative force is filled with the fervor of the social reform movements of the mid nineteenth century. Eidlitz and his friend Frederick Law Olmsted often found themselves in sharp

disagreement with more patrician practitioners like Hunt, who was suspicious of their more populist ideas. While later Beaux-Arts practitioners began to address the concerns of the city as a social problem, for Hunt the Beaux-Arts was a means of elevating artistic production—not for the benefit of the public at large, but for the sake of the art itself.[40] Through his association with controversial political figures like Fernando Wood and Andrew Green (head of the Central Park Commission), his work on public works projects, and clients like the influential Broadway Tabernacle Church, Eidlitz found ways to put his private aesthetic strategies to a more public use.

It was one thing to try to develop an architecture appropriate to time and place by writing about it and quite another to try to find clients willing to assist in the process by funding the actual building campaigns. Eidlitz was always conscious of the potentially difficult relationship between architect and client and consciously manipulated his image and interests in the pursuit of work. Speaking at the second annual dinner of the AIA in January 1859, Eidlitz described the difficulties of obtaining, and keeping, architectural commissions:

> The architect is not only expected to convert vulgar material, such as stone, pig iron and lumber, into frozen music, but he must also deal with men—the most difficult substance to mould into harmonious form. . . . It is not surprising, therefore, the architect, of whom so much is expected, should develop all the noble virtues of man under the infliction of severe trials. He is meek and patient as a lamb with the weak, and bold as a lion with the strong; economical with the poor, and lavish with the rich. . . . He is patriotic with legislators who have State-houses to build, and cosmopolitan with the projector of a library. . . . He is utilitarian with the merchant, proud with the banker, investigating with the scholar, ecclesiological with the clergyman, a pedagogue with professor, practical with the mechanic, and poetical with the literary. . . .[41]

Eidlitz well understood that the process of actually erecting a building was a joint one. No matter what the driving idea of his design was, he needed to be able to sell it to his audience.

Like most New York architects, Eidlitz did find a niche. Hunt worked largely with the wealthy, patrician segment of New York (witness the Vanderbilt mansions) as did George B. Post; neither devoted much energy to church design. Jacob Wrey Mould apparently sought out the rich and famous; Frederick Clarke Withers worked largely for Episcopal congregations and their parishioners.[42] Eidlitz had a wide-ranging practice and professional life, and we may never know the full extent of his varied endeavors. But his ideal client was clearly someone similar to himself: a self-made man, practical and frugal, but sensitive to the potential of art and architecture to create a better world.

Eidlitz, despite his high ideals, was closely attuned to the economic side of architecture. His business school background perhaps encouraged this eye toward the financial: he advised the AIA's treasurer to invest the group's dues in a successful bid to increase their available capital.[43] He also accepted payment from the Brooklyn Academy of Music partially in stock, making him a part owner of the venture when it opened, a choice that undoubtedly proved lucrative in the long term.[44] Especially early in his career, he was also willing to take on projects simply to make money. His work on Iranistan, P. T. Barnum's mansion in Bridgeport, Connecticut (1846–48), certainly fell into this category (fig. 3.4, color plate 4, page 3). Only a few images of the building remain, and documentation about the particulars of the arrangement between Eidlitz and the wealthy and irascible showman Barnum is absent, but the house cost a reported $150,000. With Eidlitz's typical fee at 5 percent of the total budget in the 1850s, his payment was well worth the trouble.

The most likely story behind this commission is that Barnum saw John Nash's Royal Pavilion in Brighton (1815–21) and became enamored of it. He purchased drawings in England and brought them back to the United States, where he searched for an architect to build his dream home. How he settled on Eidlitz is unknown; perhaps he sought out Richard Upjohn, the best-known architect in New York, who referred him to his young colleague. Barnum never acknowledged Eidlitz as his architect, and Schuyler recalls Eidlitz telling how, "in a spirit of mischief," Eidlitz rang the doorbell of Iranistan and, when Barnum answered, inquired after the architect's name. Upon being told the design was the result of a major competition that had earned the winning architect a $10,000 prize, Schuyler reports that Eidlitz retorted: " 'No it didn't,' . . . whereto the showman . . . softly queried 'Is your name Eidlitz?' "[45]

Regardless of how the arrangement began, Eidlitz clearly delivered what the client wanted: Iranistan was an orientalizing pile with a 90-foot central onion dome surrounded by several smaller domes, minarets, scalloped horseshoe arches, and windows with multicolored panes. The interior continued the fantasy, with the onion dome containing an enormous divan for lounging in "oriental" fashion and taking in the views of New York across Long Island Sound through diamond-shaped windowpanes. As the recent reconstruction of Iranistan's library at the Barnum Museum in Bridgeport shows, other rooms were furnished in a riot of colors and textiles with opulent furnishings by the French-born New York cabinetmaker Julius Dessoir. A perspective sketch of the mansion graced Barnum's personal stationery, and it is reported that Jenny Lind, upon seeing its image on a letter from Barnum, was finally convinced to come to America:

"Do you know, Mr. Barnum," [Lind] said, "that if you had not built Iranistan, I should never have come to America for you?" Mr. Barnum, much surprised, asked her to explain.

"I had received several applications to visit the United States," she continued, "but I did not much like the appearance of the applicants, nor did I relish the idea of crossing 3,000 miles of ocean; so I declined them all. But the first letter which Mr. Wilton, your agent, addressed me, was written upon a sheet headed with a beautiful engraving of Iranistan. It attracted my attention. I said to myself, a gentleman who has been so successful in his business as to be able to build and reside in such a palace cannot be a mere 'adventurer.' So I wrote to your agent, and consented to an interview,

"IRANISTAN," BRIDGEPORT, CT., THE RESIDENCE OF P. T. BARNUM.

which I should have declined, if I had not seen the picture of Iranistan."

"That, then, fully pays me for building it," replied Barnum.[46]

In the wake of Iranistan's public success—its burning in 1858 was covered widely in the press—other mythical Arabian palaces did eventually sprout in the region around New York, including Mould's design for the painter Albert Bierstadt's Malkasten (1866–68), a name that literally means "paint box" in German, but also alluded to the euphony of eastern geographical lexicons. Frederich Church's Olana, designed by Church with another of Eidlitz's friends, Calvert Vaux (1870), continued the tradition of the fairyland oriental villa into the 1870s.

3.4 Iranistan, Bridgeport, Connecticut, 1848. *Frank Leslie's Illustrated Newspaper* (January 2, 1858).

Eidlitz's fanciful essay in Moorish design, derided by Schuyler as "the architectural expression of Humbug," was not outside of his interest or he would have turned the commission down, as he did later at Brick Presbyterian Church in New York when the congregation resisted his desire to build Gothic.[47] What young architect would decline a commission from one of the wealthiest and most famous men in America? But it must frankly be acknowledged that Eidlitz was doing "work-for-hire," meaning the building's concept was decided before he took the job. Though Iranistan was obviously not a direct copy of the Brighton Pavilion, and while its general

3.5 Broadway Tabernacle, 34th Street side, showing the Sixth Avenue El in the foreground. Collection of the New-York Historical Society, neg#30915.

form, with its emphasis on constructed ornament and polychromy, were compatible with Eidlitz's developing architectural sense, it also, like most of Eidlitz's house designs, did not present an opportunity to explore his own ideas extensively.[48] Projects with a public component, like churches and government buildings, allowed Eidlitz more room to explore his ideals than did private commissions.

Fortunately for Eidlitz, New York in the 1850s and '60s was the perfect place for him to pursue not only his livelihood but also those ideals. In addition to his aesthetic innovations, Eidlitz brought a sense of social responsibility to his work: architecture had a duty to society both to uphold its ideals and to uplift its spirits. Architecture had the potential to go beyond the merest shelter and to educate and improve the growing masses of Americans. New York was a hotbed of social reform, leaving Eidlitz with no shortage of allies in his quest to improve the public's taste in architecture and art. In church architecture, the Reverend Stephen Tyng, for example, was a perfect match for Eidlitz, for the two shared a fervent desire to use the design of St. George's to communicate religious reform through its Low Church, antimaterialist message. Tyng's son, the Reverend Stephen Tyng, Jr., continued in his father's footsteps in presenting Eidlitz the commission for the Church of the Holy Trinity in New York (1873), for which he also demanded a sanctuary focused exclusively on the minister.

The Broadway Tabernacle, the first and largest Congregational church in New York City, commissioned Eidlitz to design a new home in 1858, no doubt in part because of his success in his Connecticut commissions. Founded in 1836 as a liberal antislavery Presbyterian church on lower Broadway at Catherine Lane, by the mid-1850s the real estate proved too valuable to maintain the church's home there. Though their original building had played host to Sojourner Truth and Frederick Douglass, the need to move uptown pressed more strongly than a sense of institutional history. Under the Reverend Joseph Parrish Thompson, the church moved to Herald Square, at Broadway and 34th Street, and subsequently began an active campaign that quickly expanded the number of Congregational churches in the city and in Brooklyn to more than twenty (fig. 3.5, pages 4, 5). The church at Broadway and 34th served, much as St. George's did, as the figurehead for this expansion, and Eidlitz designed an extravagant and immense Gothic building for them. The presentation drawing, which has survived, shows a pinnacled, towered, and buttressed cathedral soaring majestically above the well-heeled pedestrians below, commanding the square and the surrounding neighborhood. While not on the enormous scale of Renwick's St. Patrick's Cathedral, which was begun in 1858, and still plainer than Trinity

3.6 Broadway Tabernacle under construction in 1858. *Marc Eidlitz, Builder* (1904).

Church or Renwick's Grace Church (1846–48), the flying buttresses and openwork spire of the proposed Tabernacle show Eidlitz was conscious of the greater degree of architectural competition in the city than in Connecticut, and elevated the sophistication and detail of his design for his urban clients.

The Tabernacle as built, however, lacked most of the finer detailing included in the original design and became a more solid, sober presence on the city street, more fitting for a Congregational church. Marc Eidlitz was the contractor, managing the laying of the stonework (fig. 3.6). Because of its site and budget concerns, the building was compacted, its tower drawn into the body of the church and the rounded apse reapportioned into a separate chapel, office space, and meeting rooms. The sanctuary, which held about 1,600, was a squarish 76 feet wide by 90 feet long. The openwork spire was omitted, creating a stubbier 135-foot tower. The original proposal called for the nave roof to rise above that of the aisles, supported by flying buttresses; the buttresses were omitted, and the peak of the roof over the aisles, naves, and transepts was kept on the same level, undoubtedly a

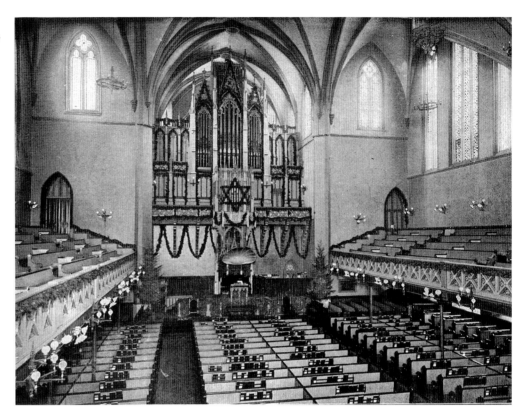

3.7 Broadway Tabernacle, nave looking toward pulpit as decorated for Christmas services. Susan Hayes Ward, *History of the Broadway Tabernacle Church* (1901).

major cost-saving alteration. A new scheme of clerestory lighting, in the form of miniature gabled windows in the roof, almost like the eyebrow windows that would later be typical of H. H. Richardson's work, appeared in the final scheme. The ashlar masonry, level roof line, and dense composition ground the building, making it appear lower and heavier than the original scheme. The sole remaining frivolity was the elaborately carved gables over the front entry. The building cost about $75,000.[49]

It was in the interior that the tension between the congregation's competing desire for a grand building worthy of their urban setting and for a building that symbolized the no-nonsense, puritanical philosophy of the Congregationalists emerged. As with so many of Eidlitz's buildings, only one image remains of the interior sanctuary, meaning many details will never be known (fig. 3.7). But the photo that remains shows that the same basic arrangement Eidlitz used in the Connecticut churches appeared again: wooden galleries with windows in the walls high above them and a simple recess for the pulpit. In the ceiling and roof treatment,

the Tabernacle differed from its country cousins. Instead of the rustic open trusswork of a meetinghouse, the 80-foot ceiling was elaborated with groined vaults and tracery originally supported by three massive piers of New Brunswick stone, removed in a renovation. Though the walls were kept a buff color, Louis Cohn, Eidlitz's later collaborator at St. George's and the Church of the Pilgrims, painted the structure, though the colors are not known.

Acknowledging that the church was perhaps grander than absolutely necessary, at its dedication a church official remarked that "it does not accord with our views of worship under the Christian dispensation, nor with the usages of our body, to attach sanctity to a material structure." On the other hand, he was also able to admit that the building had a "chaste and almost severe simplicity, which imparts an air of grandeur and beauty to the whole structure."[50] As the symbol of the new presence of the Congregationalists in the city, the Tabernacle fulfilled its purpose perfectly: it drew attention to the church and provided the setting for numerous antislav-

3.8 Currier & Ives, *Great Riot at the Astor Place Opera House*, published 1849. LC-USZC2-2532.

ery and women's suffrage rallies. Its warren of parlors and Sunday school rooms, described in an 1859 pamphlet as the "*home* of the church," provided meals to the hungry and education to the ignorant through the prodigious mission work of the church. Among the most prominent members of the Broadway Tabernacle was Major General Oliver Howard, known as the "Christian general," who after the Civil War helped establish a university for African-Americans, now known as Howard University in his honor. The Broadway Tabernacle was a church where worship was not simply about church attendance, but about active engagement in social change, whether it be hunger, education, immigration, issues of race and integration, poverty, orphan relief, or any of the other myriad issues that occupied the nineteenth century's social reformers.

As New York emerged as a "major world metropolis" in the 1840s and '50s, with new status as an international economic and cultural center, the city began to experience its first major social upheavals and political crises.[51] The causes and sources of the unrest were varied, a combination of immigration, industrialization, and the resultant economic and social stresses. But the Astor Place riots of 1849 dramatically illustrated the tensions that the rapidly growing city, and country, had to face (fig. 3.8) . The riots, which left 23 dead and as many as 100 wounded, resulted from a rivalry between two Shake-

spearean actors, the British William Charles Macready and the American Edwin Forrest. Macready affected an upper-crust British persona and scorned what he saw as the uncouth nature of Americans unable to appreciate his refined acting; Forrest, a native-born American, acted with a wild, passionate abandon appealing to the working classes and equally despised Macready and his followers' pretension. Their rivalry became the fodder of newspaper articles and editorials, escalating into a public outrage that Macready, who publicly insulted the taste of masses of Americans, should be allowed to take the stage at the Astor Place Opera House. On the evening of Macready's performance of May 10, 1849, a crowd of some 15,000, incited by Forrest's bitter remonstrances, gathered to protest. The police proved unable to control the crowd, who pelted them with stones, and the militia were called in, resulting in the first incident of American troops firing on its own citizens. The resulting civilian deaths caused even more violence that dispersed only after three days of rioting. The incident tore the city apart, exposing the deep class divisions between the working class, who supported Forrest, and the emerging upper classes, who supported the more cultured, European Macready.[52]

In the wake of the Astor Place riots, many began to think seriously about how to address the seemingly uncontrollable mobs of New York, laying the foundation for much of the development of the philosophy of entertainment and mollification of the middle and lower classes for the rest of the nineteenth century. Barnum's American Museum and Frederick Law Olmsted's plans for Central Park were both responses to the urban crisis of what to do with a disgruntled, uncouth, and uneducated public in order to keep them from attacking New York's institutions of power and wealth.[53] In other words, the Astor Place riots sparked a new wave of thinking about bread and circuses for modern America. On the one hand, cheap plebeian amusements both distracted and offered their own form of scientific education. And on the other, the edification of a simple country escape in the park provided the contact with nature that was essential to the spiritual well-being of the city dweller (figs. 3.9, 3.10). In government, the insti-

3.9 "The Poor of New York," *Frank Leslie's Illustrated Newspaper* (November 18, 1865). Paired with "The Rich of New York," these scenes of contrasting poverty and wealth were typical of the editorial art of the Gilded Age.

3.10 "The Rich of New York," *Frank Leslie's Illustrated Newspaper* (November 18, 1865).

tution of voting gangs that united groups of immigrants and working-class men in support of competing candidates ushered in the age of the political machine that culminated in the Tammany Hall corruption of Boss Tweed's New York.

Eidlitz grappled with the issues raised by the Astor Place riots, focusing especially on education as well as the need for an egalitarian economic system and an honest and forthright government. Eidlitz firmly and optimistically believed that architecture was a potential means of social reform for a people whose economic and practical achievements had outstripped their cultural sophistication:

Here [in America] we behold a nation sprung into manhood in a day, endowed with all the intelligence of an old community; in possession of the mechanic arts, an extensive commerce, and daily increasing wealth; with the most perfect development of religious and political liberty, eager to acquire and encourage the only thing they have not—works of architectural art; ready and willing to appreciate them, endowed with a stock of general education and common sense, prone to pursue the right direction, if that direction is only pointed out with a proper degree of intelligence. . . .[54]

For Eidlitz, the solution lay in providing both good architecture and good education. Education meant, on the one hand, the provision for institutionalized instruction, as with his Grand Central School. But it also meant designing good buildings. The public was starved for edifying architecture, and each project Eidlitz built, particularly his churches and civic buildings, presented a new opportunity to educate and uplift the masses. Through the fifty years of his career, Eidlitz was both consistent and persistent, evincing an unwavering belief in the responsibility of the architect to educate and improve the taste of clients and the public at large. Eidlitz's view was, however, far from romantic and far from liberal in the sense that we mean today. His reform sense, while sincere, was like most in the Gilded Age, paternalistic and condescending. As his understanding of nature as inspiration for design was based in a scientific optimism, his understanding of how to improve society was based in a rationalizing sensibility that saw people in aggregate rather than as individuals. His goal was the advancement of society rather than the amelioration of individual tragedy.

Eidlitz shared this jointly altruistic and patronizing view of the ability of art, architecture, and science to uplift and edify the public with many other men in pre–Civil War New York: from Barnum and Olmsted to Peter Cooper, founder of the Cooper Institute, and Jacob Astor, founder of the Astor Library. But instead of catering to their baser tastes, as P. T. Barnum's attractions often did, Eidlitz's camp chose to focus on improving them. Public libraries, public parks, and new opportunities for public education flourished in nineteenth-century New York, sponsored by the city and by wealthy patrons like Astor and Cooper. Eidlitz

was an ally of Olmsted and Vaux as they fought for their ambitious plan for Central Park, protesting Olmsted's removal from superintending the park in 1876 and later writing, with civic pride, "Central Park is the great achievement of New York City."[55]

The "nature" that was Eidlitz's muse both inspired rational aesthetics and gave birth to modern science, a science that could, like art, bring vast improvements to the world. He embraced the role model provided by Goethe as a scientist-artist uniting the disparate fields. Science, technical experimentation and innovation, equally as much as art, was a way for Eidlitz to advance his agenda. As his bank designs suggested, he was interested in fireproofing from a technical point of view. He dabbled at being an inventor and filed for three patents in the 1850s and '60s—first, for the "burglar-proof" safe, and second, for a complex photographic process designed to prevent counterfeiting. For the third, he was the American assignee for French photographer Alphonse Poitevin's photolithographic process.[56] Eidlitz had an early and technical interest in photography: he was also, along with Peter Cooper, one of the signers of the original constitution of the American Photographical Society in New York in 1859.[57] The photographs of Eidlitz and his family from the late 1860s were probably taken by Eidlitz himself. His interest in applied science was lifelong: in 1899 he published his final work, *On Light*, an astronomical treatise based on his observations of one of Jupiter's moons and his attempt to confirm James Bradley's use of stellar aberrations to measure the speed of light.[58]

In addition to his own experimentation, Eidlitz also sought out professional collaborations with engineers as part of his agenda to improve society. During the late 1850s, Eidlitz pursued a scheme for an elevated railway to serve the undeveloped northern areas of Manhattan in partnership with John Serrell, brother to the better-known General Edward Wellman Serrell, both of whom were civil engineers who worked on railroads and suspension bridges. The general was a Civil War veteran who had designed some of the earliest suspension bridges in North America; his brother John also designed suspension bridges and was a consultant for

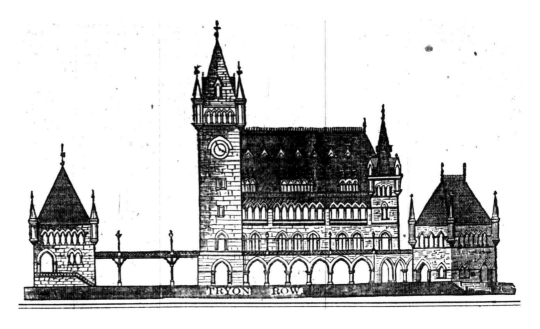

3.11 Serrell & Eidlitz, "Tryon Row," part of the Viaduct Railway proposal, probably intended to connect at the base of the Brooklyn Bridge. *New York Daily Tribune* (June 7, 1871).

the design of the Brooklyn Bridge. Eidlitz probably met the Serrells through the meetings of the Polytechnic Association of the American Institute, which were held at the Cooper Institute; Edward Serrell's father was also a business associate of Peter Cooper's.[59] In 1859, John Serrell and Eidlitz first presented the scheme to the state legislature in Albany. Although it, along with many other plans during the 1860s, was rejected, the plan received new life when in the late 1860s Peter B. Sweeny, the "brains" behind the municipal corruption and graft of the Tweed Ring, took it up.[60] Eidlitz and Serrell became consultants to the city, and some have suggested that they were actually party to Sweeny's scheme to defraud the city of funds through the building of the "Viaduct Railway." More likely, though, was that Sweeny decided to promote the Eidlitz-Serrell plan instead of the many other proposals because it was composed largely of masonry, a material for which it would have been easy to create false orders and payments. While Eidlitz believed his skills were worth a handsome salary, he was far too ethical to be involved in explicitly underhanded schemes of acquiring that remuneration.[61]

With the demise of the Tweed Ring in 1871, the scheme eventually came to nothing, but not before Eidlitz and Serrell devoted themselves to working out the engineering, economics, and design of the railroad and its stations, which were to be financed both by the city and by rents derived from letting out the space underneath the elevated tracks to shopkeepers. Eidlitz's designs for the railway stations were his only designs that so obviously recalled the Prague rooflines of his youth. Their steep pitch and finialed corners, marking the transition from one quarter of the city to another, obviously quote the medieval gateways of Prague (figs. 3.11, 3.12). Eidlitz's sense of the vernacular informed his design once again; the Charles Bridge towers had since the fourteenth century functioned as effective markers, anchoring either end of an elevated transit. The design was probably for the station that was meant to be at the foot of the new Brooklyn Bridge, making the quotation of the Prague bridge gatehouses even more appropriate in Eidlitz's mind.

Schuyler chastised Eidlitz for pursuing such "lucrative and utilitarian employment," but for Eidlitz these kinds of pragmatic projects provided further justification of his own down-to-earth architectural philosophy.[62] The Viaduct Railway project was the literal meeting of art and science. Would Hunt or Post have designed a mere railroad? A prosaic bridge? For Eidlitz, the mundane quality of the scheme and its need for technical expertise made it immensely satisfying. Like Olmsted, he was a man of the world, flirting with many professions while

always coming back to his own. Combined with the fact that it gave him the opportunity to permanently mold the entire city of New York, not just one building on one corner, the project suited him perfectly.

Eidlitz worked best with clients who had a similar vision, with men like Cooper and Astor who believed that New York and America would be a better place if its cultural and governmental institutions were respected by and open to the public. Unlike most nineteenth-century American architects, Eidlitz built very few private residences and none with the baronial aspect of those built for the robber barons of the Gilded Age such as the Vanderbilts or J. Pierpont Morgan (fig. 3.13). Instead, he kept his practice focused on the infrastructure of the new American society, following a traditional European model of practice, designing major public landmarks, especially government offices and churches and only a few commercial buildings. Through these commissions, Eidlitz hoped to exercise a beneficial influence on the public at large; any architect who undertook such important work without understanding its seriousness "destroy[ed] the property and labor of his fellow men [and] lower[ed] the moral standard of the community."[63]

New York businessman William A. Booth was a repeat client across many years. He was a director of the American Exchange Bank (1857–60) and a donor of funds for the First Congregational Church in Stratford (1858–59) who also hired Eidlitz to build his home in Stratford (1857), a later home in Englewood, New Jersey (1868), and probably also the orphans' home for the Children's Aid Society in New York (1872), for whom both Vaux and Eidlitz provided facilities. Booth, on the commission to investigate the fraud associated with the Tweed Ring in 1870, may also have been instrumental in bringing in Eidlitz to finish the Tweed Courthouse in 1876. Booth was precisely the kind of man Eidlitz admired: self-made, risen to wealth from adversity, wide-ranging in his professional capabilities, and interested in charitable works. Booth was born in Stratford and raised with his four siblings by his mother after the death of his father at age five. He spent his youth laboring in the fields but still attended school during the winter. As soon as he was able, he left for New York, where he founded a sugar-refining concern, Booth & Edgar, which quickly became profitable. From there, Booth became involved in banking, insurance, shipping, and railroads. Though wealthy, Booth was also extremely practical and demanded economy and efficiency from his investments. Never liking to waste money, in 1852 he built his own house rather than pay someone else to do it. He was also a religious man, attending Stratford's Congregational Church during his summers in Connecticut and the Fourteenth Street Presbyterian Church in New York while in town. Like many successful nineteenth-century businessmen, Booth felt that the accumulation of wealth presented an opportunity to mold society in a better image, and so he dedicated himself to charitable works as well.[64] Eidlitz was perfectly suited to work with Booth, who clearly would not have tolerated an architect with pretentious tastes or sensibilities. Eidlitz's practical business background and preference for honest, straightforward design gave Booth confidence that his money would not be wasted on extravagance or incompetence.

While practicality was certainly an appealing aspect of Eidlitz's architectural persona for all clients, for others his belief in the edifying nature of architecture was clearly compelling. In Springfield, at the dedication of the new Eidlitz-designed City Hall, Dr. J. G. Holland, for whom Eidlitz also designed a house, boldly proclaimed the mission of the new building in words that echo Eidlitz's:

> It is a treasure house of fresh and original architectural combinations; and it has done, is doing, and is to do, a most beneficent work, in elevating, liberalizing, and let us trust, in revolutionizing the architecture of this city. It has become a suggester, a prompter, an educator. It has elevated the standard of architecture, public and private. It has set people to talking, definitely and critically, upon a subject in regard to which, hitherto, they have said nothing, and known but little.—It is a thing of positive power and positive influence; and will inevitably, and must necessarily, enrich the local expression of the great art of which it is so proud an offspring.[65]

Eidlitz's City Hall, designed and built in 1853–55 and destroyed by fire in 1905, was one of the most vigorous statements made in the American *Rundbogenstil* (fig.

3.14). The building survives only in photographs of its exterior and in detailed descriptions of its interior. In the functional-structural design of the building's massing and in the careful consideration of its ornament and polychromy, Eidlitz strove for a building appropriate to the people and city of Springfield. As a small but then prosperous town with a central place in colonial and national history, due largely to the Springfield Armory, established in 1777 to manufacture weapons used in the American Revolution, Springfield aspired to an artfully designed municipal building that would not only house the requisite administrative functions, but also symbolize the citizens' American spirit.

The main body of the sandstone and brick City Hall was organized into three bays, with the center entry defined by a three-arched portal reminiscent of St. George's. The great assembly hall on the *piano nobile* (the main floor, above ground level), which reportedly held 3,000 and had a 40-foot ceiling, was clearly visible on the exterior, marked by immense round-arched windows in a similar manner to Alexander Saeltzer's Astor Library (fig. 3.15). Had the building been composed solely of this symmetrical three-bay mass, it would be a fine and faithful example of Rundbogenstil. But Eidlitz appended a 130-foot bell tower with a cross-gabled pinnacle to one side of the building that broke the symmetry of the composition. The tower was obviously planned according to its own purpose and not as a subordinate to the main wing. Its proportions did not match, and its windows lined up with its interior stair landings and not with the stringcourses or windows of the main wing. The resulting asymmetry had a vernacular quality of detached parts recombined according to functional concerns—the tower could almost have been a later addition, like the mismatched towers of medieval cathedrals such as Chartres, rather than part of the original conception of the building. The façade's decorative details also had a medieval sensibility, with crenellations and decorative brickwork marking the cornice and vegetal column capitals on the *piano nobile*.[66] The overall composition made it clear how the interior spaces functioned.

Eidlitz's ideas about structure and function did not

3.14 Springfield City Hall, Springfield, Massachusetts, 1853–55.

3.15 Alexander Saeltzer, Astor Library, New York, 1849, with additions by Thomas Griffith, 1859 and Thomas Stent, 1879. Marc Eidlitz was the building contractor for the second addition. *Marc Eidlitz and Son* (1904).

end with the overall massing and composition, however. In the interior of the Springfield City Hall, the architect continued his search for an expressive form language appropriate to the building's central place in the social and political community. The assembly hall, as the centerpiece of this "revelation," was one of the first intensely polychromed interiors in America. Exposed iron girders and painted wooden trusswork supported the ceiling of the great hall, about 75 feet across and 125 feet long. The effect was surprising and unusual, causing a com-

mentator to note wryly that the supports were arranged in "so graceful a manner that they soon become familiar, and their slender lines cease to give offense to the eye, whatever may be their first effect." The novelty of the design was heightened by the color scheme that Eidlitz devised to highlight the construction of the building. The lines of the ceiling were painted in brilliant red and blue, as were the railings of the galleries and their supporting brackets; at the meeting of the ceiling and walls was a "fancifully colored" cornice supported by "columns of color" between the great arched windows. Figural frescoes of George Washington and the Goddess of Liberty, painted by the German muralists Stowe and Borgelt, adorned the wall behind the ceremonial stage, and the windows themselves had a slight red tint to enhance the warmth of the color scheme. The invocation of Washington, as the foremost of the founding fathers, was particularly appropriate because he had designated Springfield the site of the National Armory in 1794. It is possible that the City Hall's crenellated corner tower may have been intended to evoke the imagery of fortification, in keeping with the town's national military significance.

Holland spoke passionately about how the new building was "the exponent of the wants of the city." It served as more than a "receptacle for the . . . varied machinery of a healthy municipal life," becoming a "teacher of new and beautiful architectural ideas." The City Hall was a "revelation" whose "walls are broader than they seem—they inclose [sic] the hearts of a city—a common floor beneath them, a common roof above!" Holland declared "every room is a stanza, every fresco a line, whose illuminated initial letters are arched windows and carved desks and cabinets. There is no paucity of forms and fancies,—no barren, brainless iteration of common places."[67] William Thackeray, author of *Vanity Fair*, while on a literary tour of the United States, reportedly said the hall was the most beautiful he had seen in the U.S. and more beautiful than any in England except for one, which went unnamed.[68] The combination of exposed structure highlighted by polychromy in primary colors and broad expanses of wall space given over to a combination of repetitive geometric patterns and large narrative mural history paintings provided a vivid and unprecedented experiment in expressiveness.

The key for Eidlitz was finding the right clients, like Booth and Holland, and the right commissions, like St. George's, the Broadway Tabernacle, and the Brooklyn Academy of Music. Where other Gilded Age architects found their clients at their clubs, Eidlitz tended to seek out political connections, and by the 1870s he had made deep inroads into the Democratic machinery. The Viaduct Railway proved extraordinarily important in this respect. The investors in Eidlitz and Serrell's plans included, in addition to Booth, William Tweed and Peter Sweeny, Manton Marble, editor of the *New York World*, and Peter Cooper.[69] In 1876, Eidlitz was a vice president of the citizens group formed to promote the

mayoral candidacy of Andrew Green, who had quickly become more than a park commissioner and was in 1871 the comptroller who oversaw the reconstruction of the city's finances after the ouster of Tweed and Sweeny. His fellow campaigners included Booth and such New York luminaries as Royal Phelps, Theodore Roosevelt, Sr., and William Cullen Bryant.[70] Green had been a lawyer in Samuel J. Tilden's firm in the 1840s; Tilden would later become governor of New York (1874–76) and a champion of Eidlitz and H. H. Richardson's design of the New York State Capitol. Eidlitz presented a copy of his 1881 book *The Nature and Function of Art* to his "friend" Simon Sterne, a New York lawyer who was a key figure in the breakup of the corrupt Tweed Ring in 1871.[71] This connection, in addition to that with Booth, most likely assured him of the 1876 commission to complete the New York County Courthouse, now better known as the Tweed Courthouse. He was connected with Peter Cooper again through the American Photographical Society—they were both founding members of the group. He knew his son Edward Cooper through his membership in the General Society of Mechanics and Tradesmen of New York City. To Edward, he gave another copy of his book, inscribed "from your friend Leopold."[72]

But most indicative of Eidlitz's search for allies was his earlier professional association with Fernando Wood, the mayor of New York from 1855 to 1858 and again from 1860 to 1862. For Wood, Eidlitz worked on multiple commissions: Wood's house (ca. 1860), the temporary structure for celebrating the visit of the Prince of Wales (October 11–13, 1860), the refurbishment of the New York City Hall after an 1858 fire, and probably the initial plan for the Viaduct Railway from 1859.[73] Wood was another self-made man who entered politics with a vision of taking on the powerful clique that ran Tammany Hall and bringing power to the common man.

What Wood actually accomplished, however, is subject to much debate. During his tenure in office, he fanned the flames of ethnic and class divisions by fighting for secession from the Union rather than siding with abolitionists in the Civil War. The 1863 New York draft riots, though they took place during the Republican

RIOT IN NEW YORK. REAR OF THE CITY HALL. ATTACK OF THE MUNICIPAL UPON THE METROPOLITAN POLICE.

3.16 "Riot in New York. Rear of City Hall. Attack of the Municipal upon the Metropolitan Police." *Frank Leslie's Illustrated Newspaper* (June 7, 1857).

mayoralty of George Opdyke, are often ascribed in part to Wood's previous anti-Union positions. Wood had used the gang warfare between Bowery Boys and Dead Rabbits, immortalized in Herbert Asbury's tale *The Gangs of New York* (1927), to solidify his power. New York's state government even took sides against Wood, attempting to remove him from office in 1857 by creating a new police division, the Metropolitan Police, that battled with Wood's own police force, the Municipal Police, on the steps of City Hall, surely a low moment

in city history (fig. 3.16). Despite the widespread looting and assault and his eventual removal from office, Wood was reelected mayor in 1860.

While his tenure as mayor of New York was marred by corruption, some have argued that Wood's nascent populism also made him a "city builder" and an "urban progressive" who "championed the interest of the working class and immigrants and sought to avoid incipient class conflict by urging businessmen to develop a social conscience that placed human rights over property rights."[74] Eidlitz's connection with Wood is intriguing and, in light of Eidlitz's own antislavery position, must have been based on a pragmatic understanding of how New York politics operated. Schuyler's posthumous declaration that Eidlitz could tolerate politicians because of a shared desire to "leave monuments of public utility behind" is no doubt an accurate assessment.[75] Despite the corruption of Wood's administration, which was surpassed in degree by the mayors of the 1860s and 1870s, Eidlitz's interest in the betterment of the working class dovetailed with many of Mayor Wood's social policies. While there is no surviving evidence to show the exact nature of their relationship, the two men clearly had a professional connection through about 1860. While far from the kind of royal patronage an architect would have sought in Prague or Vienna, Wood's political patronage provided Eidlitz with the validation he sought far more than a commission from a wealthy client would have.

In his preference for civic commissions, Eidlitz was clearly out of the mainstream of architects by 1870. Commercial architecture and the emergent skyscraper became the commission of choice in the decades after the Civil War, but Eidlitz persisted in his old model

of practice. Architects like Hunt and Post embraced the new mercantile spirit of the age with great success. Hunt's ten-story New York Tribune Building (1873–75), whose awkward proportions were roundly dismissed on aesthetic grounds, showed that Hunt had a keen understanding of the formal implications of the new commercial architecture (see fig. 4.16). The Tribune Building was an immensely successful building, not because of its appearance or formidable engineering, but because it commanded substantial rents for its owner.[76] But Eidlitz never executed a commercial commission on the scale of Hunt's. Instead, he continued with his belief in architecture as a profoundly social art that had a responsibility to educate the public. In the 1870s, he became preoccupied not with the development of the skyscraper, but with the development of a language of public, governmental architecture that espoused the ideals of American democracy.

4

ARCHITECTURE AS CRITIQUE

The New York State Capitol Commission

EIDLITZ, DESPITE HIS CLASHES WITH THE AIA, ENTERED THE 1870S riding a wave of accomplishment. With the accolades for Temple Emanu-El ringing in his ears, he began the next phase of his artistic career with his creative acumen at its sharpest. He permanently shifted his design idiom away from the German *Rundbogenstil* of his earlier years. By the 1860s, Eidlitz's work had become more polychromatic, more overwhelming to the eye—the color and ornament that had been typical of his interiors in the 1850s became absolutely central to his design conceptions. Temple Emanu-El freed Eidlitz from any earlier sense of restraint and pushed him toward a greater emphasis on color and pattern, marking the final stage in Eidlitz's development of a mature conception of the organic ideal in design, a union of mass, structure, materials, and ornament. The New York State Capitol commission (1876–83), while it ultimately doomed Eidlitz's career, was the culmination of all of Eidlitz's previous study and his most successful experiment in organic architecture.

But before his work on the capitol began, a handful of work from the early 1870s outlined the new direction his work would take. The Dry Dock Savings Bank and the Decker Brothers Building, two new commercial commissions, show Eidlitz's move toward the High Victorian Gothic that seized New York in the 1870s (fig. 4.1). Frederick Clarke Withers and Calvert Vaux's Jefferson Market Courthouse and Jail (1873–77) is perhaps the best-known American example of the polychromy and picturesque asymmetry that typify the movement's principles (fig. 4.2). The building is a collection of disparate and variously scaled parts, with the jail, market,

Opposite: See page 110.

4.1 Dry Dock Savings Bank, New York, 1873–75. *AR* (October 1908).

4.2 Frederick Clarke Withers with Calvert Vaux, Jefferson Market Courthouse and Jail, New York, 1874. Photograph by Cervin Robinson, 1960. HABS NY,31-NEYO,65-1.

and courthouse bound together by bands of red and buff brick highlighted by carved stone details in the pediments and along structural seams. The tower that crowns the complex looms clumsily overhead, a brooding sentinel in a neighborhood that, in the 1870s, was "bad, mean, and unsavory."[1]

Since the 1850s, Eidlitz had of course already experimented with asymmetry, modeling, and the collision of disparate masses as a means toward an expressive, organically derived architecture. The bulky tower and squat body of the Dry Dock Savings Bank clearly continue that interest, making the bank a solid and seemingly eternal urban presence. But comparing this turreted, multidimensional building with the American Exchange Bank of just twenty years earlier (see fig. 2.11) shows just how far Eidlitz had gone in the direction of surface ornamentation and polychromy. The walls of Dry Dock still have the rigid, flat quality of Eidlitz's earlier work, but the surfaces are striated, mottled, and colored with sharp contrasts equivalent to the contrasts in scale exhibited in the mass of the building.

The façade of the Decker Brothers Building (1869–70), a narrow five-story shop front built on the west side of Union Square as a salesroom for pianos but which

4.3 Decker Building, New York, 1870. *AR* (October 1908).

also served as the first home for Brentano's bookstore in its basement, has the same sense of planarity overlaid with a dressing of stone and brick (fig. 4.3). In both cases, the surface ornamentation visually divides the building into its constituent parts so that one can read the building clearly as it grows from a solid base at the street to a more elaborate, more finely modeled profile at the top. The play of scale, from the broad doorway at the first level to the interlaced pointed arches over the windows to the miniscule dormers in the mansard roof, is heightened by the use of alternating light and dark voussoirs that contrast with the darker brick surface of the wall. The building reads as a skeleton of white arches

outlining the large voids of windows recessed behind their frames. These visual effects were not lost on contemporary viewers; one review of the building specifically noted that "the variety of ingenious forms adopted for windows in the several stories, the distinction and meaning of the ornamentation, the tasteful combination and contrasts of different stones and brickwork, all exhibit traces of artistic thought and skill."[2] Though the building's ornament could be called Gothic, Romanesque, or the more exotic Moorish, it again defied stylistic conventions. Schuyler, always a keen observer of Eidlitz's work, put it beautifully: its "combination of brick and stone and the mild polychromy of the stonework . . . gave the Venetian look to a front in which the detail owed nothing to North Italy."[3] In 1892, John Edelman, Louis Sullivan's mentor and dear friend, designed the eleven-story replacement for Eidlitz's building that still stands today on Union Square West, a more refined and restrained reinterpretation of the Venetian-Moorish strands in Eidlitz's original.

But it was the Church of the Holy Trinity that was the most astounding design in Eidlitz's new phase. Sited at the corner of Madison Avenue and 42nd Street, directly on top of the old Jacob Wrey Mould–designed chapel, and half a block from the new Grand Central Station, Holy Trinity combined expressive asymmetrical massing with bold polychromy (figs. 4.4, 4.5). Dubbed by detractors as the "Church of the Homely Oilcloth," the stone and brick diaper work in blue, yellow, and brown tones, set with black mortar, was laid in contrasting patterns in different portions of the building. Along the clerestory level, a pattern of dark X's contrasted with an infill of lighter diamonds; on the front façade at the gallery level, the pattern was inverted, with lighter X's and dark diamonds. In the gabled peak, the same motifs reappeared at a different scale, the diamond angles, sandwiched into horizontal bands and directly echoing the proportion of the steeply pitched roof, neatly fitting into its apex. The pointed arches over the windows were defined by contrasting dark and light stone voussoirs, using a different palette than the skin of the building. The single tower on the 42nd Street corner doubled the height of the building, with stubby Gothic columns sup-

4.4 Church of the Holy Trinity, New York, 1872–74. View of the front façade on Madison Avenue, ca. 1890. The bulbous mansards of the Grand Central Depot are visible at rear. Milstein Division of United States History, Local History & Genealogy, The New York Public Library, Astor, Lenox and Tilden Foundations.

4.5 Church of the Holy Trinity. View along 42nd Street toward Madison Avenue. *AR* (September 1908).

porting an enormous, nearly vertical slate-roofed cupola shaped like a witch's cap that drew on Prague's pinnacled peaks (see fig. 3.12). At the rear of the church, again on the 42nd street side, another smaller tower with a similar profile emerged awkwardly from the nave, marking the separate entrance to the chapel and meeting rooms. Dubbed "continental Gothic" by the *New York Times*, the building did share the slate-roofed polychromy of St. Stephen's in Vienna, but certainly nothing else.[4]

Seating about 1,900, the church was commissioned by the Reverend Stephen Tyng, Jr., son of Eidlitz's first client at St. George's. Holy Trinity was even more aggressively Low Church Episcopalian than St. George's and located in a part of town that by the 1870s was more associated with the downtrodden than the wealthy. Holy Trinity was at the vanguard of the evangelical movement and had as its object, according to one writer at the time, "the evangelization of the masses of New York and vicinity—the vicinity being the *rest* of the United States." The younger Tyng, a lawyer and a graduate of Williams College, was charismatic and ambitious, and Holy Trinity had an extensive program of missions as well as a "school for evangelists," which trained young men and women to venture out into the streets of New York to shepherd converts to the church. The church, to increase its appeal, hosted a broad range of social and spiritual activities. It held sewing classes and mothers' meetings,

4.6 "Sunday Afternoon Temperance Meeting," at the Church of the Holy Trinity. Dr. Tyng proclaims in the foreground to an audience of the dispossessed in one of the church's meeting rooms. *Harper's Weekly* (April 28, 1877).

4.7 William Butterfield, All Saints Church, London, 1849–59. *Builder* (1853).

fed the poor, and hosted temperance meetings. Holy Trinity's emphasis was on the individual's knowledge of Christ rather than the minister as a mediating force. As Tyng, Jr. put it, "Our design is to accept such only as have an experimental knowledge of Christ as a personal and all-sufficient Saviour." Henry Ward Beecher, leader of Brooklyn's immensely successful Plymouth Congregational Church, expressed skepticism of Tyng's methods, viewing his army of trained evangelicals as taking "short cuts" to the ministry.[5]

But the church was for a time, before Tyng's untimely resignation in 1881 to become an insurance executive in Paris, exactly the magnet Tyng and his supporters wished it to be (fig. 4.6). Peter Cooper was among the supporters of Tyng's mission, giving money to the church and giving them space to worship in the Cooper Union while construction disrupted the use of their sanctuary.[6] The interior continued Eidlitz's emphasis on unified interior volumes, but this time the "preaching box" took on the shape of an ellipse rather than the traditional rectangular nave. To preserve the integrity of the ellipse, two enormous wooden trusses ran the longitudinal length of the building, providing support to the steeply pitched roof while leaving the geometry of the floor plan undisturbed.

The vibrancy of the church, so unlike the sobriety of St. George's and the Broadway Tabernacle, had little precedent in New York. Its only relative was Mould's All Souls Unitarian Church, a more stridently colored composition that Eidlitz admired for its experimentation but ultimately found unsuccessful because its ornamentation undermined perception of the overall structure.[7] Instead, Holy Trinity may trace its roots to some of the applications of associationism in England. Urban churches in London took on bold forms and bold colors, as art historian George Hersey has argued, to attract the attention of the uneducated and the poor, who were thought to need something shocking and opulent to raise their interest and attention. All Saints, William Butterfield's red and black brick extravaganza on Margaret Street in "bohemian" London, was an exemplar of this attempt to use architecture as a symbol of both the church's power and its attraction (fig. 4.7). As the Bishop of Exeter explained, "Where the congregation consists mainly of the poorest orders, there we commonly observe a love of a majestic and even elaborate service. The ornaments of their church . . . gladdens while it elevates their minds."[8] Clearly, at Holy Trinity the desire for Low Church severity was balanced against the need to bequeath a lavish gift to the poor.

These works allowed Eidlitz to explore ideas that received their fullest expression in the controversial designs for the New York State Capitol at Albany (fig. 4.8). In 1875, he—along with Henry Hobson Richardson and Frederick Law Olmsted—was called in to take over the design and construction process. A storm of criticism immediately erupted; the AIA vehemently protested the involvement of the new Advisory Board, as the trio was called. But despite the negative publicity that ensued, the capitol project consumed Eidlitz's practice for the next decade, as he dedicated himself almost exclusively to this single project alone. His Assembly Chamber and its Golden Corridor were the masterpieces of his career and represented his most mature exploration of the relationship between structure and ornament, but they were extremely short-lived. In the wake of structural difficulties that plagued Eidlitz's vaulting, his signature contributions to the building were destroyed by a most unsympathetic remodeling in the late 1880s.

While the convoluted building campaign of the capitol building is not an unknown story in American architectural history, when viewed within the context of Eidlitz's career it takes on a new significance. Biographers of Olmsted and Richardson have briefly treated the Albany episode, unanimously concluding that the controversy had no lasting negative impact on either man's career. Similarly, Hunt's biographers have treated the controversy lightly, passing over it as a minor disappointment.[9] Accompanying the long-term and very successful recent restoration efforts at the capitol building,

the events surrounding the building's history have been reconstructed from a more objective point of view.[10] Restoration of Eidlitz's vaulted ceiling is currently under discussion, sponsored by the New York State Commission on the Restoration of the Capitol, though ironically, in view of Eidlitz's insistence on the honesty of materials, in lightweight artificial materials and not in the original stone.

But despite these investigations, the importance of the capitol controversy in Eidlitz's career and in the development of the American architectural profession has been underestimated. No other series of events so sharply and publicly divided architects against each other until the construction of Louis Sullivan's Transportation Building at the 1893 Chicago World's Exposition.[11] Eidlitz and Richardson, and to a much lesser extent Olmsted, were excoriated both for their designs and for their professional behavior by the AIA, led by Richard Morris Hunt, George B. Post, Carl Pfeiffer, and Richard Michell Upjohn (who inherited his father's practice). While Richardson, who had been in active practice only about ten years and was still at an early stage in his career, recovered fully from the episode, Eidlitz, who had been practicing for thirty years, was deeply scarred. A look at the capitol controversy serves as a means of understanding how the tensions between progressivism and conservatism that had been building in Eidlitz's debates with the AIA since the late 1850s finally came to a head and left his career and reputation in a shambles. That the AIA had both the power and the desire to inflict this upon a fellow practitioner says equally as much about the direction the profession was to follow in the late nineteenth century.

THE CAPITOL COMMISSION
The New York State Capitol had been slowly coming to life since 1867 under the guidance of architect Thomas Fuller. But budget overruns, construction delays, and mounting concern over the quality of the design caused the New York legislature to reconsider the award of the commission to Fuller. In 1875, after an expenditure of over $4 million, the building had only reached its second story (fig. 4.9). After a series of committee hearings,

4.8 New York State Capitol at Albany, 1867–99. Thomas Fuller, Leopold Eidlitz, H. H. Richardson, and Isaac G. Perry, architects. Fellowcrafts' Photo Shop, 1915. LC-USZ62-59216.

4.9 The progress of construction of the New York State Capitol at Albany when Eidlitz, Richardson, and Olmsted were called in to critique the design in 1875.

Eidlitz, Richardson, and Olmsted were asked to write a report detailing what their plans would be if they were to take over the project. The Advisory Board's report, which subjected Fuller's design to a scathing review, came out in 1876. Shortly thereafter, the Eidlitz & Richardson firm, formed specifically to deal with the capitol design, officially acquired the commission to complete the building.

How the trio of Eidlitz, Richardson, and Olmsted came to work together has never been firmly established. Lieutenant Governor William Dorsheimer was an established patron of Richardson's, and Olmsted, the designer with Calvert Vaux of Central Park and the sanitary commissioner during the Civil War, was a well-known manager of public works projects. Eidlitz's connections, though, have been harder to pin down. He had long been a friend to Olmsted and had sided with him against Hunt in an earlier controversy in which Olmsted had fought to keep Hunt's architectural designs from being built within Central Park.[12] Eidlitz's connections to New York City government and his history of testimony before the state legislature on issues of building code regulations made him a known quantity.[13] Schuyler suggested that Manton Marble, the editor of the *New York*

World, so admired Eidlitz's work that he successfully lobbied his friend, then-Governor Tilden, for his inclusion on the commission.[14] Marble knew Eidlitz from their business association surrounding the unbuilt Viaduct Railway scheme; Tilden was also closely connected with Andrew Green, whom Eidlitz supported in his run for mayor of New York City. While the specifics that brought about the arrangement may never be known, the three quickly established a cordial working relationship, with Richardson reportedly saying of Eidlitz: "I never met a man who had architecture so completely at his fingers' ends." Eidlitz returned the compliment, protesting that "Richardson has far more copiousness of invention than I."[15] Richardson even named his son, born in 1876, Frederick Leopold William Richardson in honor of the collaborators.

The contrast between Fuller's and Eidlitz & Richardson's initial designs, which were published in the *American Architect and Building News* in March 1876, was marked (figs. 4.10, 4.11). Fuller's was an ornate Second Empire monster, piled high with pilasters, paired columns, entablatures, pediments, swags, and mansard-roofed towers. Eidlitz & Richardson, despite the fact that two stories of Fuller's building had

4.10 Thomas Fuller, design for the New York State Capitol at Albany, 1867. *Harper's Weekly* (1869).

4.11 New York State Capitol Building perspective, 1876, as proposed by the Advisory Board of Eidlitz, Richardson, and Olmsted. This drawing shows Eidlitz's hand; the final building shows Richardson's. *AABN* (1876).

already been completed, suggested building a Gothic and Romanesque fantasy topped by an enormous slate-roofed dome. While the existing footprint of the building could not be changed, they clearly intended to abandon Fuller's classical overture. The Eidlitz & Richardson composition was more substantial and less fussy, emphasizing the mass of the building more than the encrustation of details on its surface. On the interior, Eidlitz and Richardson clearly divided the commission, following Eidlitz's usual practice, with Eidlitz designing the dome, the Assembly Chamber, and two staircases on the east side of the building and Richardson designing the Senate Chamber and the great entry staircases on the west side (fig. 4.12). Olmsted designed plantings for the Golden Corridor and landscaping for the capitol grounds; the latter was never executed.

The most unusual feature of the design was Eidlitz's Gothic dome (fig. 4.13). These drawings were the most advanced of the interior schemes at the time of publication and showed a marriage of the skeletal structure of Brunelleschi's Florence dome with a Gothic sense of

structural ornamentation. Similar to but more archeological than Eidlitz's conception was Sir Gilbert Scott's 1872 scheme for the Reichstag in Berlin, which was rejected but published in the *Builder* (London) in August 1875, perhaps too late to have had a direct influence on Eidlitz's initial designs (fig. 4.14).[16] The idea of a Gothic dome had been earlier floated in England by E. M. Barry in his design, also rejected, for the 1867 New Law Courts. The creation of a Gothic dome, a form foreign to medieval builders, was the final step in secularizing the Gothic form language; for Eidlitz, unlike Scott or Barry, it was also a step toward proving its relevance to modern-day life. The Gothic, as Eidlitz showed again and again, was about structure and not about historical precedent. The dome at the capitol was about the expression of unified interior space, of public service contained beneath an overarching and embracing roof.

These early Eidlitz & Richardson schemes, however, were not those eventually built. At this stage, Eidlitz had clearly done most of the work: the design for the exterior is far more in keeping with his polychromatic work of the 1870s than with Richardson's more sober and more elegant compositions. The polychromy of the Church of the Holy Trinity bears a marked similarity to the proposed capitol. By contrast, Richardson's Trinity Church in Boston (1872–77) was nearing completion, showing his emphasis on symmetry and the subordination of ornament beneath the mass of the building (fig.

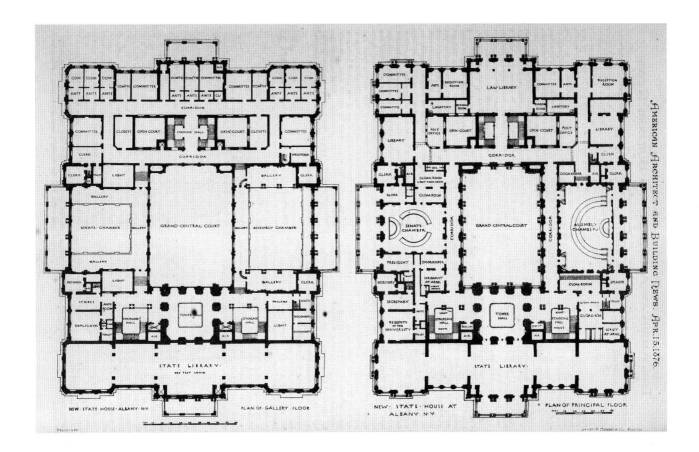

AMERICAN ARCHITECT AND BUILDING NEWS. APR. 15, 1876.

4.12 New York State Capitol plan, as proposed by the Advisory Board of Eidlitz, Richardson, and Olmsted, later modified. *AABN* (1876).

4.15). Protests over the too-Gothic appearance of the capitol design caused modifications that produced the more restrained Richardson design that was actually built, without the dome, and moving toward a French Romanesque-Renaissance conception of ornament. Despite the more graceful Richardsonian feeling of the new design, traces of Eidlitz's Gothic detailing remained, especially in the gabled windows.

The reaction to the publication of the Advisory Board's designs was swift and vitriolic and focused on two major themes: the design itself and the professional behavior of the architects. On the former issue, the completion of the upper stories of the building in a style different than that of the first two stories gave affront. Hunt, in 1876, composed a letter of protest to the New York State Senate on behalf of the Albany and New York chapters of the AIA in which he declared that "the Chapter finds that the projected work is designed in direct antagonism to the received rules of art. . . .

This design is false in principle, an agglomeration of incongruous forms, its details are inharmonious, and the result must be bad. . . ."[17] When this early protestation did not secure the resignation of Eidlitz & Richardson, Hunt and the New York AIA continued their critique. In public testimony before the legislature and in articles published in the *World,* the *Times,* the *Tribune,* as well as in the *American Architect and Building News*, the New York Chapter of the AIA, led by Hunt, called for either the completion of the exterior of the capitol according to Fuller's classical designs or the resignation of Eidlitz & Richardson. Citing "narrow-mindedness and blind devotion to a favorite style" as the reigning defect of the new architects' plans, they formally declared that were the building "allowed to be erected without formal

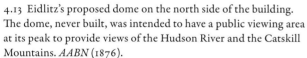

NEW STATE CAPITOL AT ALBANY.
SECTION THROUGH THE PROPOSED DOME.

HELIOTYPE.   JAMES R. OSGOOD & CO., BOSTON.

4.13 Eidlitz's proposed dome on the north side of the building. The dome, never built, was intended to have a public viewing area at its peak to provide views of the Hudson River and the Catskill Mountains. *AABN* (1876).

4.14 Sir Gilbert Scott, proposed design for Berlin Reichstag, 1872. Unbuilt. *Builder* (1875).

4.15 H. H. Richardson, Trinity Church, Boston, 1872–77. Photograph by Jack E. Boucher, 1987. MA 1215-2.

protest, it would be a perpetual reflection upon the architectural skill of the generation in whose time it was erected."[18]

Even architects who had been friendly with Eidlitz in the past chose sides in the new debate. Detlef Lienau, who had amicably served under Eidlitz on the AIA's Committee on Papers, had stated in 1859 that "the difference in our views will not separate us in the pursuit of our common interest, which is the good of our profession, and the elevation of our Art."[19] But in 1877, nearly twenty years later, Lienau was one of the group of five architects who traveled to Albany to testify before the Ways and Means Committee of the New York legislature about the "propriety"—meaning "impropriety"—of the new design for the capitol building proposed by Eidlitz & Richardson. Accompanying him as representatives of the New York Chapter of the AIA were Napoleon LeBrun, Henry Dudley, George B. Post, and, of course, Richard Morris Hunt.[20]

Others joined in to lambaste Eidlitz & Richardson's judgment, and many interesting epithets were created to critique the new design. One of the most memorable, authored by the Rhode Island Chapter of the AIA, warned against acceptance of the new design because it would spread the "evil influence of mongrel architecture."[21] The crux of these critiques centered on this "mongrel" idea, a common theme in nineteenth-century discussions of art and science that reflected a larger and growing concern about the mixing of races, ethnicities, religions, and nationalities.[22] In the case of architecture, it was not that any particular style (the Gothic, Romanesque, or Renaissance) was necessarily preferable—though increasingly codes of appropriateness guided stylistic choices—but that the combination of any element of one style with any element of the others was akin to heresy. Eclecticism in general was acceptable. A Romanesque city hall down the street from a Renaissance state capitol, for example, was unobjectionable. But exceeding the bounds of any historical style, defying its quantified limits, within a single building was forbidden. This supposed, of course, that the defining characteristics of any particular style were agreed upon by all architects and further implied that experimentation was unwelcome.

The second cause for outrage was the belief that a professional breach of etiquette had occurred: Once an architect began work on a design, the AIA contended, he was forever in charge of that design. No one had the right to modify his plans once begun. Indeed, the first reaction of the AIA to the Albany situation was to add a new clause to its bylaws in 1876, sponsored by Richard Morris Hunt, specifically stating that an architect held control of his own designs.[23] It was considered to be a moral outrage that Eidlitz, Richardson, and Olmsted had dared propose changes at all.

This was not the first time the AIA had taken up this position against a fellow practitioner. In 1871, for example, the Philadelphia Chapter of the AIA had closed ranks against Frank Furness, the chapter's founder, because he had taken over the commission for the Philadelphia House of Correction from James Windrim. Though Windrim had quit the job in hopes of being rehired at a higher rate of pay, he accused Furness of unprofessional behavior and convinced the AIA to join him in giving Furness a "stern and public drubbing."[24] Furness, for his part, continued his work on the jail and disassociated himself permanently from the group whose Philadelphia Chapter he had helped to establish. What was new in the Albany case was just how public the drubbing became. Other chapters of the AIA were asked to join with the New York and Albany chapters in officially protesting their actions. All chapters, including Chicago, Philadelphia, Rhode Island, and Cincinnati, with the notable exception of the Boston AIA, signed on.[25] The reassignment of the contract to new architects, regardless of the faults of the original designer, became a point of deep offense not just to Fuller, but also to the profession as a whole.

Another issue gave the Albany controversy a new and particularly devastating punch: the *American Architect and Building News* (*AABN*), widely acknowledged as the first truly successful architectural periodical in America, began publication in January 1876, providing a national forum for the airing of the AIA's grievances against Eidlitz & Richardson. In March 1876, only two months into its existence, the *AABN* began its coverage of the capitol news, and it had difficulty maintaining a professional objectivity. There was confusion about whether or not the journal was supposed to support the AIA's point of view, and there was some pressure for the editor, W. P. P. Longfellow, a Boston architect who taught in William Ware's Beaux-Arts architecture program at MIT, to choose sides.[26] To his credit, he resisted and at first attempted to call the competition as he saw it. But his judgment wavered. At first, he thought Eidlitz & Richardson's designs a vast improvement over Fuller's, and the *AABN* stated, "The gratification which people who really care for architecture will derive from what these architects have done must be mixed with the regret for the loss of what the Albany Capitol might have been had they, or architects of their rank, had charge of it from the beginning."[27] But as the depth of the AIA's displeasure became known, he began to equivocate. Just a month later, the *AABN*'s front page took a different tack and chastised the Advisory Board, warning them that

> the thing for a person or board to do when called on to amend the design of another man is . . . to do so with as little destruction of its unity as possible; and the work which has already been done, if it is to be retained, should not be subjected to any needless indignity. When whole communities worked only in one style, and knew the practice of no other, it was natural that whatever additions they had to make to a building should be made in the only style they knew; but in our time, when there is no style understood to the exclusion of others, and with experts presumably capable of working in all, the case is altogether different.[28]

As the official publication of the AIA, the *AABN*'s issues in 1876 and 1877 were filled with letters from chapter presidents protesting the building, making the journal's coverage of the issue essentially one-sided and not in Eidlitz & Richardson's favor. While the AIA's rebuke of Furness had remained a Philadelphia issue, their castigation of Eidlitz & Richardson was decidedly national.

Regardless of the venue, the crusade against the Advisory Board's design consistently hammered away at these two basic points, design propriety and profes-

sional decorum. The Advisory Board's responses to the critiques of their peers were few and, considering Eidlitz's usual writing and speaking habits, unusually brief. Richardson's biographer Mariana Van Rensselaer suggested that his silence resulted from his personal affront at the actions of the New York AIA, of which he was a member. The AIA had failed to consult any of the architects involved before launching their public attacks, and Richardson found this deeply offensive.[29]

Olmsted, too, an honorary member of the AIA, was disturbed by the group's actions and composed a letter to Hunt, never sent, complaining bitterly of their actions.[30] At the first sign of the trouble, he had sought the advice of Charles Eliot Norton, the newly appointed first professor of art history at Harvard and a well-known and widely respected cultural figure and intellectual. The two corresponded across many months in 1876 and 1877 about the matter, with Norton siding with Olmsted and against the New York AIA, calling their protest "a foul blow and a weak one. . . . I certainly do not find . . . any 'direct antagonism to the received rules of art.' If they are antagonistic, it may be to certain canons of building laid down by some architects of the Renaissance, canons deduced not from principles of art, but from what were assumed to be classical models."[31] Norton's conclusions reassured Olmsted that Eidlitz & Richardson's designs were in fact preferable to Fuller's, and he continued to seek Norton's counsel during the ensuing debates. After Hunt, this time accompanied by James Renwick, Jr., traveled again to the capitol for yet another round of public testimony in 1877, Norton wrote, "I wonder, though without surprise, at the ill feeling which the protesting architects display; and at their consequent unfairness of statement and insinuation. They are doing much to injure the repute of the profession."[32] He wondered in particular that Hunt and Renwick should feel comfortable criticizing others on the grounds of stylistic purity.[33] Norton was quite right on this count, as Renwick's Church of the Covenant in New York (1863–65), with its combination of Byzantine round arches and Gothic pointed arches, was far from an architecture designed according to "the received rules of art." Hunt's New York Tribune Building (1874–76), with its mansard roof, awkward tower, and Neo-Grec brick detailing, also took liberties with style that could be construed, depending on one's point of view, as "mongrelizing" architecture (fig. 4.16). In Norton, the three capitol designers had a progressive thinker as an ally against the stylistic conservatism of their colleagues.

As for Eidlitz, in the absence of his papers, one can only imagine the nature of his personal reaction, which was likely a mixture of anger, contempt, and condescending humor. Privately, all three agreed that the real reason for Hunt's and the AIA's fury was merely professional jealousy. But whatever their private speculations and feelings, the Advisory Board did not publish an official response to the initial criticism. It is likely that Eidlitz, Olmsted, and Richardson largely held their tongues to prove their professional natures by not engaging in the undignified fray. Their pay from the State of New York was exceedingly generous and perhaps made the sting of the criticism more bearable: the Eidlitz & Richardson firm received $20,000 per year for their work for the duration of the project, divided equally between each.[34]

The collaboration between Eidlitz and Richardson was probably strengthened by the controversy, as the two men, so different in temperament and origins, had little in common to begin with and, in recognition of this, simply divided their work. Richardson, a southern gentleman from New Orleans who had studied at Harvard and in France before permanently settling in the Northeast after the Civil War, began his life with all the advantages of class and money. Common ground with Eidlitz came more from intellectual than social sources. Richardson, while never a theorist, had a deep affection for Emerson and things transcendental that gave the two a meeting point from which to develop their camaraderie in the face of the AIA's critiques.[35] As Schuyler reported, their journeys on the overnight steamer up the Hudson River from New York to Albany and back were filled with dynamic conversations among Eidlitz, Richardson, Olmsted, Dorsheimer, and himself: "There was Richardson, with his headlong precipitate enthusiastic discourse, suddenly brought up, as at a crisis of the rhapsody, with a proposition from Eidlitz, which, to impose

4.16 Richard Morris Hunt, New York Tribune Building, "Newspaper Row," New York, 1873–75. *AR* (1895).

itself as axiomatic needed but to be stated."[36] The two architects shared a view of history as a dynamic process rather than as an arbiter of design: neither Richardson's Romanesque nor Eidlitz's Gothic at Albany have any clear relationship to historical precedent, instead abstracting the essence of each. They surely appreciated the authentically medieval character of their designs, in which the history of the building, its change from one architect to the next, could be easily read in its walls.

Despite the extremely public complaints of their fellow architects, the team saw their designs implemented largely unchanged, though they did make one concession. By official act of the legislature, Eidlitz &

well as Italian High Renaissance.[37] Furthermore, the design of the interior courtyard façades continued in Eidlitz's more Gothic mode, since the interior walls were not subject to the legislation.

Ultimately, though, the controversy seems mostly to have made the architectural profession look rather foolish to the outside world. The letters to the editor, the articles, and the critiques were all published in many New York newspapers. And after a full year of controversy, in the eyes of the public, and even in the eyes of the profession, it became nothing more than classicists versus Gothicists. Olmsted's private contention that professional jealousy on the part of certain unnamed New York architects had spawned the entire debate was echoed in the press as well. Articles in New York newspapers tended to show that the public was intrigued more by the controversy over the design than by the design itself, about which it understood or cared little. Eventually, the *American Architect and Building News*, after itself fanning the flames of the debate for more than a year, observed in 1877 that

> if architects show serious disagreement in matters which they seem to think important, the public will lose its respect either for the matter in dispute or for the professional opinions of architects, or both. We doubt if any occurrence in this generation has done more to weaken the general confidence in architects as architects, among those who have witnessed it, than this unlucky quarrel.[38]

Ironically, it was the very attempt to establish and enforce professional standards of design and conduct that made architects look foolish. The dramatic and public posturing over an issue that did not seem exceptionally important to the masses ultimately ended up making the AIA look more like a social clique than a professional organization.

The opening of the first completed portions of the interior in 1879 did nothing to further the legitimacy of the AIA's scathing critiques of the design. Though New York's governor, Lucius Robinson, reportedly hated the new capitol design passionately, refusing to attend the

4.17 The Assembly Chamber, New York State Capitol, as completed in 1879. Aaron Veeder, photographer. Robert N. Dennis Collection of Stereoscopic Views, Miriam & Ira D. Wallach Division of Art, Prints & Photographs, The New York Public Library, Astor, Lenox and Tilden Foundations.

Richardson were required to complete the exterior of the building in an Italian Renaissance style. Richardson was clearly responsible for the majority of this second phase of the exterior design, and he interpreted the term "Renaissance" rather loosely, however, and we know from a statement made by Richardson to Olmsted that he wryly decided that French Renaissance would do as opening ceremonies, the public on the other hand was enchanted with Eidlitz's Assembly Chamber, Golden Corridor, and Assembly Staircase (figs. 4.17, 4.18, pages 6,7). (Richardson's portions of the design were completed later.) The Assembly Chamber reportedly had the widest span of any stone vault ever constructed and was painted in patterns of gold, red, and blue. Eidlitz designed the lamp standards and furniture for the room as well, and chose red carpet and upholstery. The stained glass was also executed in red, blue, and gold. It was the tour de force of Eidlitz's career and received glowing notice in *Harper's* and *Scribner's* among many others.

It even elicited grudging praise from hostile quarters. Eidlitz's old rival and Hunt's protégé Henry Van Brunt acknowledged Eidlitz's accomplishment at the capitol, writing that as far as Gothic designs were concerned, there was "no better and bolder composition to be found anywhere, none with more refinement and elaboration of execution, and none with more ingenious and beautiful detail." Van Brunt, however, greatly disagreed with the propriety of even considering the use of Gothic at the capitol and condescendingly wrote as well that "one hardly knows whether to admire [Eidlitz] for the boldness of his convictions, or to be amazed at his want of sympathy for what we have been accustomed to regard as the obvious proprieties of design."[39] He further cautioned Richardson, whose Senate Chamber was still in process, to pay more attention to the style of the exterior of the building when designing for the interior. Eidlitz's Chamber, though stunning, was, he warned, a jewel indifferent to its casket, inappropriately and unnecessarily at odds with the exterior and the rest of the building. The "war of styles" continued.

The flames of controversy were destined to rage anew in 1880 when the ambitious vault that Eidlitz designed for the Assembly Chamber had begun to show signs of cracking. It was with a somewhat ghoulish delight that the profession once again took up its attack on the capitol building. Letters again began to appear in the New York newspapers and in the *AABN* proudly proclaiming that they had been right to criticize the design all along—and especially now that the vault was showing signs of instability. Safety, as opposed to style, was an

4.18 Golden Corridor, New York State Capitol. Opened 1879. This space was dismantled in 1888 and now no longer exists in this form. The planters were designed by Frederick Law Olmsted. *AR* (November 1908).

issue that the public could really get behind. This time, Eidlitz could not count on Olmsted and Richardson to back him up. Both had moved on to other places and things. Desperate by the late 1880s for a show of support from his colleagues, Eidlitz seemed nevertheless to recognize that after all his years of fighting, he was truly on his own. In 1887, after years of being dogged by the controversy, he wrote to Olmsted imploring him for help, but also declaring, "I am willing as I have been on former occasions to fight this battle alone. . . ."[40]

The criticism began from within the legislature. Benjamin C. Butler, a legislator from Warren County who had been opposed to Eidlitz & Richardson's designs from the beginning, assailed Eidlitz's designs in January

4.19 Richard Michell Upjohn, Connecticut State Capitol, Hartford, 1875–85. Perspective drawing, 1875. *New York Sketch Book of Architecture* (1875).

4.20 A view of the foundation pit, showing the soil and stone on which the New York state capitol was built.

1881, saying that the Assembly Chamber and Golden Corridor amounted to nothing more than "architectural quackery."[41] Butler, no doubt coached by his old New York AIA friends, wished longingly for a building like Richard Michell Upjohn's pure white marble Connecticut State Capitol Building, rather than the show of color and drama in Eidlitz's "oriental grandeur."[42] Ironically, Upjohn's Capitol Building was quite as much a hybrid as Eidlitz & Richardson's, with its classical white marble, its Renaissance paired columns, and its Gothic pointed arches (fig. 4.19). Butler, nevertheless, recommended completely abandoning the cracking Chamber and starting anew with a more mechanically, ornamentally, and fiscally responsible architect. One imagines he would have suggested Hunt or Upjohn for this new endeavor.

A new Advisory Board was formed to investigate the capitol in 1882. This time, Eidlitz—instead of Fuller—was on the receiving end and George Post, Charles Babcock, and W. P. Trowbridge were called in by the legislature to second-guess his design; this first report recommended that "the architect be instructed to remove all of the stone vaulting . . . and to supply

the place of the groined ceiling with a construction of wood."[43] They couched their criticisms in terms of professionalism, citing the incompatibility between Fuller's foundation and Eidlitz's vault designs as the source of the problem. Uneven settling had occurred because of the great weight of the vault and the shifting nature of the soil, and without more substantial foundations, they were uncertain that the vault could be stabilized (fig. 4.20). Adding to the difficulty was Eidlitz's original recommendation that the attic above the vault be kept warm to ensure that the tie rods did not shrink and swell with the weather; Post, Babcock, and Trowbridge found this to be a thoroughly impracticable arrangement. These men—of whom the first two had just four years earlier so vehemently and publicly promoted the idea that an architect's work should not be tampered with by other architects—now published a report declaring Eidlitz's design faulty because he placed his construction on a foundation designed by a different man for different purposes. An article written by H. W. Fabian and published in the *AABN* subjected the vault to a series of calculations and culminated in the statement that "absolute security can be obtained only by tearing down the whole vault and building another in its place."[44]

Eidlitz, of course, disagreed. To Fabian he wrote a brief reply stating that his calculations were incorrect because based on incorrect figures regarding the loads of the vault and the lines of its springing.[45] With the sup-

4.21 Since the removal of Eidlitz's vault, the Assembly Chamber has had a flat, wooden ceiling. The view here is from 1913 and clearly shows how the new ceiling cuts off the profile of the pointed arches in the galleries. LC-USZ62-95464.

port of Olmsted and Richardson, Eidlitz also authored a report in 1882 that detailed the errors of the Post, Babcock, and Trowbridge investigation. Their calculations, he believed, did not support their conclusions. Instead of proving that settling had occurred, he believed their measurements showed that the vault and foundations had construction errors that could be corrected. With these corrections and proper maintenance, the vault would be perfectly safe.[46]

For several years, the legislature apparently followed neither the recommendations of Post and Babock nor of Eidlitz, and the ceiling simply continued to deteriorate. By 1888, chunks of stone began to fall, and Eidlitz wrote an urgent letter stating that "by reason of the long neglect above referred to, we deem it our duty to respectfully protest against the further occupancy of the north wing of the Capitol in its present condition."[47] Eidlitz urged the legislature to make repairs immediately. Yet another commission was formed to investigate the Chamber's structure, this time headed by Richard Michell Upjohn, joined by two engineers, John Bogart and Thomas C. Clarke. The team reached the same conclusion that Eidlitz had already reached, namely that the Chamber in its present state was not safe. Their recom-

mendation of how to proceed, however, differed greatly from Eidlitz's. They, as had the previous commission, recommended dismantling the vault immediately and replacing it with a coffered wooden ceiling.[48] This time, work proceeded quickly and the vault was removed. But even this unambitious remodeling did not escape a storm of controversy, as the contractor clandestinely used plaster rather than oak in the new ceiling, pocketing the enormous difference in cost.[49]

Which side of the story was correct is nearly impossible to determine now since the removal of the vault has left little evidence to study (fig. 4.21, page 7). And while this second episode in the Albany controversy may have left Richardson and Olmsted unscathed—they were both by this time no longer attempting to practice in New York City, having moved to friendlier Brookline, Massachusetts—Eidlitz's reputation was indeed permanently affected. What should have been the crowning glory of his forty years of practice was instead destroyed. The irony of this situation, that Eidlitz's work was ruined because of the advice of an expert board of his peer architects, just as he had ruined Fuller's, cannot have escaped the AIA. The *AABN* declared that "the future reputation of the designer of the Assembly Chamber must rest upon the memory of those who have had the privilege of seeing his work before its demolition."[50] The message was clear: whatever its merits may have been, Eidlitz's design was gone and would soon be forgotten, thus closing the chapter on the controversy once and for all.

What is striking about this second episode is that the New York AIA members were perfectly willing to close ranks and attack a fellow architect, breaking the principles that they had themselves just enacted. Professionalism, as viewed through this six years of controversy, ultimately seems to have meant that the opinions of the reigning members of the New York Chapter of the AIA on any architectural question were to be obeyed by all practitioners. From the view of Eidlitz, Richardson, and Olmsted, the AIA had become a group intent on creating a regulated sameness of attitude and allegiance. Though Eidlitz had had the foresight to quit the group in 1869, he could not escape its condemnation and its growing influence.

The design of the capitol at Albany is a watershed event in American architectural history. The controversy that Eidlitz became embroiled in represents a transitional moment, a moment when intolerance for certain practices and ideas in architecture became the accepted norm. While the 1893 World's Columbian Exposition in Chicago represented the ultimate triumph of Beaux-Arts planning and the City Beautiful movement, the rejection of Eidlitz's Grand Central School, followed closely by the New York State Capitol debacle, were the first steps toward the White City. The quest for uniformity and classicism in design, though lost in the experimental Romanesque and Gothic at Albany, would by the end of the century triumph.

THE DESIGN

One of the most unfortunate results of the controversy over the capitol is that it overshadowed the design itself. For Richardson, who went on to build many other important commissions, his Senate Chamber (completed to great fanfare in 1881) and Great Western Staircase are perhaps justifiably considered less interesting than

his epochal Trinity Church in Boston (1872–77) and Marshall Field Warehouse in Chicago (1885–87). But for Eidlitz, the Assembly Chamber, Assembly Staircase, and Senate Staircase were truly the culmination of decades of thinking, writing, and building. During the years Eidlitz worked on the capitol designs, from 1875 to about 1883, he also prepared the final manuscript for his major published work, *The Nature and Function of Art, More Especially of Architecture*, which appeared in 1881. Eidlitz intended the capitol design and his book to be his ultimate statement about architecture, conceived jointly in stone and in words. Considered together, the two works demonstrate Eidlitz's mature conception of an organic architecture that married structure, ornament, and populist ideals.

As with his designs in the 1850s and '60s, to focus exclusively on the Gothic elements of the Assembly Chamber is to miss its expression of Eidlitz's organic ideal. Despite Van Brunt's characterization of the Assembly Chamber as "unrelenting Gothic," the great hall makes Eidlitz's aversion to a Gothic *revival* most evident.[51] His Dry Dock banking floor was here inflated to massive scale, but still maintained the same spatial organization: a single great vault supported by four piers, creating one unbroken space beneath. The medieval Gothic had created space through the repetition of bays: a cathedral, while containing a great volume of space, does so by creating that space in series, one bay at a time, with the pattern of ribs recurring over and over. The overall effect is one of repetition and subdivision. Eidlitz's Assembly Chamber did have some trappings of the Gothic: pointed arches, ribbed vaults, and stained-glass windows. But the underlying effect was decidedly different. Eidlitz's early concern for the creation of unified internal volumes received its greatest expression in the Assembly Chamber. There was one great square stone vault with four massive ribs that covered the entire space. There were no bays, only four massive piers supporting the entire load. The spatial effect was decidedly more Roman than Gothic, with its emphasis on spanning an immense undivided space.

A comparison with the interior of Pugin and Charles Barry's House of Lords (1844–52) makes this distinction clear. In London, the space is completely English Gothic in character. The meeting space derives its form from a Gothic chapel, its longitudinal arrangement culminating in a focus on the throne standing in the place of the altar. Even when stripped of its Gothic details, the room would still derive its organizational concept from Gothic sources. Eidlitz's Assembly Chamber, though, used a Gothic vault but did not resemble any traditional Gothic spaces. A contemporary reviewer noted that it was more like a "model, life size, of a stupendous cavern in the rocks, at sight of which one ought to be struck with awe."[52] Eidlitz could have conceived of no greater compliment to his work than to have it compared to a naturally occurring cave, formed by forces of nature itself.

One could argue that the emphasis on stone construction was purely Gothic in intent, but Eidlitz was in fact attempting to push the limits of stone technology in the new industrial era. As the era of the skyscraper dawned in the late 1870s, it is somewhat ironic that the creation of this great vaulted space actually required a great deal of technical expertise and inventiveness. After the vault's removal, he became quietly obsessed with its failure, publishing a decade later a paper proposing standardized formulae for determining the strength of pillars.[53] Eidlitz created the widest-spanning vault in the Americas by embracing a thoroughly technical analysis of load distribution and by utilizing cast-iron tension rods in new ways to reinforce the strength of the vault. This feat was even more impressive given that there was a lack of skilled stonemasons in the United States, a problem that had already prevented the construction of a stone vault in Renwick's St. Patrick's Cathedral.[54] No such construction feat had been attempted in America, and Eidlitz marshaled the latest developments in engineering, material technology, and mathematics to secure his design.

The Assembly Chamber vault is also the greatest expression of Eidlitz's conception of a universal interior space, which he defined anew in *The Nature and Function of Art*. In it, Eidlitz wrote about "cells" as the generative forms for architecture: "The monument, to be a work of fine art, must be an aggregation of single cells, each of which is a complete organism in itself."[55]

The Chamber, then, was an enormous cell, designed, like so many of Eidlitz's other interior spaces, without specific regard to the building's exterior or to the other spaces within. The biological analogy was apt: the vault of the Assembly Chamber was like a rib cage, containing the heart of democracy within. This "cell" imagery may be a general reflection of the currency of biological analogy in the post-Darwinian late-nineteenth century. But it may also reflect Eidlitz's reading of Karl Marx's *Das Kapital*, in which the author used a cell-beehive analogy to describe labor and the practice of architecture:

> Labour is, in the first place, a process in which both man and Nature participate, and in which man of his own accord starts, regulates, and controls the material re-actions between himself and Nature. . . . A spider conducts operations that resemble those of a weaver, and a bee puts to shame many an architect in the construction of her cells. But what distinguishes the worst architect from the best of bees is this, that the architect raises his structure in imagination before he erects it in reality. At the end of every labour-process, we get a result that already existed in the imagination of the labourer at its commencement.[56]

In using the metaphor, Eidlitz intentionally used language that had visual, economic, scientific, and artistic connotations.

The "cell" of the Assembly Chamber was created to have a transportative visual effect. While he seemed to aim for the poetry of Goethe in some of his earlier religious spaces, in this secular space his ideas seem more closely related to the ideas of empathy explored by German aesthetician Friedrich Theodor Vischer. Vischer's theories centered on the idea of an *Einfühlung*, or empathy, between the observer and the built form. Through objective means, such as composition, massing, and ornamentation, an architect manipulated the subjective emotional response of the viewer.[57] To Eidlitz, this suggested a new phenomenological approach to design in which the architect could, by study of the history of architecture, learn what devices produced certain responses. Eidlitz wrote: "Architecture deals with ideas,

4.22 View across the Assembly Chamber, towards one of the massive fireplaces nestled into one of the dark corners beneath the seating galleries. The branching light standards designed by Eidlitz are also clearly visible here. Paul A. Chadbourne, *Public Service of the State of New York* (1882), vol. 1.

4.23 The Assembly Chamber showing William Morris Hunt's mural *The Flight of Night* in the tympana above the light streaming through clerestory windows. The desks in the foreground were designed by Eidlitz. Aaron Veeder, photographer. Robert N. Dennis Collection of Stereoscopic Views, Miriam & Ira D. Wallach Division of Art, Prints & Photographs, The New York Public Library, Astor, Lenox and Tilden Foundations.

and with ideas only. In the forming of a structure, it attempts to depict the soul of the structure, not merely to minister to the physical wants of its occupants."[58] The Chamber was the soul of the building, constructed to elicit the noblest feelings in its inhabitants.

The ornamental scheme for the chamber received no less attention than its structural conception. Ornament, for Eidlitz, "demonstrat[ed] function." His position, again, was similar to Ruskin's call for all ornament to be related to structure, but Eidlitz's argument was more the scientist's than Ruskin's. For Eidlitz, ornament was "the modelling of masses" and it began with the "arrangement of the masses themselves."[59] To this end, Eidlitz

arranged the subsidiary spaces of the Chamber in such a manner as to emphasize the immense size and openness of the central vaulted meeting floor. The contrast between the dark and close spaces beneath the visitors' galleries, warmed by immense fireplaces, and the lighter, open space in the center of the room was marked (figs. 4.22, 4.23). The stained-glass round-arched windows, grouped in threes reminiscent of the entry portal at Eidlitz's first commission at St. George's, filtered colored light into the room; the carpet was a deep red. The vault was incised with bands of geometricized vegetal ornament, the incised areas filled with red.

As with Eidlitz's earlier decorative schemes at Springfield City Hall and the Brooklyn Academy of Music, the Chamber's banding and arabesques seem related to the English Gothic Revival mode of Pugin. The palette was of the same bold, saturated reds, blues, and greens, and the subject matter, vegetal forms in geometric frames, was similar. Eidlitz designed encaustic tiles for the floors and walls of the Golden Corridor and the approach to the Assembly Chamber, which were made in England and manufactured by the Minton Company, which Pugin also used. He designed the furniture, lighting, and carpets, as Pugin had done for the House of Lords, although it should be noted that Eidlitz's chairs and desks are far simpler than those provided for the English nobles and that he tried, though unsuccessfully, to convince the legislature in 1878 to install electric lighting rather than gas.[60] The desks in particular, manufactured by Weller, Brown & Mesmer of Buffalo, New York, echo the ornamental concerns of the larger space, with ornament provided by the elaboration of the mortise and tenon joints and a roundel derived from the design of the Chamber's keystone.

But the differences between their approaches are equally as important. Pugin was a historicist, interested in reviving the lost past. His designs were meant to instill the present with the supposed purity of medieval endeavors. As noted, Eidlitz was certainly interested in Pugin, as he owned a copy of his 1849 *Floriated Ornament*, but he also rejected the religious piety underlying his medievalism. Eidlitz's Emersonian, agnostic side turned him toward an organic conception of ornament

4.24 A. W. N. Pugin, *Floriated Ornament* (1875), plate 26.

4.25 Relief carving divided into individual "cells" along the surface of a pilaster at the New York State Capitol.

as "modelled mass," a more objective and rational approach. The result was a more abstract and less literal design, more dependent on geometry than naturalism. The vegetal forms at Albany were rationalized, drawn from an *idea* of leaves and vines rather than by studying medieval treatises on plants or heraldry, as Pugin had done (figs. 4.24, 4.25).

Further, Eidlitz placed the ornament in ways that, he believed, would emphasize the structural work that various parts of the building did: "The object of decorating the surfaces of building material is . . . to give artificial texture to it, which shall reenforce its apparent capability to resist pressure."[61] A rough-hewn stone appeared stronger to the observer than a smooth-hewn stone; the object of ornament was to duplicate this kind of perception in the viewer. The "closely packed" horizontal bands beneath the windows, therefore, implied the static, unmoving role of the vertical wall. The curving bands in the vault, composed of wide stripes and bold arabesques colliding at the ribs, showed the dynamic of lateral and downward stress. One can argue whether or not this rationale was entirely successful, but again, Eidlitz's conception of ornament was in this way ahistorical. Science and mechanics guided the art of the Chamber.

If Pugin was perhaps a starting point for Eidlitz, two other theorists helped him refine his means of expression: Goethe and Owen Jones.[62] Goethe's theory of color seems to have been of interest to Eidlitz for some time, and at Albany he explored its tenets in pursuit of a pure visual harmony. Goethe's theory provided several

4.26 Assembly Chamber, looking toward the main public entrance. Chadbourne, *Public Service of the State of New York* (1882), vol. 1.

important principles for Eidlitz: one, that colors held moral meaning simply through their physical effects on the eye and brain. Second, the effects of colors were heightened by juxtaposing pure, unmixed colors more than by mixing and creating new tints and hues. And third, that by the perfect juxtaposition of colors and "colorless spaces," one could achieve a compelling visual harmony.[63] Goethe intended his advice largely for painters, but Eidlitz interpreted his principles for architectural ornamentation.

Eidlitz believed that "the deeper the color of a structural part the greater its apparent resistance to strain."[64] This did not mean, however, that one should simply paint structural surfaces. The ultimate visual effect could be achieved by a combination of carving, paint, and exposed material, causing the viewer both to apprehend the true nature of the material and to receive an artistically inspired impression of its strength. According to his theory, in the Chamber each ashlar block at the lower part of the wall, where the load was heaviest, was incised, leaving a raised border, and the incised areas painted in a "crude," unmixed color, red (page 7). Eidlitz intended this scheme to have several effects. The color red was to produce an effect of awe and majesty on the viewer appropriate to the seriousness of the Assembly's business. Red, according to Goethe, had the most visceral impact on a viewer and was the color most easily appreciated by the uneducated, perhaps making it the most appropriate color for a room dedicated to the business of all people and not just the upper and educated classes. But too much red, Eidlitz believed, would simply be overwhelming. The blank spaces around the red left an open area for the eye to project red's complement, green, a more soothing color, thus relieving the stress that too much red could create.[65] Further, through the combination of texture and color, the ornament was to show the stability and strength of the wall. The incised carving created a rough appearance, and in combination with the deep red enhanced the apparent strength of the wall.

In the vault, the ornament differed because of the differing structural concerns (fig. 4.26). Eidlitz needed to produce a sense of both strength and lightness, and he left a great deal of exposed stone, particularly in the ribs themselves, to accomplish the former. In the expanses between the ribs, he designed several broad polychromed bands predominantly in a vermilion red complemented by ultramarine blue and accented by gilded highlights. Blue, according to Goethe, was "between excitement and repose" and tended to recede from the eye, making it the perfect complement to the intense red of the rest of the room.[66] The gilding caused the ceiling to glow during the diffuse light of day and to shimmer in the gas lighting at night. Eidlitz thus intended to dematerialize the panels between the ribs by the application of color: an intense and advancing red, cooler and receding blue, and glowing gold all working upon the eye to create an optical harmony.

Though Goethe may have supplied the framework for Eidlitz's use of color, he justified his method of creating vegetal ornament through his reading of Owen Jones, the English designer and theorist responsible both for the decoration of the Crystal Palace and a remarkable illustrated study of the Alhambra. Jones, like Eidlitz, studied the architecture of the past in hopes of seeing in its forms and structures principles that could be used to create a new architecture of the present. While Eidlitz distinctly disagreed with Jones's color theory, which permitted the mixing of primary colors into tints, he embraced his idea that to employ natural forms as architectural ornament, the forms must be conventionalized, or abstracted, to "convey the intended image to the eye without destroying the unity of the object they are employed to decorate."[67] Directly mimetic ornament would have been, Eidlitz believed, merely distracting. While in Jones's designs, and later in Sullivan's and Wright's, conventionalization produced flowing, continuous bands of vegetal ornamentation, Eidlitz interpreted the principle somewhat differently. For Eidlitz, the physical structure of the building material took precedent over the conventionalized form, meaning that the design did not move across a series of ashlar blocks—instead, the conventionalized form was contained within the block. Through conventionalization, Eidlitz tried to make plants and animals, which were by nature soft and malleable, into rigid forms that appeared capable of bearing weight:

A leaf or flower is not capable of doing actual work. . . . If this frail form is to carry loads, or serve as an outside symbol of matter which is engaged in carrying loads, then it must have an appreciable fitness. It must have sharp faceted sides, which strain back rigidly against the stone it springs from. A leaf, to become a part of a structure, in one word, must become of stone, stony. To impart to natural forms a stony or metallic rigidity, to fit them in their contour, and more especially in their sectional development, to express a performance of mechanical work, is the process of conventionalizing animal and vegetable forms when used for the decoration of architectural organisms.[68]

In the Chamber, this resulted in the compartmentalized and subdivided ornament that adorned the walls and vaults. The vegetal ornament never obscures the structure of the building and in fact makes the subdivision of the unified space back into its constituent building blocks easier for the viewer to discern. The parts never blend together. Eidlitz instead emphasized the ri-

gidity of the structural parts by maintaining the strict divisions between rib and vault, between the ashlar blocks, between supporting beams. Unlike Furness's contemporary Pennsylvania Academy of the Fine Arts (1871–76), another tour-de-force of polychromy, or Sullivan's later designs for the Auditorium Building (1886–90), Eidlitz's ornament never finessed the structure beneath. For Schuyler, this meant that the ornament and structure never merged as fully as they might have. But this would not have disturbed Eidlitz. The major role of ornament was rational: to make the structure of the building more knowable.

William Morris Hunt's murals, commissioned by Eidlitz to fill the two tympanae beneath the vault and above the windows, completed the ensemble. Eidlitz contacted Hunt by letter, explaining the commission and the role of the murals in the Assembly design. His decision to contact Hunt, the brother of his adversary Richard Morris Hunt, must have been political in nature, designed to appease Hunt's objections to the project. But it was also well in keeping with Eidlitz's approach to democratic design: the much earlier Springfield City Hall included figural and not just decorative painting. Hunt specifically wrote that he planned his compositions and subject matter "in accord with the conception of the architect," and Schuyler again recalled a great rapport between the men.[69] Hunt, having trained in Dusseldorf, was perhaps

more open to Eidlitz's German idealism than was his brother, and declared him to have "a great brain and a great heart."[70]

Hunt's paintings, about 16 by 40 feet, painted directly onto the stone walls and now heavily damaged and hidden behind the dropped ceiling, touched on two allegorical subjects, both of which emphasized the idea of history as a continuous and evolutionary process, well in keeping with Eidlitz's own subjective and theoretical preoccupations (fig. 4.27, and see 4.23). One was the *Flight of Night*, depicting Anahita, the Persian goddess of night, driving her horse-drawn chariot to escape the rising of the dawn sun, accompanied by a sleeping mother and child. The other was *The Discoverer*, a depiction of Christopher Columbus in a small boat surrounded by Faith, Hope, Science, and Fortune that can be read as an allegory of the creation of modern democracy. They were painted in brilliant colors, a departure from Hunt's usual palette, a response both to Eidlitz's palette and the need for the murals to be visible in the dark upper reaches of the vault. The murals have been subject to many interpretations—Hunt never specifically communicated the exact meaning he intended—from something as simple as the depiction of East and West to the more complicated idea that they represent the triumph of civilization.[71] It is likely that Eidlitz understood the content in much the same way that his friend the art

critic Clarence Cook did, as a depiction of the triumph of light over darkness, of science over ignorance.[72]

But ornament and structure also had a subjective role to play that depended on its ability to communicate directly. Eidlitz wrote:

Now Architecture is a species of language. . . . Literature, music, painting, and sculpture will convey to posterity a bright record of modern civilization and mental development. Yet the history of the Reformation, of the discovery of America, of the great advance of constitutional government and of individual liberty, of the developments of science, the mechanic arts, agriculture, and trade, within the last five hundred years, is

nowhere expressed in Architecture. Architecture alone is silent.[73]

At Albany, Eidlitz's intended for architecture to speak again, and to speak of the achievements of the modern age. The Chamber is an early Hegelian *Gesamtkunstwerk*, emphasizing a union of the arts and sciences, with light, furnishing, structure, and ornament all designed of a piece. The great vaulted space was open and uncluttered, symbolizing the clarity and all-embracing nature of the elected Assembly. The vault itself was a powerful and enduring form (in intent, at least), symbolizing the permanency of the democratic institution. The murals created an evocative narrative of history, culminating in

4.29 Senate staircase, showing the wheel-of-life stone tracery. *AR* (November 1908).

the creation of the capitol itself. The ornament, created on the basis of laws of perception (and not the "received rules of style"), showed how the union of art and science, ornamentation and construction, the subjective and the rational, could create a perfect, harmonious vision. This was a message not just about architecture, but about society, government, and education that Eidlitz hoped would resonate with the legislators and the constituents who viewed their actions from the galleries. In the Assembly Chamber, Eidlitz finally created a space that embodied the societal ideals to which he aspired. As Cook wrote, the room was "conscience embodied."[74]

Though the didactic qualities of the Assembly Chamber remained exclusively symbolic, the lessons taught by

Eidlitz's Senate Staircase were overt. The creation of a Gothic dome and a single immense Gothic vault showed the flexibility and viability of the structural principles, and the staircase showed that the medieval ornamental language was equally viable. Starting at the base of the staircase and moving all the way to its top, Eidlitz conceived of a series of relief sculptures depicting a hierarchical evolutionary scheme. The subject is the realm of vertebrate creatures. The first creature, depicted as the base of the first arch, is a trilobite, an invertebrate Paleozoic creature nearly ubiquitous throughout the world. One imagines that as the excavations for the foundations of the capitol were made, trilobite fossils (common in the Albany area) emerged from the depths of sandstone.

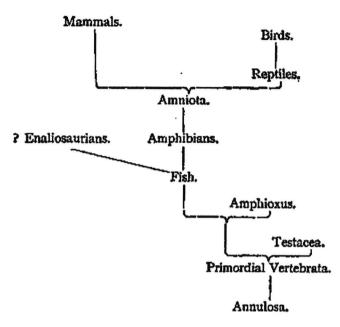

4.30 Haeckel's hierarchies, as diagrammed in Oscar Schmidt, *Doctrine of Descent and Darwinism* (1875).

From that primordial beginning, the creatures moved gradually through reptiles and fish, fowl, and finally, mammals (figs. 4.28, 4.29). Nature, which provided the rational guidelines for the development of architecture, also provided subjective content for its ornamentation.

At first glance, the decorative scheme seems to be merely a medieval bestiary, with the animals tracking up the stairs like visitors from an illuminated manuscript, oddly chosen to continue the Gothic feel of Eidlitz's portions of the building. The other elements of the staircase, after all, were a fantasy of Gothic roses and tracery, recombined in striking positions above the handrails, emphasizing upward movement. But the staircase, while clearly endowed with a wealth of formal inventiveness, also has a more direct message about the union of science and art and about the evolution of the highest form of governance known to man, democracy. The staircase was dubbed in the nineteenth century the "evolutionary" staircase, but it does not depict a strict line of evolution according to the well-known theory of Charles Darwin. Instead, the order of the animals shown seems to follow the hierarchy of animal development promoted by many nineteenth-century scientists.

In Albany in 1851, for example, the Swiss geologist Arnold Guyot reprised his successful Boston lecture series "The Earth and Man," in which he suggested four periods of development in which the "organic process" created first invertebrates and fish, next fish and reptiles, third mammals, and fourth man. He tied this scheme of development to the Christian conception of the days of creation.[75] Guyot went on to establish the first courses in geology at Princeton in 1855.

The theories of Ernst Haeckel, the greatest supporter of Darwin in Germany, were also well known in the United States. Haeckel created a hierarchical system that placed emphasis on the relative sophistication of whole phyla of animals (fig. 4.30). Discredited today because his strict hierarchical accounting of species formed part of the foundation for Nazi social Darwinism, in the nineteenth century he was respected for his thorough and painstaking zoological investigations. The stairwell depicts not a linked evolutionary relationship between each of the animals, but the relative importance of their group. Thus, the primoridal invertebrates are at the base, surmounted by fish, amphibians, reptiles, birds, and then mammals.[76]

Medieval cathedral ornament had always been didactic in nature, used to propound creation stories, lives of the saints, and to advance specific theological interpretations. Nineteenth-century scholars had abundantly rediscovered this fact, and Eidlitz continued the didactic medieval tradition at Albany, using his stairway sculpture to tell a secular creation story. Eidlitz adhered to no religion by this point in his life, but this did not mean he did not perceive a universal order defined by science. Sensitive to the spiritual needs of man, Eidlitz provided a new framework for understanding his place in the universe. The circular rose tracery beneath the risers referred, perhaps, to the age-old concept of the order of the "spiritual cosmos," which Eidlitz reinterpreted in a new secular setting, using a quasi-spiritual, quasi-scientific hierarchy to again place man in his proper place above beasts.[77] Where he had attempted with the Assembly Chamber's ornament to use advances in the science of perception to create a pure visual harmony, in the staircase he sought to portray those advances

through direct iconographic means. Architecture, as Eidlitz had preached since the 1850s, was a means to reach the minds and hearts of men.[78]

TWEED COURTHOUSE

Perhaps nowhere more than at the New York County Courthouse, better known today as the Tweed Courthouse, did Eidlitz pursue this didactic vision of architecture. John Kellum, the courthouse's original architect, had died in 1871 at the moment that the corruption surrounding the building's construction was finally proven and revealed. Even after spending upward of $8 million on the building—an incredible sum, particularly for a building of such relatively small size—it remained incomplete, the money diverted to corrupt city contractors and politicians at the behest of Boss Tweed.[79] Both Eidlitz and his brother Marc were personally involved in the swirl of committees and citizens' groups that formed to investigate and reform the corruption endemic to Tammany Hall. Marc was a member of the Committee of Fifty, a group formed in 1877 to promote changes to city administration. Eidlitz, with his connections both to city government through Fernando Wood and to citizens' reform groups through Peter Cooper, Simon Sterne, and William Booth and the Commission of Seventy, eventually won the commission to complete the

4.31 John Kellum and Leopold Eidlitz, New York County Courthouse, better known as the Tweed Courthouse, Chambers Street entrance, New York, 1861–81. Photograph by Irving Underhill, 1919. LC-USZ62-62789.

4.32 Tweed Courthouse, meeting room in Eidlitz's new south wing. *AR* (November 1908).

building in an economical and honest manner, though Calvert Vaux had also been considered for the job.[80] In 1876, the project began construction.

Eidlitz's contribution consists of two major portions of the building: the south wing, now known as the Eidlitz wing, and the central rotunda. The south wing was a new addition to Kellum's original plans which had called, instead, for a massive ceremonial stair on the south side of the building. Eidlitz wisely recommended eliminating this redundancy; the north side of the building already consisted of a major ceremonial entrance (fig. 4.31). The south side of the building is within 200 feet of the rear of City Hall, and a major stair there would have been useless. Instead, Eidlitz supplied office and meeting space (fig. 4.32); and rather than Kellum's proposed dome, Eidlitz proposed a large skylight as both a more economical and a more practical means of admitting light into the warren of offices that had already been completed.

4.33 Tweed Courthouse, showing Eidlitz's Romanesque south wing abutting Fuller's neo-classical building. Photograph by Walter Scallin, Jr., 1979. HABS NY,31-NEYO,116-4.

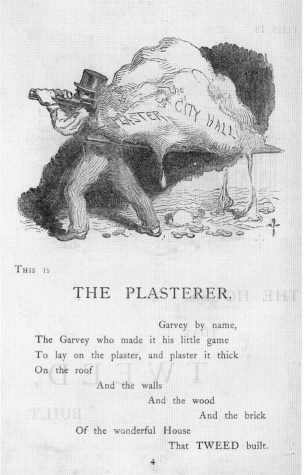

THIS IS
THE PLASTERER,
TWEED
BUILT.

THIS IS

THE PLASTERER,

Garvey by name,
The Garvey who made it his little game
To lay on the plaster, and plaster it thick
On the roof
    And the walls
        And the wood
            And the brick
Of the wonderful House
        That TWEED built.

4

Had Eidlitz merely changed the plan and program of the nearly completed courthouse, the commission might have gone unnoticed. But Eidlitz was not content to stop there, as the applied cast-iron Renaissance pediments, pilasters, and festoons of Kellum's design were highly offensive to him. Though he was willing to complete the portico on the north entry according to Kellum's original designs, for the rest of the building Eidlitz radically changed both the style and materials. He did not, however, remove any of Kellum's classical detailing, instead appending his own Rundbogenstil and Romanesque structure and ornamentation. As in all of Eidlitz's work, what appeared to many to be an insipid eclecticism is far more substantive.

On the exterior, Eidlitz's Romanesque south wing abuts Kellum's Renaissance building with no transi-

4.34 Tweed Courthouse, detail of the construction in the rotunda showing Eidlitz's brick abutting Fuller's cast iron. Schuyler reported that on a visit to the rotunda with Eidlitz, the architect said, "'Is it possible for anybody to fail to see that this,' pointing to the new work, 'performs a function, and that that,' pointing to the old, 'does not?'" Eidlitz's juxtaposition of structural brick with Kellum's applied cast-iron and plaster ornament could not have made his point more obviously.

4.35 "The Plasterer," a character lampooned in W. J. Linton's satirical poem *The House That Tweed Built* (1871).

tion attempted whatsoever (fig. 4.33). On the interior, in the rotunda, the Rundbogenstil use of economical brick in vivid colors of orange, black, and cream, clashes visibly with the ornate applied pediments (fig. 4.34, color plate 10). The immense skylight above, of cast iron and stained and frosted glass, introduced figural, conventionalized ornament, with its squirrels and flowers coursing its edge. The result, to contemporary eyes and after a magnificent restoration completed in 2001, is a stunning and unprecedented translation of the spirit of medieval structure and ornament.[81]

Eidlitz's design was a built critique both of the ethical corruption of the building campaign and of Kellum's designs. A 1871 satirical poem entitled "The House that Tweed Built," invoked the image of the plasterer as the central metaphor for corruption:

This is
THE PLASTERER,
Garvey by name,
The Garvey who made it his little game
To lay on the plaster, and plaster it thick
On the roof
And the walls
And the wood
And the brick
Of the wonderful House
That TWEED built.[82]

Throughout the poem, the plasterer lays on more and more plaster, disguising the cheapness of the building beneath its spongy layers and charging more and more exorbitant prices for his chicanery (fig. 4.35). Eidlitz's building, unpainted and unplastered, revealed all of its parts. Every brick, every stone, and every piece of iron could be visually counted and accounted for. This was the ultimate in structural honesty and symbolically answered the call for economic honesty as well. His polychromed brick and carved stone were also a stern rebuke to the hollow cast-iron columns and pediments that Kellum had applied to the original structure. In Kellum's building, cast-iron supports were hidden beneath plaster that was covered again with hollow cast-iron ornamentation. Layer upon layer was necessary to achieve the final result. In Eidlitz's design, what the viewer saw *was* the structure of the building. The brick of the rotunda was not a veneer, but the actual supporting material. The stone of the columns supported the weight of the floors above (fig. 4.36). Nowhere was the distinction between

4.36 Tweed Courthouse, detail of rotunda showing the fine carving and masonry work.

artifice and structural honesty more obvious than in the Tweed Courthouse.

But was Eidlitz's design art? In 1876, Eidlitz was already under fire for the audacity of his and Richardson's plans for the State Capitol, and the profession could tolerate his design for Tweed even less. The *American Architect and Building News* was the forum for continued assaults on Eidlitz: "Of course no attention was paid to the design of the existing building and within and without a rank Romanesque runs cheek by jowl with the old Italian, one bald, the other florid."[83] The contrast between Eidlitz's design and Kellum's was, and is, startling to say the least. Where Richardson had smoothed over the most glaring incongruencies between Fuller's and the Advisory Board's designs, at Tweed, it seemed, Eidlitz did everything he could to make them obvious. This was the final straw for his peers. He had been clearly out of step for decades, but this flaunting of convention had gone too far. Between the Albany controversy, the failing vault, and the Tweed redesign, Eidlitz's professional reputation was in ruins.

As with the criticism about his capitol design, though, Eidlitz would have cared little. That he raised the ire of his fellow architects with his design only proved that his statement needed to be made: as long as the profession could defend designs like Kellum's and Fuller's, it was in need of reform. Twenty years earlier, he raked Henry Van Brunt over the coals for his youthful essay on cast iron—the Tweed Courthouse was the built equivalent of that earlier diatribe, an essay in brick and stone that attempts to shame the tawdriness of the adjacent cast iron. What Eidlitz again failed to consider is that, while his message may have been worthy, such blunt and heavy-handed critiques were unpersuasive.

In an era when architectural ornamentation had become increasingly meaningless to everyday men, as its designers became more and more absorbed with an archeological sense of style, Eidlitz attempted to create a new iconography based on traditional form and structure. His effort was quite different than earlier attempts to forge new national iconographies by creating tobacco and corn capitals at the U.S. Capitol Building in Washington, D.C., or the French desire to create a new national order to supplement the existing classical orders. The "evolutionary" staircase and the harmonized colors of the state capitol were meant to act directly on the minds of viewers, enlivening their thoughts and bringing them into the modern world, where art and science worked together. He was not seeking entirely new forms, but a way to make old forms meaningful again. When Eidlitz, in conversation with Richardson, said "in true Gothic, so long as you find two stones together, you find architecture," he meant it literally.[84] The immense vault at Albany, the simple bricks at Tweed—this was architecture. As much as Eidlitz wrote and talked about architecture, he believed the best way to educate the public about it was to build, and build well and honestly.

5

THE NATURE AND FUNCTION OF ART

DURING THE YEARS EIDLITZ WORKED ON THE CAPITOL DESIGNS, HE
also prepared the final manuscript for his major published work, *The Nature and
Function of Art, More Especially of Architecture*. The book appeared in 1881, just
as the cracks began to appear in the vault of the Assembly Chamber in Albany. A
huge undertaking, just shy of five hundred pages, it was a labor of determination
and love. When Eidlitz began writing in the 1850s and 1860s, the intellectual tenor
of his writing was certainly unusual for American practitioners. By the early 1880s,
others had begun to share in the probing and insightful nature of his inquiries,
but none approached the breadth and profundity of Eidlitz's book. *The Nature
and Function of Art* was published by the respected London firm of Sampson Low,
Marston, Searle & Rivington, also the publishers, posthumously, of Sir Gilbert
Scott's memoirs in 1879, of the South Kensington Museum's applied art collections
in 1881–82, and of Louisa May Alcott's novels in Britain.[1]

With the publication of *The Nature and Function of Art*, Eidlitz cemented his
claim as a leader in the intellectualization of American architecture. While Eidlitz's
compatriot H. H. Richardson had already emerged as the uncontested master of
built form by the 1880s, celebrated by critics and his fellow architects alike, he wrote
nothing on the subject of architecture, leaving his powerfully eloquent buildings
as the sole statement of his beliefs about design. In the field of architectural theory,
the written companion to visual form, though, Eidlitz remained at the forefront.
Whereas in the 1850s, when Eidlitz began to write, European architectural theory

Opposite: See page 159.

5.1 One of the photographs in Eidlitz's personal collection shows the Cathedral in Regensburg, Germany, which was completed during the nineteenth century: the towers were built in the 1860s and the spire was completed by 1872. Avery Architectural and Fine Arts Library, Columbia University in the City of New York.

5.2 Another print from Eidlitz's collection, showing a small unidentified Gothic palazzo in Venice. The collection features buildings in Continental Europe, especially Italy, Germany, Spain, and France. Avery Architectural and Fine Arts Library, Columbia University in the City of New York.

was still arguably in its adolescence, by 1881, the early work by English aesthetes like Ruskin and Pugin had been supplemented by the rigorously academic and encyclopedic writings of Viollet-le-Duc, whose *Diction-naire Raisonné* began publication in 1854 and continued through the 1850s, and of Gottfried Semper, whose mas-

terwork *Der Stil, oder, Praktische Aesthetik* (On Style, or Practical Aesthetics) was published in 1878–79. Both Viollet-le-Duc and Semper had the same goal as Eidlitz: to create a comprehensive theory of architecture that would transcend current practice by delving deeply into its fundamental meanings and sources.

For Eidlitz, though, practice came before theory.[2] The basis for that practice is in some ways typical for the time. Eidlitz, like many other architects, collected photographs that helped to form a shared visual literacy (Figs. 5.1 and 5.2). But it was Eidlitz's reading and his autodidactic impulse that set him apart. His books and essays are, above all, a written justification for his designs. *The Nature and Function of Art* provides a window into the mind of an architect that shows exactly what he was trying to achieve through building. Eidlitz was perhaps the most intellectually driven architect of nineteenth-century America, but he was not a theorist *per se*; he was an architect who wrote. The true significance of the book thus lies not in its lengthy philosophical musings, but in the fact that Eidlitz systematized the experience of his forty-year career into a working method for organic design.

Even more to the point, Eidlitz intended the book to be a comprehensive and final answer to the critics who had denounced his design at Albany. Without the impetus given him by that bizarre and tumultuous publicity, he would probably not have attempted to systematize a design theory at all; nothing in his brief earlier forays into theory indicated that he had a desire to engage in anything more than episodic and self-contained position papers that appeared in the *Crayon*. When Russell Sturgis and Peter B. Wight, who both knew and admired Eidlitz, cofounded the art and architecture periodical the *New Path* in 1863, one might expect, for example, that Eidlitz would have been a natural contributor, but he was not.[3] *The Nature and Function of Art* answered his critics on two levels: first, and most specifically, it answered the stylistic complaints that Richard Morris Hunt and the AIA had voiced. While he had remained silent in 1876, in 1881 he wrote: "It occurs sometimes that monuments are begun in a manner which does not in fact express or promise to express the ideas which they are intended to commemorate. May we in this case change their 'styles'? . . . The sooner you stop it and begin to relate facts as they are, the better it is for the good of the monument and the interests of its builders."[4]

But second, and more importantly, the book overall was an attempt to prevent such future outbreaks of professional discord from recurring. Because the controversy showcased such outwardly irreconcilable differences in the profession, and such ignorance and malleability on the part of the public, Eidlitz attempted in his book to define fundamental truths about beauty, taste, and style and write them down so that both the lay person and the architect could read and comprehend them. In other words, he sought, as he wrote in the introduction, "To devise remedies which shall arrest the decay

of art, and especially of architecture, to arrive at a clear understanding of its nature and function, and to mature a system which shall direct its practice in the right channel. . . ."[5] The book was surely intended as a transcendent philosophical inquiry, but, more important, it was also a remedy directed at a specific historical moment in America in which architecture, it seemed to Eidlitz, had begun to drift substantially off track. Eidlitz was not primarily a theorist, but an architect who attempted to explain the manifesto of his designs through words: his written and built work are two sides of the same coin.

THE NATURE AND FUNCTION OF ART

Even a cursory evaluation of the book's title gives some hint of the message within: an exploration of Eidlitz's long-standing interest in architecture as a union of art and science (Fig. 5.3). "Idea" and "matter," the terms he had used to describe the inherent dualism of architecture, were translated into "nature" and "function." Eidlitz conceived of architecture as a dialectical interplay between nature and function, or put differently, between its spiritual purpose and its material form. For Eidlitz, every aspect of architecture could be condensed into these two opposing aspects of design. Striking a balance between ornamentation and structure, between the subjective and the objective, was the architect's task.

The structure of the book reflected Eidlitz's didactic agenda. In Part 1, "Present Condition of Architecture," Eidlitz surveyed contemporary theories and histories of art and architecture, sifting through them to find the errors and benefits of their positions. He looked largely, though not exclusively, at architectural writers popular and widely read in the United States like John Ruskin and James Fergusson.[6] His intent was to discover the sources of his clients' and the public's notions about architecture—by ferreting out why the public thought the way it did, he hoped to better devise a means of correcting its taste, and more fundamentally, its conception of architecture as an art. Informing this query was a Marxian realization that art was becoming more and more a luxury and that, consequently, the art of architecture needed to be justified and explained:

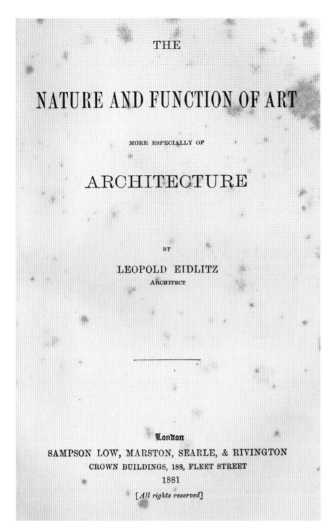

THE

NATURE AND FUNCTION OF ART

MORE ESPECIALLY OF

ARCHITECTURE

BY

LEOPOLD EIDLITZ

ARCHITECT

London

SAMPSON LOW, MARSTON, SEARLE, & RIVINGTON

CROWN BUILDINGS, 188, FLEET STREET

1881

[*All rights reserved*]

5.3 Title page, *The Nature and Function of Art, More Especially of Architecture* (1881).

. . . the conclusion reached by taste and common sense with reference to art is that . . . it performs no function in the social economy excepting, perhaps, that it affords the aforesaid pleasurable emotion; and, as this pleasurable emotion is of a transient character and of intangible value, it remains to be concluded that art is superfluous, and can well be dispensed with. . . . But for a few individuals who wield considerable influence in society, and who unaccountably seem to perceive in art not only a needful civilizing influence, but also a value measurable in money, common sense would inevitably abolish it from the face of the earth.[7]

In other words, Part 1 assessed the current aesthetic relationship of architecture to society so that a viable means of improving that relationship could be devised; in his next work, *Big Wages and How to Earn Them*, Eidlitz concentrated specifically on the sociopolitical and economic conditions that affected the building trades.[8]

Having conducted his social analysis, Eidlitz set out in Part 2, "Nature and Function of Art," to create a common basis for understanding art in the present day. He did this, again, by sifting through theories of art and beauty put forth by others, from Plato, Socrates, and Aristotle to Hogarth, Lord Shaftesbury, Winckelmann, Baumgarten, Kant, and Hegel. Though there are a number of passages that illustrate the form of Eidlitz's consideration, one in particular is indicative of the omnivorous quality of his deductions and their combination of both original and derivative thinking. Eidlitz, like so many writers and artists before him, sought to define beauty. His purpose was to formulate a position on this abstract concept that would make it easier for architects and their clients to understand each other and that would also make it easier to achieve beauty as an end result of design.

In defining beauty, Eidlitz first cataloged the definitions found in Hegel, the "German school of aesthetics" (which referred to Hegel), Socrates, Plato, Aristotle, Baumgarten, Kant, Keats, and then returned to Hegel again. Eidlitz covered an immense amount of territory in a mere four pages, his resulting conclusion being that in order to be beautiful, architecture must represent a subjective idea. In other words, architecture depended both on the built object and its ability to embody a transcendental symbolism. He based his conclusion on the fact that all the philosophers he considered had broken art into a dichotomy between the physical object and the resulting emotion with more or less emphasis placed on one or the other and with different conceptions of how one translated to the other. Eidlitz was less concerned with the specific mechanism of beauty than with achieving it as an end result and therefore found little value in allying himself with any one position—thus, Eidlitz could embrace both Hegel and Kant despite the fundamental differences in their concepts of how beauty is perceived. It sufficed for him to extract the essence of the philosophical debate by acknowledging the dichotomy of the physical and emotional components of architecture.[9]

The goal in considering these diverse authors was to be as intellectually thorough as possible; Eidlitz wanted to display publicly the vast intellectual terrain he had covered. He also took a scientist's position: he needed to know what truths had already been established in order to proceed with his own experiment: "Scientific men profess a readiness to discard every theory of this [fallacious] kind the moment it is disproved. Art should follow this example by elaborating ideas in their progress, instead of tenaciously holding to them after they have been virtually discarded."[10] A scientific conception of beauty in art, one that, while acknowledging the inherent mysteriousness of the concept, was nevertheless measurable and reproducible, was his goal:

> It will be objected, no doubt, that science cannot be cited as a parallel to art, the one being a matter of mathematical demonstration, and the other an emotional element of human work. This is precisely the error committed in modern art analysis, and it may be directly traced to the fact that the *expression* of emotion and emotional results are not accomplished by means which are emotional. There is more mathematical consideration involved in the formation and modelling of an arch or a buttress than in the computation of the atmospheric pressure or the velocity of light. And the true value of a corbel or of a capital, the depth and density of their carved ornament, and their respective treatment in color depend upon a series of mechanical considerations which must be thoroughly understood by the architect before he can make these symbolic features true works of art.[11]

Eidlitz's conception of beauty was informed by the understanding that the process of creation was inherently mechanical: the application of science preceded the apprehension of beauty.

Part 2 concluded, therefore, with a "science of beauty" that posited equal status to science (the material) and art (the subjective) as benefits to mankind: "Science teaches man to think logically; and art acquaints him with true human thoughts."[12] The world was plagued by an imbalance between the search for material progress and the cultivation of subjective values. Architecture in the late nineteenth century had become "bad art" which, while it could appear sophisticated, was in fact shallow and no longer communicated higher societal ideals. In this, we can see that Eidlitz was particularly influenced by Hegel's conception of art as a medium for understanding ideas. Eidlitz, in using Hegel's definition of "beauty absolute as the shining of the idea through the sensuous medium" and then referring to Hegel's divisions among the arts, was referring to the *Lectures on Aesthetics*, which Hegel had delivered in Berlin in the 1820s and which were published posthumously in the late 1830s. One could argue that Eidlitz's entire conception of architecture was Hegelian in nature: that his desire for an architecture of ideas, of space, of mass, of modeling, and of color was a romantic synthesis, an early *Gesamtkunstwerk*, that united Hegel's divisions of the arts (architecture, sculpture, painting, music, and poetry) into one. Eidlitz's "science of beauty," therefore, sought to acknowledge and change the situation that made "bad art" possible: "The knowledge conveyed by art is almost entirely overlooked; and to make this knowledge potent, to secure its cultivating influence to humanity, its existence must be brought out in the clearest light."[13] Architecture, as Eidlitz had attempted to show at the Albany capitol, could, through a union of the arts and the sciences, represent both material and spiritual progress.

The book culminated in Part 3, "Nature of Architecture," in which Eidlitz brought these abstract matters to bear on contemporary practice. Eidlitz moved from a general discussion defining architecture to a series of discussions of specific elements of building, with chapters including "Form and Construction," "Proportion," "Treatment of Masses," and "Style." The result was a wide-ranging discussion of the design process, moving in general from the broadest idea to the most specific, and including a mix of philosophical and specific recommendations about practice. On the one hand, Eidlitz described the best method for creating a good bond in brickwork, and on the other he asked, and attempted to answer, the provocative question "How is an idea to be expressed in a structure?"[14] Eidlitz discussed materials, his theories of color, ornament and conventionalization—anything germane to the actual process of creating architecture. He concluded the book with a chapter on his pet subject, architectural education. Eidlitz still believed that a complete overhaul of the training of architects was necessary before architecture could reconnect with its clients and users. A change in architectural education was the only way that the imbalance between "material" and "subjective" concerns could be redressed. The book thus ended on a practical, pragmatic note; the abstract musings of the first two sections led him to a concrete conclusion about the need for reform of current practice.

As remarkable as Eidlitz's earlier forays into theory had been, his book was even more ambitious and more out of keeping with the usual literary projects of American architects. The profession finally had a viable publication of its own, the *American Architect and Building News*, begun in 1876, but American architectural writing by practicing architects, though far more copious, remained similar in character to that of the 1850s. It tended to be practical, concerned with such issues as fireproofing (which Eidlitz himself wrote about, too, in the 1870s), building codes, architectural competitions, and buildings in progress.[15] There, were, to be sure, other more humanistic topics covered, including exhibition reviews and surveys of the architecture of other countries in Europe and Asia.[16] In the *Inland Architect*, a Chicago-based journal begun in 1883, two years after the publication of Eidlitz's book, there were more complex theoretical discussions of the cultural origins and meanings of architecture.[17] The most ambitious literary project of the period was Henry Van Brunt's English translation of Viollet-le-Duc's 1863 *Entretiens sur l'Architecture*, accompanied by an appreciative and insightful introduction, which appeared in 1875, with portions also serialized in the first volume of the *AABN* in 1876.[18] But all of these articles—books like Eidlitz's 493-page tome were not attempted by practicing American architects in

the 1870s—were brief musings compared to *The Nature and Function of Art*.[19] The book was intended for this particular American circumstance in which there was a great deal of architectural knowledge, more to be sure than there had been in the late 1850s, but still very little analysis of its deeper implications and meanings.

There is a certain consistency between Eidlitz's earlier writings for the *Crayon* and the book. In many cases he returned to the old arguments as if they had taken place just yesterday. About cast iron, the source of so much ill will twenty-five years earlier, he wrote: "A mania for iron buildings, which is now happily dying out everywhere, was merely an attempt at a spurious cast-iron imitation of modelled and carved marble, granite, or sandstone. . . . It would take a long time, also, before a respectable iron architecture could be developed; but as a cheap display is its sole object, and it has been demonstrated that there is no economy in it, it has been wisely abandoned."[20] The intervening decades between his and Van Brunt's papers on cast iron had done nothing but prove, to him, his initial correctness. Emerson's transcendentalist vision of the union of art and nature had become even more pronounced in his later work. Emerson wrote: "The creation of beauty is Art. The production of a work of art throws light upon the mystery of humanity. A work of art is an abstract or epitome of the world." And Eidlitz still echoed him, saying, "Now the work of the creative force, as seen in nature or in art, is the beauty we talk about. . . . Beauty is the measure of creative force in the abstract."[21] And, of course, Eidlitz's insistence on an overhaul of education as the seed for reform in architecture also remained.

In terms of style, Eidlitz retained his general enthusiasm for the Gothic, although his earlier support for the *Rundbogenstil* had faded, reflecting, perhaps, the course of Germany's own "battle of styles" that had pitted the refined *Rundbogenstil* classicism of Gottfried Semper against the Gothic Revival of August Reichensperger.[22] But he had also moved further beyond the frustration he had expressed with historical styles in 1858, continuing his search for a new style, based in the principles, not the forms, of the past: "[The architect] must utilize every advance made up to the present time, not in the production of completed architectural forms, but in the *causes* of forms [emphasis added]."[23] Here he sounded a call similar to Viollet-le-Duc's, who had defined style as "the manifestation of an ideal based on a principle" and had projected a future architecture based on the rationalized structural principles of the medieval age.[24] Eidlitz, while sympathetic to Viollet-le-Duc's cause, seems to have considered him little more than a kindred spirit. Eidlitz, by comparison, placed much greater emphasis on the "creative force," similar to the art historical idea of *Kunstwollen*, and always believed that the functional, mechanical basis of architecture required refinement through the individual genius of artistic expression.[25]

In this emphasis on the art of architecture, Eidlitz again appeared to echo John Ruskin, who distinguished clearly between mere functional building and higher achievements.[26] Though he admired Ruskin's enthusiasm for and careful observation of architecture, Eidlitz nevertheless attacked his confusion of form and principle. Ruskin improperly, he believed, created a theory of art based on his observation of forms rather than on the analysis of the structure and principles that underlay those forms: "A frank inquiry . . . might have led the author to the conclusion that the laws and principles of past practice are either not known to him, or that the laws and principles of past practice are erroneous laws."[27] This confusion of formal inquiry and a deeper structural analysis resulted in a fundamentally flawed position. Furthermore, Eidlitz found outright laughable Ruskin's reliance on biblical proscriptions for his recommendations about contemporary use of materials. After quoting a passage in which Ruskin had used the Bible as support for his contention that iron was unsuitable for contemporary building, Eidlitz wrote: "This would sound like blasphemy or drivelling in the mouths of most persons. Mr. Ruskin's personal character and peculiar methods of thought exonerate him from such an accusation."[28] Despite his dissatisfaction with Ruskin's theoretical framework, Eidlitz did sympathize with his desire for architecture and ornament to unite in a truthful evocation of the human spirit.

Eidlitz repeatedly attacked other writers' positions on style as a means of placing his own and, as if the contro-

versies of his own career were not enough, he joined the fray on other widely-debated issues of the day. James Fergusson, the widely-read English architectural historian, for example, was too much of a formalist who denied the meaning of buildings. Paraphrasing Fergusson, he wrote: ". . . in the introduction to his history of architecture, speaking of architecture as an art, and defining its position among the sister arts, [he] concludes that a building can tell no story, and that it can express an emotion only by inference. If this were really true, then architecture would not be a fine art in any sense of the word."[29] Eidlitz used his critique of Fergusson's analysis of the cathedrals of Cologne and Milan as an opportunity to join the decades-long fray over the proper means of completing Gothic cathedrals in the modern age. In 1840 a new campaign was mounted to finally finish Cologne Cathedral, which had stood incomplete since the thirteenth century. The design of the cathedral, completed in 1880, was based on surviving medieval documents that required supplementation and reinterpretation by contemporary architects, primarily Ernst Zwirner. The same was true for the Milan Cathedral, which had also remained unfinished since its beginnings in the fourteenth century, but which finally saw completion in the mid-nineteenth century. Though both cathedrals were examples of late Gothic construction, their vastly different structural and ornamental programs highlighted the flexibility and diversity of the Gothic form language (Figs. 5.4 and 5.5). Nineteenth-century critics and historians wrote prolifically about the campaigns to complete each building.[30]

Eidlitz's treatment of the subject is particularly interesting and shows quite clearly his insistence on a continuous process of argument and counter-argument as the basis for clear architectural theory. First, he quoted extensively from the criticism of both buildings written by Fergusson, and then compared that analysis to passages on the same subjects written by the German art historian Franz Kugler. The purpose of this close analysis of text was to show the irrationality of Fergusson's critique and the eminent logic of Kugler's, which Eidlitz argued was based on a functional-structural, rather than a stylistic, reading. Eidlitz then supplemented Kugler's analysis

5.4 The completed Cologne Cathedral, ca. 1900. Part of the Detroit Publishing Company's "Views of Germany," 1905. LC-DIG-ppmsca-00808.

with his own, and closed the section with a quote from Kugler's pupil, the great art historian Jacob Burckhardt, that cemented the superiority of German art critics who, like Eidlitz, were "in search of ideas embodied in material forms." This is a particularly ponderous and slow-reading portion of the book, but it was crucial to Eidlitz's need to position himself intellectually.[31]

Sir Gilbert Scott, the preeminent Gothic Revival architect of England, came closer to defining a defensible pro-Gothic position by virtue of his practical experience as an architect. Eidlitz admired Scott (he had nominated him for honorary membership in the AIA in 1859), calling him "a man to be counted among those foremost in the profession of his country, broad, liberal, and free from prejudices. . . ."[32] He quoted from Scott's *Remarks on Secular and Domestic Architecture*, and though he agreed with Scott's general admiration for the Gothic as the "most free and unfettered of all styles," he was dissatisfied for what he saw, again, as too much of a focus on specific forms: "And so Sir Gilbert loves architecture, not as a system arising out of a principle, but as an aggregation of forms."[33]

French theory still held little attraction to Eidlitz, who seems to have clung to a Germanic distaste for things French, aptly captured by Schlegel, writing in 1805: "The most famous buildings in Paris are all modern, both in date and style, and have no decided character, except a superficial imitation of antiquity, confined, feeble, and, by many ingenious adaptations made to suit every variety of taste."[34] The influence of French architecture theory, from Durand to the Neo-Grec, came only secondhand, through Hübsch's and Bötticher's writing. Gottfried Semper, the most important German theorist of the latter part of the nineteenth century, is also still notably absent from Eidlitz's consideration. This absence is harder to account for but can perhaps be ascribed to his distaste for Semper's neoclassicism or his

5.5 Panoramic view of the Piazza and Cathedral, Milan, Italy. Notman Photo Co., 1909. LC-USZ62-122904.

lack of popularity in the United States. Eidlitz would certainly have been aware of Semper's books and essays, but because he tended to grapple with texts well known to his American audience, this may have been reason enough to ignore a theorist who clearly grappled with the same issues.

However, there were notable changes in his thinking as well. Because the landscape of architectural and aesthetic theory had changed since the 1850s, Eidlitz explored new generations of European writers, the most important of which, again, came from English and German sources. Since his *Crayon* articles appeared, the Gothic Revival had developed toward the High Victorian Gothic, with its emphasis on polychromy and emotionally charged compositions rooted in the aesthetic tenets of "associationism." From the German side of things, Eidlitz expanded his earlier interest in expressing ideas through building in the new theories of empathy that emerged from the expanding field of aesthetics. Both developments, in associationism and in empathy theory, were extremely important for Eidlitz, who found in these literary fronts additional fodder for his own continued interest in "expression."[35]

The idea of expression, which Eidlitz discussed in the 1850s in terms of symmetry and massing, received new attention in *The Nature and Function of Art*. He discussed and analyzed the effects of color, space, ornament, and "modeling," a term that replaced "expression" as Eidlitz's key concept in architectural form. Taken together, the fuller investigation of the varieties of architectural effects, pursued so dramatically in the Assembly Chamber at Albany, marked a new phase in Eidlitz's theory, one in which he finally began to define a full working method for architects.

ORGANIC FUNCTIONALISM

At the heart of Eidlitz's pursuit of a theory of architecture was the reconciliation of art and science as *equal partners* in an era of increasing specialization. This was a direct response, on the one hand, to the rise of an engineering architecture that required only builders and mechanics, and on the other to an artistic architecture that relied on stylistic precedents without consideration

of their meaning to the present-day. Other mid-to-late-nineteenth-century architects, such as H. H. Richardson, were concerned with similar ideas but, as Eidlitz recognized, pursued them in a purely artistic way; Richardson, despite his many imitators, did not explain or evangelize his working method as Eidlitz did.[36] While Richardson may have provided the forms that inspired a new conception of American architecture, Eidlitz's greatest contribution was his attempt to create an organic working method.

To achieve the reunion of science and art, a union that Eidlitz believed was first embodied in the medieval building traditions, he used his organic, biological conception of architecture to merge structure and ornament into a readable, meaningful composition. One passage in particular, though rather long, crystallizes the way Eidlitz finally established his guiding principle. Quoting it in full reveals both Eidlitz's peculiar thought process and the ponderousness of his language:

Now if a structure is devoted to physical needs, it becomes the mechanical housing of a mechanical operation, and is, therefore, a work of mechanic art; but if the structure is devoted to spiritual acts, or to acts relating to moral principles, to the fundamental laws of human relationships, to the end that we may sustain the life of humanity, protect and guard it, then it becomes an arena for these spiritual acts and thus an integral part of a scheme by which is performed an act expressive of an idea. In the first instance we are concerned with the mechanical perfection of the structure only, which means that each part shall do the mechanical work imposed upon it, and insure the stability of the whole. The organic parts of a structure considered in this light form its skeleton bones and sinews; and in their creation no special note is taken of the ultimate expression of mass and form. It is not attempted to make visible to the observer that mechanical work is done well, done with ease, grace, or elegance; nor is it necessary that in a structure devoted to the supply of mere physical needs, the variety of functions performed by its occupants shall find expression in a corresponding variety in the form and relation of its cellular organization. Mere economy and mechanical certainty of ultimate performance are all that is demanded of the author of a work of mechanic art.

But where a structure becomes related to a human group or groups, or is a housing of the same, and these groups are in motion—motion determined by emotions (a process of reaction of the mind upon the body) in consequence of physical acts performed, which illustrate an idea—then this housing or structure, by its own grouping, must express the groups contained within it. In the length and breadth of its single cells, or groups of cells, it must indicate the purpose of each group, and the range and scope of action permitted to the persons forming it; and in the altitude of single cells, it must express the degree of dignity, absolute and relative, attached to individual groups. Furthermore, the methods of construction must express the elegance, boldness, and dignity of the idea represented by the structure; while modelling and decoration must correspond with the character of the construction selected.

If in a structure these conditions are complied with, it may be said that the structure as a whole, and in its parts, betrays emotions the result of physical acts illustrative of an idea, and that it is a work of fine art.[37]

This passage is the crux of his architectural philosophy, both built and written. The basic tenets of an organic and functionalist architecture are here: form, structure, and ornament derive from a biological sense of fitness to purpose. By linking "emotion," to "physical acts," to "ideas," Eidlitz interwove the core issues of idealist philosophy into his theory. The framework for measuring and balancing these abstract concerns were the laws of nature, which supplied all the guidance an architect needed to perfect both the mechanics and the emotions of his building.

Eidlitz was a functionalist, but not in the sense that the European modernists of the 1920s and 1930s would bring to the word. Architecture was about structure and form, but it was also about social meaning, tradition, and the human condition. Function, for Eidlitz, was more than meeting the physical and technical needs of a building program. Architecture, as Eidlitz said, was a language that could communicate ideas; art and ornament was the means of drawing those ideas out. People should learn by looking at buildings—about themselves, their society, and their ideals. Eidlitz's critique of the Roeblings' design for the Brooklyn Bridge is indicative of his position. Though he admired the bridge's forceful massing, he felt it was crude and unfinished and offered to complete the design by "modelling" the great masonry piers to better reflect their various mechanical functions.[38] The combination of the rational and the subjective to form "an idea in matter" was always Eidlitz's goal.

The true significance of the book lies in Eidlitz's laying out of a means of creating this architecture. In another long passage that echoes the one above, he lays out the steps to creating an organic architecture:

[The architect] must submit to this argument: If I thoroughly understand the idea which I am to illustrate by expressing it in matter; if I understand the emotions pertaining to it, I must evolve first the single cells which will correspond to the groups of persons who are to inhabit his monument, with a view to represent the fundamental idea, and I must then select from the whole range of known methods of construction that which answers the physical relation of matter as it presents itself in this arrangement of single cells, and which, by its degree of boldness, elegance, or of simplicity and directness of expression, will correspond with the emotion to be depicted. When this is successfully completed, and the masses of the proposed monument are determined, I will so model and carve and color them that the meaning of every part of this structural organism shall become more apparent, and its ability to perform mechanical functions shall be more clearly demonstrated. I will use for this purpose any or all known decorative forms, or will devise others by conventionalizing any suitable forms found in nature or art, so long as the forms so used will answer the purpose for which they are used, viz., to heighten the effect and express more clearly the function of parts in performing their assigned mechanical work. Now when all this is done, it is not probable that the completed form arrived at, either in the monument as a whole, or in any part of it, will be at all like any architectural form heretofore produced; it will not be the form of any style; it will be a true original development, which may not upon first trial seem very promising to its author, but which, when persisted in by the individual architect, and then by a generation of architects, will show true progress in art.[39]

Here, after nearly forty years of practice, Eidlitz described his working method as an architect. First, to contemplate the program as a practical and symbolic problem; second, to lay out the main interior space, followed by the subsidiary spaces; and from this to determine what method of construction best served both spiritual and corporeal matters. Next, the architect designed the ornament and color scheme with an eye both to "effect" and to "function."

Key to this conception of architecture was the architect's control over the entire building process, from engineering to ornamentation. Architects needed mundane mechanical knowledge but they also needed to be philosophers capable of analyzing the building's relationship to its users. Sculptors and painters fell under the architect's control: ". . . carved-ornament and color decoration, to effect the object intended, must be designed by the author of the monument, the architect."[40] From Eidlitz's earliest work, St. George's Church, to his last major work, the Assembly Chamber, there is a remarkable consistency of approach. He started with the idea of the building and found a means to use space (unified, unobstructed volumes), construction (cantilevering and vaulting), and ornament (conventionalized forms) to express it. In his Congregational churches, the idea of the building was determined largely by his clients, who had pronounced ideas about appropriate architecture. In his secular buildings, he was freer to interpret the idea that drove the construction: from the "barbaric" fantasy of the Brooklyn Academy of Music to the democratic symbolism of the Assembly Chamber. He considered use before style, construction before ornament, and moved from the interior space to the exterior skin, continually striving to integrate symbolic

and prosaic functions. Every part of a building had a meaning to impart. Eidlitz's conception of the organic was a means of making sure that the proper balance between them was maintained.

Throughout *The Nature and Function of Art*, this idea of balance and ecology of form is repeated. The cellular metaphor, so important in Eidlitz's conception of interior space, is both a literal and a metaphorical image. It positioned the architect as a scientist, analyzing program and incorporating it at every stage of construction and design. This holistic process was opposed to what Eidlitz saw as the shallow design methods of most of his contemporaries. He was critical of the quick generative *esquisse* method of the Beaux-Arts because it placed formal composition before a full understanding of the building's idea and even before its constructional necessities, corrupting the relationship between structure, design, and expression. His focus on the proper relationship among a building's constituent parts was, of course, not exactly new. But he attempted to push past what he saw as the limiting and formalist Renaissance focus on proportion and precedent; architecture focused on these issues was concerned with artifice only and denied its true potential for expression.[41]

Eidlitz's distrust of Renaissance aesthetic concerns also responded to his fear that architecture was losing its meaning to contemporary men. The archeological rehashing of Gothic details and the Beaux-Arts classical monument did not allow design to transcend its sources. Eidlitz's organic method eliminated this quandary by suggesting a way to free the designer from the tyranny of style. Through organic functionalism, an architect could finally translate his abstract, symbolic characterizations of architecture into physical reality. The omission of illustrations in the book is intentional: organic architecture did not look like anything in particular. It was a way of thinking, a way of understanding space and form.

RECEPTION

Eidlitz's book, like his designs for the New York capitol, was largely misunderstood and disregarded in his day despite his best intentions. But the book contains some of the most interesting architectural writing of the

American nineteenth century and, despite its shortcomings, deserves to be seen as its most ambitious and intellectual investigation of the principles that underlie the generation of architectural form. While there is much in the book that is merely derivative and repetitive, Eidlitz's earlier explorations of nature and the spiritual, and of science and the mechanical, reached their culmination in an original and fully rendered theory of organic architecture. *The Nature and Function of Art*, however, still remains an obscure book. Some of this neglect is due to the book's extremely long, repetitive, and dense prose. Eidlitz, for example, defines the human creation of art using twenty principles; Frank Lloyd Wright, himself never known for concision, first defined organic architecture in eight.[42] Pithy, Eidlitz was not. Instead, his writing was imbued with the heavy and formal structure of his native German tongue, making it difficult going even for dedicated readers.

Eidlitz's diminished professional reputation in the wake of the controversy and subsequent structural failure of the Assembly Chamber certainly had some affect on the book's reception as well. Its publication in 1881 coincided with the final debacle of the State Capitol, the cracking of the Assembly Chamber vault. When published, it received a scathing review in the *New York Times*, whose reviewer complained bitterly that "there is a great deal of sound and sensible matter in the book, but one only gets at it by allowing Mr. Eidlitz to buttonhole you and talk philosophy for a length of time quite disproportionate to the ideas eventually brought forth. Mr. Eidlitz has no mercy."[43] William Ware was later to note evasively when asked to comment upon *The Nature and Function of Art*, "I do not think his writings were thought to add materially to his reputation."[44] From his evident disdain, one assumes Ware had not even read the book.

In the thirteen years that had intervened since Eidlitz's active participation in the AIA, the world of New York architecture had continued its process of stratification, and Eidlitz, even more than in the 1850s, did not fit neatly into a particular camp. Though he was obviously anti–Beaux-Arts, it was difficult to align him with any group by 1881. He appeared still to be an ardent Gothic

Revivalist, yet he openly attacked its greatest proponent, John Ruskin. He practiced as well in a Romanesque mode, but did not quite fit the increasingly popular Richardsonian mold. And while he lavished great care on the development of color and ornament for his designs in keeping with Victorian eclecticism, he claimed also to be a strict functionalist with no use for mere decorative architecture. The positions appeared inconsistent and perhaps even unintelligible to Eidlitz's peers.

Eidlitz's old rival Henry Van Brunt, for example, published a devastating and certainly biased review in the *Nation*, calling the work "harmful, unphilosophic, and misleading."[45] Van Brunt believed that Eidlitz "follow[ed] in the main the lines laid down by the greatest writer of the century on the theory of architecture, M. Viollet-le-Duc, and he accepts without hesitation and with all their consequences the purist dogmas of Pugin, Ruskin, and the other modern literary reformers of art. . . ."[46] But contrary to Van Brunt's assessment, Eidlitz was not interested in belatedly joining the Ruskin, Pugin, or Viollet-le-Duc bandwagon and presenting a simple, dogmatic solution to the problem of modern architecture. Van Brunt's assessment is more accurate when applied to an architect like Frederick Clarke Withers, whose motivation for design clearly derived strictly from the mainstream of the English Gothic Revival: Pugin, Ruskin, and a touch of Viollet-le-Duc provided all the framework for his successful career designing churches and country houses.[47] Eidlitz, however, read far and wide and synthesized diverse elements from every major writer of the nineteenth century. The book reads more as a series of disparate lectures than a narrative with a single unifying theme.[48] It is a fluid, dynamic, and difficult text. Trying to pin it down as a mere reflection of the ideas of Ruskin or Viollet-le-Duc, as Van Brunt did, missed the book's point entirely.

One of the common critiques of *The Nature and Function of Art*, offered by both Van Brunt and Charles Henry Hart, who published a positive if hesitant review in the *American Architect and Building News*, was that it needed pictures to show just what Eidlitz meant by "an idea in matter."[49] Both felt that had Eidlitz included a series of drawings, a visual handbook to show how to use

5.6 Cyrus L. W. Eidlitz, Dearborn Station, Chicago, 1883–1885. The Dearborn Station still stands today though its tower has lost its steeply gabled roof. *AR* (April 1896).

his principles to create a new language of architecture, it might perhaps have been more persuasive. Words alone did not support his case. This particular criticism also misses the overriding point of the book, which is that architects must learn to think critically about the act of building and its meaning rather than relying on a visual library for inspiration. If Eidlitz was specific at times about the proper way to build, his real point was much broader than whether or not a cornice should be composed of iron or brick: he hoped to "show how Architecture may again become a living and creative work."[50]

Despite the skepticism of his New York peers, there were a few architects who found the veins of gold in Eidlitz's book. It was in Chicago in the 1880s, a locale still largely independent of the strictures of the AIA, that

interest flourished. There the Western Association of Architects (WAA), led by John Wellborn Root and Daniel Burnham, maintained a fierce independence from their East Coast rivals. The AIA and its local Chicago Chapter were far less influential than the much larger WAA until 1889, when the groups finally merged after much tense negotiation.[51] In Chicago, far from the infighting of Eidlitz's New York, *The Nature and Function of Art* found a receptive audience.

Root, one of the most articulate and gifted of the architects practicing in post-fire Chicago, clearly read and absorbed Eidlitz's ideas. Though Louis Sullivan is better known as the theorist of the so-called Chicago School, Root, the designer of the provocatively monolithic Monadnock Block (1889–91), was his equal in intellectual matters.[52] An old associate of Peter B. Wight's in New York before both moved to Chicago in 1871, Root may first have become familiar with Eidlitz through Wight, who admired Eidlitz's early work.[53] H. H. Richardson, who built the seminal Marshall Field Warehouse in Chicago (1885–87), is another potential conduit. But knowledge of Eidlitz in Chicago can also be ascribed to his son Cyrus Eidlitz's commission to design the city's Dearborn Station from 1883 to 1885 (fig. 5.6). At this point in Cyrus's career, the two worked together as a team, and though records do not definitively indicate that they traveled to Chicago for the commission, given Eidlitz's earlier insistence on traveling to St. Louis as part of his design process for Christ Church, it is extremely likely that at least Cyrus and probably his father as well visited during the early 1880s. It is quite possible, therefore, that Eidlitz actually met with Wight and Root in Chicago.

Root was twenty-seven years Eidlitz's junior, but they were absorbed with the same issues: defining the concept of style, exploring the relationship between nature and architecture, and forging a new path for architects. In 1888, he published an article, "Broad Art Criticism," in which he appropriated a key concept from Eidlitz's *Nature and Function of Art* about beauty and "creative force" in a work of art or architecture. "What is a work of art?" Root asked. "The answer most nearly true seems to be that given by Mr. Leopold Eidlitz."[54] Eidlitz was surely delighted at Root's confidence in his assertions.

Root quoted two passages, the first in which Eidlitz asserted that beauty in art was in proportion to the "creative force" one could perceive in it. This was another way of phrasing Eidlitz's long-standing definition of architecture as an "idea in matter," emphasizing the idea of "expression" that was so central to Eidlitz's architecture. The more powerful the idea, the more beautiful the artwork or architecture. Second, Root quoted one of Eidlitz's biological and scientific analogies to prove the complexity of measuring "creative force." In physics, to measure the effort a man takes in carrying a burden, one needed to measure the weight of the burden and of the man, the distance and any incline traveled, any tools used to lighten the load, etc. Eidlitz proposed that the

same exacting methods be applied to the criticism of art and architecture, and Root agreed.[55] Root's subsequent arguments read like a précis of Eidlitz's earlier conception of organic functionalism: "As far as material conditions permit it to be possible, a building designated for a particular purpose should express that purpose in every part. The purpose may not be revealed by conventional means, but it must be so plainly revealed that it can be escaped by no appreciative student."[56] In other essays, Root seemed to echo Eidlitz as well. In 1890, he wrote, "It is certainly true that before architecture can ever attain vital expression the building must be viewed by the architect as an organism, having within it elements as vital functions, as well defined and as consistent with themselves as in any of the organisms created by nature."[57] Root called both for rationalism in design and for "vital expression" as well. Here was the successor to Eidlitz's quest for a new poetic conception of architecture modeled on the laws of nature.

Sullivan also must have been aware of *The Nature and Function of Art*, if not through reading it himself, then through Root and their discussions of architecture. While there is no evidence as direct as Root's quotation of him, Narciso Menocal has shown that Sullivan's writing at times directly echoed Eidlitz's.[58] His concern for a "heroic architectural anthropomorphism," Menocal believes, comes directly from Eidlitz and his organic conception of buildings as having souls, ideas, and expressions.[59] This is a critical link, for its shows Eidlitz and Sullivan, though they were both protofunctionalists, never conceived of an architecture defined solely by construction. Echoing Greenough and Eidlitz, Sullivan wrote, "Form ever follows function," but like Eidlitz, that function always contained a poetic element. And Sullivan believed, also like Eidlitz, that ornament was the key to a building's soul.[60]

This understanding of ornament, that it had something noble to communicate, directly contradicted the Beaux-Arts conception of ornament that Eidlitz's New York peers like Hunt and Post espoused. Their insistence on correctness, on the "received rules of art," had nothing to do with emotive expression. If architecture was a language, as Eidlitz believed, one needed to

CLERGY HOUSE.
St.GEORGE'S CHURCH.

← FRONT ELEVATION →

5.7 St. George's Memorial House, New York, 1886–88; front elevation drawing ca. 1886.

use it, not just to say something, but to say something relevant and powerful. This belief in the language of architecture set Eidlitz, Root, and Sullivan apart from those architects who relied on an academic or historical sense of propriety to guide their designs. Ironically, while the Beaux-Arts Revival eclipsed the underlying richness of Eidlitz's organic theory and designs, it was the modernist movement that made it difficult to see the richness in Sullivan's. As David Van Zanten has eloquently discussed, modernist architects and historians later recognized only the pure functionalist aspects of Sullivan's designs, failing to acknowledge Sullivan's quest for underlying meaning through ornament.[61] When the modernist movement embraced a functionalist dogma of pure structure in the twentieth century, it eviscerated

the organic experiments of Eidlitz and Sullivan and obscured the connection between the two.

DÉNOUEMENT

With his professional reputation destroyed in the wake of the Albany controversy and the poor public reception of his book, Eidlitz spent most of the rest of his professional life in the 1880s and 1890s quietly. There were intimations in the press in 1886 that he was perhaps considering a post as supervising architect for the Treasury Department, but William A. Freret, a New Orleans architect, actually filled the position.[62] Eidlitz designed a few more buildings, all on a small scale, like the Memorial House for St. George's; after forty years, the parish was still a faithful client (fig. 5.7). He also, perhaps in an effort to salvage his reputation for mechanical savvy, refurbished the Cooper Union building, which was suffering from foundation problems (1885–86). He shored up the basement and added structural support by replacing the cracking stone lintels above the second-floor windows with simple, unadorned iron beams (fig. 5.8). Later, in the early 1890s, he also renovated the top floors into studio space for the new women's art school, adding industrial sawtooth skylights to light their quarters.[63] This work found Eidlitz practicing again, as with his Viaduct Railway, in the realm of "artistic engineering."

Eidlitz's withdrawal from a prominent role in the architecture world in the late 1880s and 1890s, though, did not mean he stopped contemplating its future. Eidlitz saw architecture as connected to every facet of human life: in his second book, *Big Wages and How to Earn Them*, published in 1887, (fig. 5.9) architecture was an economic endeavor inextricably linked to labor markets and unionization. At first glance, Eidlitz's second book could not be more dissimilar to the esoteric intellectualizing of *The Nature and Function of Art*. Written under a pseudonym, and thus subject to suspicion from readers from the outset, *Big Wages* is by contrast utterly pragmatic, focused only on the day-to-day existence and earning potential of workers, especially workers in the building trades: masons, stonecutters, bricklayers, ironworkers. It appeared in the wake of a series of labor demonstrations in the spring of 1886 and was sparked by

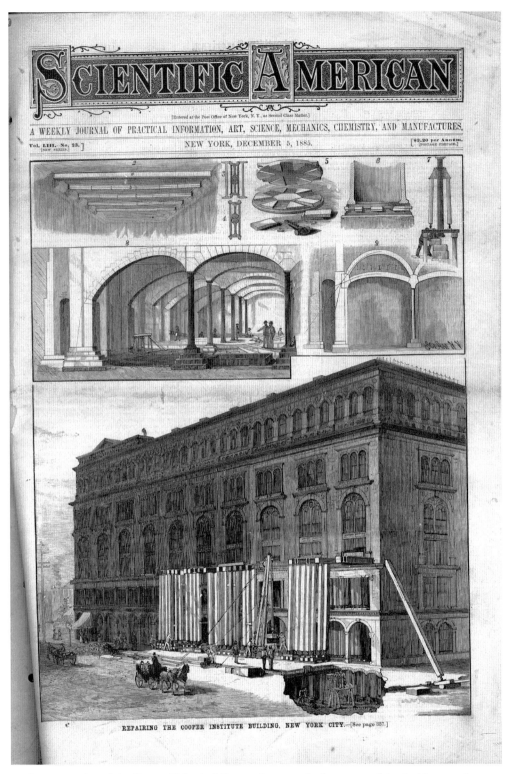

SCIENTIFIC AMERICAN

[Entered at the Post Office of New York, N. Y., as Second Class Matter.]

A WEEKLY JOURNAL OF PRACTICAL INFORMATION, ART, SCIENCE, MECHANICS, CHEMISTRY, AND MANUFACTURES.

Vol. LIII.—No. 23.
[NEW SERIES.]

NEW YORK, DECEMBER 5, 1885.

[$3.20 per Annum.
[POSTAGE PREPAID.]

REPAIRING THE COOPER INSTITUTE BUILDING, NEW YORK CITY.—[See page 357.]

5.8 Reconstruction of the Cooper Union building, as shown on the front page of the Architects and Mechanics edition of the *Scientific American* (December 1885). Frederic A. Peterson was architect of the much-altered original building in 1853–59.

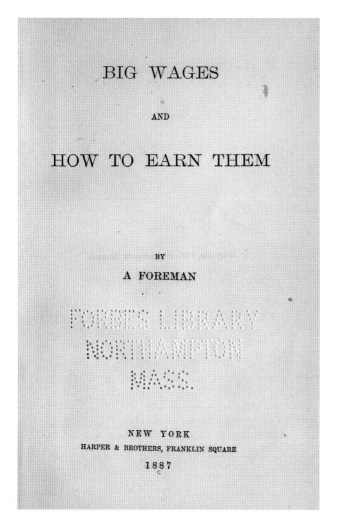

BIG WAGES

AND

HOW TO EARN THEM

BY

A FOREMAN

NEW YORK
HARPER & BROTHERS, FRANKLIN SQUARE
1887

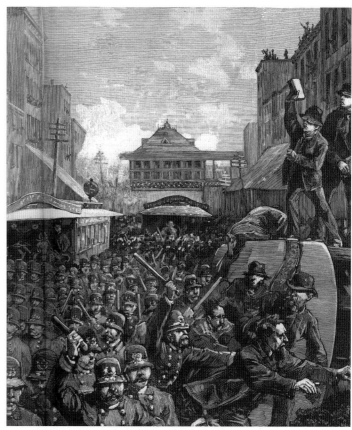

5.9 Title page, *Big Wages and How to Earn Them* (1887).

5.10 Artist's depiction of the railcar strike in New York, 1886 (detail). *Harper's Weekly* (1886).

the experiences of his contractor-brother Marc Eidlitz, as well as his own with ballooning budgets, construction delays, and striking workers (fig. 5.10). *Big Wages* was a paean to the average laborer to take pride in his individual work rather than yielding to the more homogenizing standards of labor unions. Eidlitz urged workers to rely instead on their individual ambition and honesty as guarantee of fair wages. Outside of Washington, D.C.'s Adolf Cluss, who had been an associate of Marx and a public supporter of socialism in America early in his career, Eidlitz is the only American architect to so directly address the potential impact of socialism, labor unions, and economics on architectural production. Cluss abandoned his socialism as his success in the architectural profession became secure.[64]

The book, however, shares with *The Nature and Function of Art* evidence of Eidlitz's synthetic method, of reading, sifting, and condensing the major works in the Western tradition into a form that he believed his audience could appreciate. Here rather than Kant, Hegel, Baumgarten, Ruskin, and Fergusson, we find Marx, Adam Smith, John Locke, John Stuart Mill—the great writers on modern political economy. As in art and architecture, Eidlitz embraced no one position, instead borrowing and recombining to craft a position that aligned with no particular camp. He could reject Marx's socialism while applauding his attention to the worker; he could embrace Smith's emphasis on meritocracy and the free market while rejecting his distrust of democratic government. As always, he took his cues from experts but asserted his own right to criticize and adapt their ideas to his own circumstances. History, theory, and philosophy were filtered through Eidlitz's own personal lens: if a poor Jew from Prague could become the architect of the New York State Capitol, his argument seemed to be, then anyone could do anything. The common theme throughout was his Lockian belief in labor as inherently valuable unto itself.[65]

Eidlitz's discussion of labor and wages was informed by his high status within the building trades. As an architect, he was in fact far more than a foreman. As the official linchpin between the client and the building process, Eidlitz repeatedly had to answer when building schedules fell far behind, when budgets skyrocketed, and when work contracted was of poor quality. In the economic system of nineteenth-century architecture, Eidlitz was a mediator. Carpenters, masons, and painters presented their bills for materials and labor to him; he then inspected their work, signed their requests for payment, and forwarded them to the client.[66] Eidlitz was in all respects a boss, and his perspective was one of an employer, not truly of a fellow laborer, and to present himself as such, while interesting from an intellectual point of view, was certainly disingenuous. Eidlitz was against the eight-hour workday because increased labor costs would make monumental architecture even more prohibitively expensive. He had suffered frustrations because of striking workers, and his brother Marc Eidlitz and nephew Otto Eidlitz were both outspoken public critics of unions, pushing for legislation that would outlaw and restrain their activities.[67] In Eidlitz's view, the government had a large role to play in the advancement of the building trades not as a regulator, but as a patron, as an employer of architects, builders, and tradesmen who would create the infrastructure of the modern world.

In these two books, Eidlitz suggested the dialectical relationship between the architect as an artist and the architect as a laborer. In architecture as a discipline, the pull was between art and science; in architecture as a profession, the pull was between art and money. Eidlitz's view was deeply informed by his reading of Marx, whose socialism he outright rejected, but whose

concern with the dignity of the laborer he embraced. He decried the "despotism" of union bosses as "unparalleled in the history of the world" and suggested the abolition of the current system of labor unions as economic bargaining units in favor of cooperative societies dedicated to the education and stewardship of its members.[68] *Big Wages*, sold for only 75 cents a copy, was directed to a working-class audience and received no notice in architectural circles. But reviewers in other circles, undoubtedly members of Eidlitz's privileged class, embraced his "man-to-man talk" and message of self-reliance, urging the publisher to "get this book into the proper hands."[69] In the *Literary World*, his views were characterized along with those of Henry Wood, author of *Natural Law in the Business World*, newly reissued in a cheap 50-cent edition, as "sympathetic but not sentimental;" both were crucial reading for workingmen.[70] It was an apt pairing: both works were essentially conservative in nature politically and economically, while envisioning a controlled liberalization of the social world generated by the working classes themselves. In a striking example of how conservative and progressive social criticism overlapped, Eidlitz's insistence on education and hard work as the path to the dignity of the worker closely echoed the language of the socialist-anarchist Peter Kropotkin, who in an article that appeared in America in 1888 also envisioned "a society composed of men and women each of whom is able to work with his or her hands, as well as with his or her brain, and to do so in more directions than one."[71]

Eidlitz's writing of *Big Wages* is symptomatic of the sweeping and unwavering criticism that Eidlitz had written throughout his career, and it was not long after its publication that he again turned his withering pen to architecture. In 1891, the new journal *Architectural Record* appeared as a counter to the more conservative and practice-oriented *American Architect and Building News*. Montgomery Schuyler, Eidlitz's dear friend, was one of its founding editors, and he no doubt extended the invitation to the aging architect to take up the gauntlet once more. In three articles that appeared between 1892 and 1894, Eidlitz wrote on education and on the dismal effects commercial architecture had on professional

practice, but these late works received little response from the world of architecture. In tone, they had a pessimistic ring, as if Eidlitz's earlier optimism about the future of architecture had been shaken. "The Architect of Fashion" was a scathing indictment of the architects of the day and their tendency to allow clients and profit to motivate their architectural practices: "The church, the state and society at large," he said, "are at this time engaged not so much in developing ideas as in discarding those that have become obsolete. We are in a state of transition, and just now very busy in tearing down, rather than in building up."[72]

Eidlitz's pessimism about the state of architectural affairs in New York is understandable when considered from his point of view. Even in 1894, fourteen years before his death, many of his finest achievements in New York had fallen by the wayside. The arrival of the Beaux-Arts and the explosion of the commercial and business world of New York combined to make Eidlitz's buildings obsolete. For example, a mere twenty years after it was completed in 1860, Eidlitz's New York Produce

5.11 The Temple Emanu-El, literally overshadowed by the new commercial architecture of Fifth Avenue in 1924, just before its demolition. Milstein Division of United States History, Local History & Genealogy, The New York Public Library, Astor, Lenox and Tilden Foundations.

5.12 The demolition of the Temple Emanu-El in 1927. Only the side aisles and the narthex remain. York & Sawyer's Salmon Tower, newly completed in 1927, is visible in the background. Milstein Division of United States History, Local History & Genealogy, The New York Public Library, Astor, Lenox and Tilden Foundations.

Exchange was demolished to make way for Post's monumental palazzo-inspired design. The Church of the Holy Trinity was drastically remodeled in 1892, then by 1897 was sold and torn down, with the congregation moving to the Upper East Side and into a new complex designed by Barney & Chapman. The Broadway Tabernacle was demolished in 1903, with that congregation moving further up Broadway into another sanctuary designed by Barney & Chapman.[73] The Decker Building was demolished in 1893. Fire consumed the Brooklyn Academy of Music in 1907; the Springfield City Hall burned to the ground in 1905. By the time of Eidlitz's death, St. George's (without its towers, which had been dismantled in 1889), and Temple Emanu-El were the only remaining fragments of his long career (figs. 5.11 and 5.12). But even the great synagogue fell to the wrecker's ball in 1927, to be replaced by a thirty-seven-story office tower designed by Shreve & Lamb, who would later design the Empire State Building. The rabbi, Rev. H. G. Enelow, in his final sermon expressed some regret at its destruction: "The reaction in a house of worship should be one of adoration, and certainly this great sanctuary, magnificent while retaining a delicacy of line, is awe-inspiring and prompts one to express his adoration of God." But in the end, it was just a shell, nothing more: "When we leave our temple, we leave only the building."[74] The building was dismantled, its parts distributed to friends of the buyer, Joseph Durst. The ceremonial wrought-iron gates at the entry went to Nathan S. Jonas, who used them at his estate at Great Neck, Long Island, where they became neighbor to Eddie Cantor. Lee Shubert, one of the creators of the Shubert theater empire, took the other three sets of gates to use in his theaters. The capitals, columns, and mosaics were distributed to Durst's friends in the congregation. And one column and capital in its entirety went to none other than Leopold Eidlitz—erroneously identified by the *New York Times* as the building's architect, when in fact it was his son.[75] The fate of these disembodied parts remains unknown. In the "creative destruction of Manhattan," the rise and fall of Eidlitz's peculiar architecture is all too typical.

But while Eidlitz's career tapered off during the final decades of the nineteenth century, his oldest son Cyrus L. W. Eidlitz's architectural career blossomed during the 1880s (Fig. 5.13). Especially in the early years of Cyrus's practice, the senior Eidlitz played a large part in helping his son with the commissions he won. During this period, the two shared an office at 128 Broadway; Eidlitz's younger son, Leopold Jr., appears to have been an engineer in the firm. Cyrus's Dearborn Station in Chicago and Buffalo Public Library have the combined Rundbogenstil and Gothic patterns of his father's work and clearly show the hand of the State Capitol's de-

5.13 Cyrus L. W. Eidlitz, an undated portrait. Courtesy of the Century Association Archives Foundation.

signer (fig. 5.14, see 5.6).[76] Their planning still reflects the father's expressive sense of composition: towers and bays protrude and recede, reflecting the arrangement of interior spaces. But the restraint of the color scheme and the more conventional Richardsonian Romanesque effects should be ascribed to Cyrus, who developed into a far more conventional, though skilled, designer than his father had been.

Leopold, if unable to influence the direction of the American architectural profession as a whole, had clearly intended his son to follow in his footsteps. He sent Cyrus to study architecture at the Polytechnic Institute at Stuttgart in 1871–72, when both the great art historian Wilhelm Lübke and the aesthetician Friedrich Theodor Vischer taught there.[77] While Americans did go abroad to study in Germany in the 1870s, they more typically went to Düsseldorf or Munich. Eidlitz's choice of Stuttgart for his son was in keeping with his own

views about architectural education: that the study of history and theory was the most advanced stage of learning. Cyrus had already spent time learning the mechanics of design in his father's office and had spent several years at a preparatory school in Switzerland. Stuttgart was to be the final and formative stage.

Lübke was one of the founders of German art history in the university setting. His groundbreaking studies of German medieval architecture published in the 1850s quickly made him a leading expert in the field, followed by more general and populist histories of art intended to reach the growing German middle class. Lübke's positivist approach to the study of art and architecture, in which meaning could be derived through careful study of the objects themselves, certainly appealed to Eidlitz, as did his desire to enlighten the general public about the objects and buildings that surrounded them. Lübke's combination of scholarly study and popular writing made him the kind of mentor Eidlitz would have found appropriate for his son.[78] Vischer, too, was driven by the hope of reconciling ordinary human emotion and the

5.14 Cyrus L. W. Eidlitz, Buffalo Public Library, 1887. Demolished early 1960s. *AR* (April 1896).

higher realm of art. But his means of doing so was more abstruse and more cerebral. Eidlitz embraced his theory of empathy, in which an architect could anticipate and manipulate the emotional response of his viewer through composition and ornament. The inorganic matter of building was thus invested with life. At Stuttgart, Cyrus would have had the opportunity to learn from these masters firsthand and potentially continue his father's theoretical investigations of how best to translate "ideas into matter."

Despite his father's hopes for him, Cyrus seems to have been much less taken with theory or even the lessons of medieval construction than his father, and he certainly did not fashion himself as a crusader for any architectural cause. He and his wife, Jennie Turner Eidlitz, became fixtures in East Hampton, Long Island, where they lived across the street from his sister Harriet and her husband, successful businessman Schuyler

5.15 Cyrus L. W. Eidlitz, Townsend Building, Broadway Avenue, New York, 1901–03.
5.16 Eidlitz & McKenzie, New York Times Building, Times Square, New York 1903–5. Photograph by Irving Underhill, 1906. LC-USZ62-76217.

Quackenbush. By the 1890s, when Cyrus had a more independent practice, he had abandoned his father's medieval language and turned to the Renaissance Revival that had gripped New York. His Townsend Building (1901–3) showed he had a good eye for ornamental pattern, but it was unadventurous in content or presentation (fig. 5.15). The New York Times Building (1902–5) showed the transformation complete (fig. 5.16). As the first building to connect to New York's underground subway system, it was a technical marvel. But in its overlay of Renaissance proportion with Romanesque details, it was decidedly conventional.[79] Cyrus may have inherited his father's fascination with technology, but not his beliefs about style.

The lesson Cyrus learned from his father was one of pragmatism. Perhaps weary of the controversy that dogged his father throughout his own early years, Cyrus sought a more anonymous professional image that would allow him to reap the financial benefits of his architectural expertise without the constant battles. The Eidltz name was not exactly a boon to him in this endeavor. In January 1904, Cyrus applied for membership to the AIA. His application was supported by Stanford White and William R. Mead (of the prestigious Mc-

Kim, Mead, & White firm), and he noted that he had been in practice in New York for thirty years. Nonetheless, the AIA rejected his application for membership. Cyrus in his turn rejected the eventual offer for a second vote, but he was later elected to the group in November 1905. The bad blood between the Eidlitz family and the AIA was certainly not calmed by this series of events.[80]

But Cyrus became a truly successful architect by most measures, establishing the Eidlitz & McKenzie firm in about 1907 to deal almost exclusively with the telephone building business.[81] The firm employed a mix of engineers and designers to supply the communications industry with buildings both stylish and pragmatic; Leopold Eidlitz, Jr. was probably one of the firm's engineers.[82] One the one hand, the telephone buildings needed to impress clients, but on the other, they needed to contain the miles of wiring needed to support the industry. While a worthy and profitable business, one suspects that Eidlitz would have been disappointed that his son did not continue with his own difficult quest for a truly organic public architecture.

Eidlitz's "Architect of Fashion" could easily have been an indictment of his own son. Eidlitz, in typical sardonic style, attacked architects who practiced solely in pursuit of money and social prestige without thought for the noblest principle of all, art. At the age of seventy-one, with the architectural world leaving him forgotten in the dust, Eidlitz still had an ax to grind:

> The architect of fashion is he who aspires to be the fashionable architect. Like the modern politician, the architect of fashion has no convictions, but follows adroitly in the wake of public opinion. His aim is not to be a great architect, but to do a very big architectural business, and in this he very often succeeds. . . . Of course he has abandoned all claim to immortality, to a statue in the Walhalla, or a niche in Westminster Abbey, but he enjoys life while it lasts as a highly respectable member of society belonging to the most fashionable clubs, and although at times he gets very tired of it all, because of the humiliation of constant drumming and the silent gnawing of his professional conscience, he has the consolation of success and feels sure of pre-

eminence until supplanted by an architect, even more eminently fashionable.[83]

Eidlitz had never been a fashionable architect, and with his own retirement from active practice, there was no one left to continue his decidedly unfashionable battle.

No one else from the Eidlitz office can truly be said to have taken up the mantle. Eidlitz never ran a very large office, bucking yet another nineteenth-century trend, that of the large architectural business. He, his sons Cyrus and Leopold Jr., and one or two apprentices seem to have done the majority of the work. Albert D'Oench, for example, apprenticed in Eidlitz's office in 1875 after studying architecture at Stuttgart at the same time as Cyrus. D'Oench went on to work for Richard Morris Hunt and then became superintendent of buildings in New York in 1885. Nothing indicates that D'Oench was anything other than a solid, diligent architect.[84]

Somewhat more promising was Russell Sturgis, destined to become a great architectural critic and writer, who worked for Eidlitz for a year in 1857. Sturgis had grown up on Stuyvesant Square during the construction of St. George's and doubtless sought out Eidlitz because of his admiration for that work. And while Sturgis and his sometime partner Peter B. Wight admired Eidlitz's work early in his career, penning articles in their journal the *New Path* praising his "German Gothic," that admiration seems to have faded during Eidlitz's difficult years.[85] Sturgis, for example, did not support Eidlitz at AIA meetings in the 1850s or defend his capitol designs. He also did not include an entry for Eidlitz in his major 1902 dictionary of architecture and, when he wrote Montgomery Schuyler in 1908 to correct his dating of an Eidlitz building in the *Architectural Record* articles, he did not mention to Schuyler that he had actually worked for Eidlitz.[86] Sturgis died in 1909. But by 1922, when memory of Eidlitz had evaporated in the profession, Wight at least was able to recall the originality and inspiration of his early work in an essay of reminiscences. In any case, both Sturgis and Wight had abandoned the practice of architecture by mid-career to focus on their writing, ensuring that neither would continue Eidlitz's quest.[87]

transit" was the indispensable condition of the expansion of New York, and Mr. Sweeny had the honorable desire to associate his name and memory with the satisfaction of that crying need. There was associated with Mr. Eidlitz another engineer, General Serrell, of more experience in railroad building. I have always supposed that the monumental scheme of buying a right of way through blocks, asking the public only to grant the right of crossing the streets, and thus of constructing the road at the most convenient and economical grades, instead of following the casual undulations of the terrain, was Mr. Eidlitz's own. At any rate, he entered heart and soul into the work, and was ready to point out to the frequent objector to his scheme upon the ground of its inordinate cost that the longer the city waited the costlier it would be, while some such scheme was the only real and permanent solution of the question of rapid transit. It was, in fact, according to him, a sort

of Sybilline proposition that the city, as an aggregation of landholders, was making to the city, as a municipality, a proposition becoming more "prohibitive" as the acceptance of it was delayed. To quite another class of objectors, represented, so far as I know, by the present writer exclusively, who reproached him for abandoning architecture for this lucrative and utilitarian employment, he triumphantly rejoined by enumerating the architectural opportunities in the way of bridges and stations which the Viaduct would afford. The only one of these opportunities that took shape, even in drawings, before the fall of the Ring submerged the whole project in its ruins, was a sketch for a huge steep-roofed station at the eastern end of the Brooklyn-East River Bridge, then already projected, and the southern terminal of the Viaduct or of one of its branches, which sketch got the length of publication in the illustrated papers.

NATIONAL FARMERS' BANK OF OWATONNA, MINN.—DETAIL OF MAIN MASS.
Louis H. Sullivan, Architect.

5.17 A page from Montgomery Schuyler's posthumous article on Leopold Eidlitz, illustrated by chance with a photograph of Louis Sullivan's National Farmers' Bank in Owatonna, Minnesota. *AR* (October 1908).

Montgomery Schuyler, always a critic and never an architect, was the best candidate for continuing Eidlitz's pursuit of an organic theory of architecture. As one of the founding editors of *Architectural Record*, Schuyler had a pulpit for the enunciation of new architectural principles. Schuyler's affinity with Eidlitz was through his rationalism, his cool appraisal of architecture as defined by structure and not by style. In an 1891 speech in which he defined his own approach as a critic, he

began by quoting Eidlitz, saying, "It has been said . . . that American architecture was the art of covering one thing with another thing to imitate a third thing, which if genuine would not be desirable."[88] Schuyler's 1883 analysis of the Brooklyn Bridge was deeply indebted to Eidlitz's conception of the proper modeling of mass that he had expounded in *The Nature and Function of Art*.[89] Schuyler also agreed with Eidlitz's sentiments about the shallow commercialism of the Beaux-Arts, writing sarcastically that the "classic formulas are the greatest labor saving devices of which the history of architecture gives any account."[90] But Schuyler, though he had early on been unenthusiastic about Richard Morris Hunt's work in general, could also write an admiring obituary praising him.[91] In practice, Schuyler was too much the gentlemanly connoisseur to be a modernist critic.[92] Schuyler's sympathies were clearly with Eidlitz and the organic functionalist camp in Chicago, as his articles on Sullivan showed, but he nonetheless remained unable to comprehend the implications of Eidlitz's early organic theory.[93]

In March 1908, for example, the *Architectural Record* carried Frank Lloyd Wright's seminal essay defining his own approach to organic architecture, "In the Cause of Architecture." Just a few months later, Schuyler published his three-part posthumous series on Eidlitz in September, October, and November. While their architectural work clearly derives from different principles, there is a strand that connects the two: their joint insistence on a harmonious combination of function, structure, and ornament. But Schuyler was blinded both by his distaste for Wright's "unmodelled" architecture and his own traditional compartmentalization of architecture into periods and styles.[94] Any possible connection between Eidlitz's theory and the development of a new, contemporary organic architecture was not considered because Eidlitz's era, the Gothic Revival, was over.

In a 1912 essay on Sullivan, Schuyler came closest to making a link between Eidlitz and more contemporary theory. Writing in 1912 about the People's Savings Bank in Cedar Rapids, Iowa (1911), Schuyler said, "It is, so to speak, grown from its own seed, and recalls the remark of another American architect that if one has faithfully studied and interpreted the requirements of this

5.18 An elderly Eidlitz, depicted in a scholarly pose, reading a copy of *The Photographic Times. AR* (November 1908).

structure, expressional as well as practical, and faithfully followed them out, then he does not so much 'design' his building as he 'watches it grow.' "[95] That "other American architect," though Schuyler failed to identify him, was clearly Eidlitz. Much of the rest of the article also echoed Eidlitz's pronouncements on modeling and ornament, with Schuyler's assessment of the dramatically looming Owatonna, Minnesota, National Farmer's Bank's cornice echoing his assessment of the "beetling" cornice of Eidlitz's much earlier Continental Bank.[96] But the connection between Eidlitz's theory, the foundations of Schuyler's critical apparatus, and Sullivan's architecture is never made explicit, instead only suggested by analogy and allusion: an illustration of the cornice from the Owatonna bank had actually appeared, only by chance, on the same page as Schuyler's 1908 article on Eidlitz (fig. 5.17).

Schuyler was an architectural critic, responding to architectural events. The necessarily episodic nature of his writing perhaps explains the fact that he did not make the connections that he seems so close to making. As such, his articles on Eidlitz were a look at the past in which he made no attempt to connect Eidlitz's prescient concerns to the future or even to the present. Eidlitz's major theoretical work, *The Nature and Function of Art*, received scant mention because, as Schuyler noted, "it takes an earnest reader to attack [it]."[97] And though Schuyler repeatedly affirmed Eidlitz's commitment to the idea that structure should be the generative force of all building, he missed the opportunity to show how revolutionary that concept was when combined with an integral symbolic ornament. The article was truly a eulogy, in the best sense of the word, generously praising the work of a departed friend and colleague while at the same time gently consigning it to the fading recesses of memory (fig. 5.18).

EIDLITZ THE INDIVIDUALIST

Eidlitz was a magnet for controversy not just because of his difficult personality, but because of his firm and unshakable belief in an architecture derived from rational, scientific study that could, through ornament, communicate humanistic ideals. While this does not seem a particularly controversial idea, the rhetoric of organic architecture that he used to support that belief was clearly antagonistic to many of his colleagues' sensibilities. Eidlitz practiced architecture in a time and place that ultimately came to value an intellectual and stylistic conservatism absent in his own work. The open exchange of ideas that took place in the 1850s was gradually supplanted by an atmosphere less tolerant of dialogue and difference. The rise of the AIA and a narrowly defined professionalism and the subsequent dominance of the Beaux-Arts movement in design and education all created an environment hostile to his individualistic search for an organic architecture. By the 1870s, the decade of the Albany conflict, Eidlitz's New York peers had clearly tired of his theorizing.

In the first issue of the *American Architect and Building News*, editor W. P. P. Longfellow touted "unity" as the means through which American architects could achieve a higher professional and cultural status.[98] The profession's fractured nature, he wrote, was the result of a long-standing tolerance of varying standards for education, ethics, style, and social status. If American architects truly wished to be taken seriously by their clients, by the public, and by their peers in Europe, they must embrace new, higher standards of practice and leave the days of variation and difference behind. Any practitioner who obstinately pursued an idea unpopular with his professional peers should be ridiculed as a "quack," a term that was eventually applied to Eidlitz himself. Only through the promotion of and adherence to a unified architectural profession would practitioners find success.

To Olmsted, Eidlitz had written, "I am willing as I have been on former occasions to fight this battle alone," and herein lies the seed of Eidlitz's professional downfall.[99] Going it alone, outspoken bursts of individuality—these are things the AIA was trying to discourage in the late nineteenth century. Eidlitz had been throughout his career a rabble-rouser, a thorn in the side of the more dignified and patrician Hunt and his very different vision for the future of American architecture. To Eidlitz, this was all part of the professional process that involved spirited discourse; it would never have occurred to him to be less brash and more conciliatory—just as it never occurred to him that he should reconcile his design for the Albany capitol with Fuller's that came before him. But unity in the profession became of primary importance if architects hoped to improve their position in society.

The New York establishment, embodied in the New York Chapter of the AIA, was too intellectually and socially conservative to hear Eidlitz's message or to tolerate his ideas. The generation of architects that came of age during Eidlitz's period of great activity in the 1860s and '70s flocked to the doors of Richard Morris Hunt, seeking to model themselves in his image. What resulted in New York in the 1880s and '90s was indeed an era of great unity, with Post, followed by McKim, Mead & White, Carrère & Hastings, and many others building some of the most magnificent specimens of Beaux-Arts architecture in America. Those who searched for a different architectural expression practiced elsewhere in the last quarter of the nineteenth century: Furness's bold individuality in Philadelphia, Richardson's Romanesque in Boston and Chicago, Root's and Sullivan's organic functionalism in Chicago. Though none of these practitioners were the direct descendant of Eidlitz, they followed in his footsteps, flouting convention in search of an architecture that expressed something more than a sense of archeological correctness and social propriety.

Through the years, the voices of critique and dissent have often come from those in search of a new language and function for architecture. Eidlitz's intense individuality and organic theory of architecture represents the beginning of a strain of American theory that percolates through Montgomery Schuyler and Lewis Mumford, Louis Sullivan and Frank Lloyd Wright, all vocal opponents, at times, of the American architectural system. Eidlitz's desire for collaboration, science, and practicality in education were echoed even in the plans of Joseph Hudnut and Walter Gropius when they arrived at Harvard in the 1930s.[100] In a statement that still rings true, Eidlitz exhorted his colleagues that "the dilettanteism of modern architecture must be rooted out before the art can revive and exercise a wholesome influence upon society."[101]

The trends that the modern movement would later critique—complacency, conservatism, and elitism—were sources of conflict from the beginnings of the organized architectural profession in the 1850s. The rejection of Eidlitz's polytechnic school, of his theory of organic design, and of his formal and ornamental experiments, was the result of a fundamental disagreement about the direction American architecture should take. Eidlitz took no part in the "Victorian compromise" that Lewis Mumford saw as the defining concept of the mid nineteenth century's eclecticism.[102] Instead, he fiercely defended and promoted his vision for an architecture based in an idealistic and organic conception of form and meaning. His unwavering exploration of "ideas in matter" made him an anomaly in his lifetime in New York, but ensured that the vigorousness of his endeavor would never truly fade.

APPENDIX

CATALOG OF WORKS

What follows is a chronological list of all buildings and proposed designs currently known to have been executed by Leopold Eidlitz. In the absence of Eidlitz's papers, drawings, or other office records, I first compiled the list from published sources, listed below. I have also unearthed several new designs and corrected dates and collaborators based on archival research as well as newly available full-text electronic resources. I anticipate that as more nineteenth-century sources are digitized, this list can be expanded and refined. At the end of the catalog is a brief list of works that have in the past been attributed to Eidlitz that may now be safely attributed to others. Each entry contains the following information:

- Building's name
- Collaborator (if any)
- City (and state for those buildings located outside the city of New York)
- Dates of design and construction, when distinguishable
- Whether or not the building is still extant
- Client (if not clear from the building's name)
- Brief notes about the building's design

Previously published catalogs of Eidlitz's works include:

Brooks, H. Allen, Jr. "Leopold Eidlitz." M.A. thesis, Yale University, 1955.

Erdmann, Biruta. "Leopold Eidlitz's Architectural Theories and American Transcendentalism." Ph.D. diss., University of Wisconsin–Madison, 1977.

Garmey, Stephen. "Leopold Eidlitz," *Macmillan Encyclopedia of Architects*. Vol. 2. New York: Free Press, 1982.

Holliday, Kathryn E. "Leopold Eidlitz and the Architecture of Nineteenth-Century America." Ph.D. diss., University of Texas at Austin, 2003.

Jacobs, Kenneth. "Leopold Eidlitz: Becoming an American Architect." Ph.D. diss., University of Pennsylvania, 2005.

Schuyler, Montgomery. "Leopold Eidlitz: A Great American Architect," *Architectural Record* 24, nos. 3, 4, 5 (September, October, November 1908), reprinted in William Jordy and Ralph Coe, eds., *American Architecture, and Other Writings*. Cambridge, Mass.: Belknap Press of Harvard University Press, 1961.

Stern, Robert A. M.; Thomas Mellins; and David Fishman. *New York 1880: Architecture and Urbanism in the Gilded Age*. New York: Monacelli Press, 1998.

The Catalog

ST. GEORGE'S EPISCOPAL CHURCH
Blesch & Eidlitz
New York, Stuyvesant Square
1846–48
Cornerstone laid June 23, 1846
Spires completed 1856
Extant
Partially destroyed by fire in 1865; rebuilt by Leopold Eidlitz in 1866–67. The interior was redecorated during this building campaign, with slender supporting pillars added beneath the formerly cantilevered balconies and wall painting executed by Louis Cohn added throughout the sanctuary. In 1871, the condition of the spires, which had been damaged in the fire, caused concern, and Eidlitz had Detlef Lienau, Calvert Vaux, and John Taylor (a stonemason) inspect them to certify their fitness. They recommended following Eidlitz's plan of adding an enclosing lantern to the spires to prevent frost from settling on them and causing further damage (Vestry minutes for April 13 and September 7, 1871). Ultimately the spires were removed in 1889.

SHAARAY-TEFILA SYNAGOGUE
Also known as the Wooster Street Synagogue
Blesch & Eidlitz
New York, Wooster Street between Spring and Prince Streets
1846–47
Demolished

CHRYSTIE STREET TEMPLE EMANU-EL
Renovation of existing structure and design of furnishings and ark
1847–48
New York, Chrystie Street
Demolished
Eidlitz apparently submitted drawings for refurbishment of the Methodist Church on Chrystie Street, which the Temple Emanu-El bought. It is unclear whether or not these renovations were carried out, but he did design the ark, reader's platforms, and pulpits. The congregation remained on Chrystie Street only until 1854.

IRANISTAN
The P. T. Barnum House
1848
Bridgeport, Connecticut
Destroyed by fire, December 17, 1857. The library from Iranistan was reconstructed as an exhibit in the Barnum Museum in Bridgeport.

FIRST CONGREGATIONAL CHURCH
Blesch & Eidlitz
1849
Norwalk, Connecticut
Giles Seymour, builder
Extant

FIRST CHURCH OF CHRIST
Blesch & Eidlitz
1849–54
New London, Connecticut
Extant

SOLOMON MERRICK HOUSE
1849–50
Springfield, Massachusetts, Maple Street
Demolished

WILLIAM GUNN HOUSE
1850
Springfield, Massachusetts, Maple Street
Demolished

FIRST PRESBYTERIAN CHURCH (OLD SCHOOL) OF BROOKLYN
Blesch & Eidlitz
Finished 1851
Brooklyn, Clinton and Remsen Streets
French & Dunham, masons
George White, builder
James Valentine, stonework
Extant
Later home to the Spencer Memorial Church, a liberal Presbyterian congregation and converted to co-op apartments in the 1970s.

EIDLITZ RESIDENCE
1851
New York, Riverside Drive between 86th and 87th Streets
Demolished

FIFTH AVENUE PRESBYTERIAN CHURCH
1851–52
New York, Fifth Avenue and Nineteenth Street
Demolished
In 1876, the Fifth Avenue Presbyterian Church moved further up Fifth Avenue to make way for the expansion of the Arnold Constable department store. Their new church was designed by Carl Pfeiffer. Their old Eidlitz-designed church was moved to 57th Street to be the new home of the Central Presbyterian Church. The Central Presbyterian Church then sold the building to the Madison Avenue Reformed Church in 1915.

ST. GEORGE'S RECTORY
1851–52
New York, 16th Street between Second Avenue and Stuyvesant Square

FIRST CHURCH OF CHRIST
1851–53; cornerstone laid May 28, 1852
Pittsfield, Massachusetts
Extant
My thanks to Michael Lewis and his student Johanna Heinrichs for first pointing out this church as an Eidlitz design.

CRYSTAL PALACE
1852
New York
Competition entry, unbuilt
Competition won by Carstensen & Gildemeister.

ST. PETER'S EPISCOPAL CHURCH
1853–55
West Chester (Bronx), New York, Westchester Square, now 2500 Westchester Avenue
Extant
Rebuilt to similar design by Cyrus L. W. Eidlitz in 1877 after an 1876 fire damaged the building.

SPRINGFIELD CITY HALL
1853–55; dedicated January 1, 1856
Springfield, Massachusetts
Burned January 1905

EIGHTY-FOURTH STREET PRESBYTERIAN CHURCH
1853
New York, 84th Street and West End
  Avenue
Wilson and Robison, builders
Demolished ca. 1884
A wooden "rural" church, also known
as the West End Presbyterian Church,
which Eidlitz designed for free as a service to the congregation in his community (the church was about three blocks
from his home). Eidlitz also designed
the congregation's next home, the Park
Presbyterian Church, in 1884, though
only the chapel was built to his design.

"RURAL HOME" DESIGN
1854
Published in John Bullock's *The Ameri-
can Cottage Builder: A Series of Designs,
Plans, and Specifications from $200 to
$20,000; For Homes for the People* (New
York: Stringer & Townsend, 1854).

ROBERT W. MEAD HOUSE
1854
Greenwich, Connecticut
Originally on Putnam Avenue, now at
30 Milbank Avenue
Built for Robert W. Mead, a member
of the First Congregational Church of
Greenwich and the leader in the effort
to build Eidlitz's design for that church.
Though he was not a building contractor, he served in that capacity for the
church project in order to ensure its
completion.

JONATHAN COIT MONUMENT
1856
New London, Connecticut
A tombstone in the Cedar Grove
  Cemetery.

BRICK PRESBYTERIAN CHURCH
Eidlitz, November 1856–57
Design completed in by T. Thomas &
  Son, 1857–58
New York
Extant

CONTINENTAL BANK
1856–57
New York, Nassau and Pine Streets
Demolished

SECOND CONGREGATIONAL CHURCH
1856–59
Greenwich, Connecticut
Extant
Dedication December 1858; spire com-
  pleted 1859. Spire rebuilt 1919.

AMERICAN EXCHANGE BANK
1857
New York, Broadway and Cedar Street
Marc Eidlitz, builder
Demolished

WILLIAM A. BOOTH HOUSE
1857
Stratford, Connecticut
Extant
Originally built as a home for William
  A. Booth during the periods he was
  in Stratford. The house became a
  parsonage within two years of its
  construction.

NORTH CONGREGATIONAL CHURCH
1857
Hartford, Connecticut
Project (unbuilt)

SECOND CONGREGATIONAL CHURCH
Greeneville, Connecticut (present-day
  Norwich)
1858
Extant

HAMILTON FERRY HOUSE
1858
Brooklyn
Demolished

NEW YORK CITY HALL RENOVATION
1858?
New York, City Hall Park
Extant
Reconstruction of the dome after an
  1858 fire.

PLYMOUTH CHURCH
1858–59
Brooklyn
Competition entry, unbuilt
Competition won by Charles Duggin.

FIRST CONGREGATIONAL CHURCH
1858–59
Stratford, Connecticut
Extant; exterior greatly modified

BROADWAY TABERNACLE
1858–59
New York, Broadway and 34th Street
Marc Eidlitz, builder
Thomas Wilson, carpenter
Louis Cohn, muralist
Demolished

JONATHAN NEWTON HARRIS HOUSE
1859–60
New London, Connecticut, 130 Broad
  Street
Extant

FERNANDO WOOD HOUSE
ca. 1860
New York
Demolished
The attribution is based on a drawing
by Alfred R. Waud, entitled "Mayor
Wood's Parlor," and encscribed in
Waud's hand "Leopold Eidlitz." Waud
was an artist for *Frank Leslie's Illustrated
Newspaper* at the time. The drawing
is held by the Division of Prints and
Photographs, Library of Congress.

BARON RENFREW PAVILION
1860
New York, Bloomingdale Road
Demolished
A temporary structure erected as an
outdoor pavilion for a luncheon honor-
ing Edward VII, Prince of Wales, on his
American tour (he traveled incognito as
"Baron Renfrew").

NEW YORK BLIND ASYLUM
1860
New York
Competition entry, unbuilt
My thanks to Lucille Gordon for shar-
  ing the reference to this competition.

TOMPKINS MARKET ROOF
ca. 1860
New York, Bowery and Third Avenue
Demolished

CHRIST CHURCH CATHEDRAL
1860–61
St. Louis, Missouri, Locust Street
Exterior greatly modified
Jonathan Bowen, superintendent;
John Beattie appointed supervising
  architect in 1865.
Tower added by Kivas Tully, 1911.

Designated a cathedral in 1888.
Eidlitz nominated Bowen (an architect from London) for membership in the AIA in 1860.

BROOKLYN ACADEMY OF MUSIC
1860–61
Formally opened January 15, 1861
Brooklyn, Montague Street
Destroyed by fire, 1907

NEW YORK PRODUCE EXCHANGE
1860–61
New York, Whitehall Street at Pearl St.
Solomon Banta, mason
Thomas Wilson, carpenter
Demolished 1880

NATIONAL ACADEMY OF DESIGN
1861
New York
Competition entry, unbuilt
Competition won by Peter B. Wight.

MURRAY-VERMILYE RESIDENCE
1861
Englewood, New Jersey
Demolished

BRIGHTWOOD
Dr. J. G. Holland Residence
1862
Springfield, Massachusetts, Atwater Terrace
Demolished 1940

MUTUAL LIFE INSURANCE COMPANY
1863
New York
Invited competition entry, unbuilt
Competition won by John Kellum.

BROOKLYN MERCANTILE LIBRARY
1865
Brooklyn
Competition entry, unbuilt
Competition won by Peter B. Wight.

FULTON FERRY TERMINAL
1865
Brooklyn, Fulton Street
Demolished
For the Union Ferry Company.

YALE UNIVERSITY CIVIL WAR MEMORIAL
1866
New Haven, Connecticut

Competition entry, unbuilt
Competition won by Frederick Clarke Withers.

HINSDALE PUBLIC LIBRARY
1866
Hinsdale, Massachusetts
Extant
Funded by a bequest from Mrs. Kingsley Twining, wife of the Reverend Kingsley Twining, minister of the First Congregational Church in Hinsdale.

TEMPLE EMANU-EL
Eidlitz & Fernbach
1866–68
New York, Fifth Avenue and 43rd Street
Marc Eidlitz & Son, contractor
Demolished 1927

NEW YORK LIFE INSURANCE COMPANY
1867
Competition entry, unbuilt
Competition won by Griffith Thomas.

MEMORIAL HALL, BOWDOIN COLLEGE
ca. 1867
Bowdoin, Maine
Designs rejected
Building designed by Samuel Backus in 1867.

ST. PETER'S CHAPEL
1867–68
West Chester (Bronx), New York
Extant

BROOKLYN UNION BUILDING
1868
Brooklyn, Front Street and Old Fulton Street
Demolished

WILLIAM A. BOOTH RESIDENCE
ca. 1868
Englewood, New Jersey
Demolished

CHURCH OF THE PILGRIMS, REMODEL OF INTERIOR AND ADDITION OF PARISH HOUSE
1868–70
Brooklyn, Remsen Street and Henry Street
Louis Cohn, muralist
Extant

NEW YORK MASONIC LODGE
1869–70 (October–January)
Invited competition entry, unbuilt
Competition won by Napoleon LeBrun.

VIADUCT RAILWAY FOR NEW YORK
John Serrell and Leopold Eidlitz
1870
New York
Project, unbuilt

DECKER BUILDING
1870
New York, Union Square West
Marc Eidlitz, mason
Hennessey & Gibson, carpenter
Demolished 1894

LONG ISLAND HISTORICAL SOCIETY
1870
Brooklyn
Unbuilt
Eidlitz had previously designed the Hamilton Ferry House for the Union Ferry Company, which was owned by Henry E. Pierrepont, one of the founders of the LIHS. Financial strain delayed construction of Eidlitz's design. When cash again became available to build in 1878, the Historical Society held a new competition, which George B. Post won. The building was then built according to Post's designs in 1878–80.
My thanks to Sarah Landau for sharing her research on this building.

BULKLEY SCHOOL
1870–73
New London, Connecticut
Extant in modified form

TROY MASONIC TEMPLE
Completed by local architects Cummings & Birt, who modified the design in unspecified ways
1872
Troy, New York
Destroyed by fire 1923

ST. GEORGE'S CHAPEL
1872 (begun June 25, completed November 30)
New York, East Fourteenth Street
Marc Eidlitz, builder
Demolished

MOLLER, ODELL & CO. STOREFRONT
1872
New York, Washington Street between
    Vestry and Laight Streets
C. W. Dolle, builder
Destroyed by 1882, when architect
Thomas R. Jackson designed a new
store for Isaac Odell at the same loca-
tion.

CHILDREN'S AID SOCIETY, NEWSBOYS'
LODGING HOUSE
1872–74 (begun December 11, com-
    pleted April 2, 1874)
New York, bounded by Chambers, Wil-
    liam, and Duane Streets
Richard Deeves, builder
Demolished

CHURCH OF THE HOLY TRINITY
1873–74
New York, Madison Avenue and 42nd
    Street
Demolished

DRY DOCK SAVINGS BANK
1873–75
New York, Bowery Street at Third
    Avenue
Demolished

NEW YORK STATE CAPITOL
Thomas Fuller, 1867–75
Eidlitz & Richardson, 1875–83
Isaac G. Perry, 1883–99
Albany, New York
Extant in greatly modified form
Court of Appeals, opened 1878
Assembly Chamber, opened 1879
Assembly Staircase, opened 1879
Golden Corridor, opened 1879
Assembly Parlor, opened 1879
Senate Staircase, opened 1881

NEW YORK COUNTY COURTHOUSE
John Kellum, 1867–71
Eidlitz, 1876–81
New York, 52 Chambers Street
Extant; renovated by John G. Waite
    Associates, 2002–3
Also known as the Tweed Courthouse;
now New York Board of Education
Building.

NEW YORK PRODUCE EXCHANGE
1880
New York
Competition entry, unbuilt
Competition won by George B. Post

UNION LEAGUE CLUB ADDITIONS
1880
New York
This project is described by Schuyler,
    but details remain unconfirmed.

ORIVA, YACHT INTERIOR
1881
C. S. Lee, owner
The *Oriva* was a cutter registered with
    the New York Yacht Club.

SIGMUND OPPENHEIMER HOUSE
1883–84
New York, 80th Street between Madi-
    son and Park Avenues
Extant

ISIDOR KAUFMAN HOUSE
1883–84
New York, 80th Street between Madi-
    son and Park Avenues
Demolished

HARRIS BUILDING
1884
New London, Connecticut, State Street
Extant

PARK PRESBYTERIAN CHURCH PARISH
HOUSE
1884
New York, Amsterdam Avenue and
    86th Street
Extant
The sanctuary, facing Amsterdam Av-
enue, was completed in 1890 to designs
by Henry Kilburn.

ST. GEORGE'S MEMORIAL HOUSE
1884–85
Construction 1886–88
New York, 16th Street and Second
    Avenue
Marc Eidlitz & Son, builder
Extant, used as co-op apartments

COOPER UNION RECONSTRUCTION
1884–85
New York, Astor Place
Extant

UNION SQUARE THEATER
1888
With John E. Terhune and Charles P.
    Palmer
New York, 58 East 14th Street
Demolished
Original building, 1871; fire damaged
the building in 1888, necessitating a
renovation, which Eidlitz reportedly
designed.

CENTRAL ISLIP ASYLUM BUILDINGS
1890
Central Islip, New York
Demolished

WARD'S ISLAND HOSPITAL BUILDINGS
1890
Ward's Island, New York
Demolished
Eidlitz designed two pavilions and the
superintendent's house.
In 1894, Eidlitz was harshly questioned
in the course of an investigation into
alleged graft by the administrators of
the Ward's Island Hospital during the
buildings' construction.

HUDSON RIVER DRIVEWAY
1891
New York
Unbuilt
Eidlitz's plans for a driveway and terrace
along the Hudson River from 72nd to
96th were approved by Mayor Grant's
Driveway Commission in 1891 but
never built.

*Buildings Once Attributed to Eidlitz,
Now Attributed to Others*

MRS. COLFORD JONES HOUSE
Richard Morris Hunt
1866–69
Newport, Rhode Island, Halidon Hill
Extant

BAXTER MEMORIAL LIBRARY
(RUTLAND JEWISH CENTER)
Brunner & Tryon, architects
1889
Rutland, Vermont
Smith & Allen, builders
Extant

ABBREVIATIONS

USED IN CAPTIONS, NOTES, AND BIBLIOGRAPHY

AABN American Architect and Building News
AIA American Institute of Architects
AR Architectural Record
FLOLC Papers of Frederick Law Olmsted, Manuscripts Division,
    Library of Congress
JSAH Journal of the Society of Architectural Historians
LC Library of Congress
MANY Municipal Archives of New York
MCNY Museum of the City of New York
NYHS New-York Historical Society
NYLPC New York Landmarks Preservation Commission
NYPL New York Public Library
NYSL New York State Library
NYT New York Times
RIBA Royal Institute of British Architects

Schuyler, part 1. Montgomery Schuyler, "A Great American Architect: Leopold Eidlitz. I. Ecclesiastical and Domestic Work," *AR* 24 (1908): 164–79. Reprinted in William Jordy and Ralph Coe, eds. *American Architecture and Other Writings* (Cambridge, MA: Belknap Press, 1961), 136–59. Cited pages refer to the reprint.
Schuyler, part 2. Montgomery Schuyler, "A Great American Architect: Leopold Eidlitz. II. Commercial and Public Work," *AR* 24 (1908): 277–92. Reprinted in William Jordy and Ralph Coe, eds. *American Architecture and Other Writings* (Cambridge, MA: Belknap Press, 1961), 159–74. Cited pages refer to the reprint.
Schuyler, part 3. Montgomery Schuyler, "A Great American Architect: Leopold Eidlitz. III. Capitol at Albany," *AR* 24 (1908): 365–78. Reprinted in William Jordy and Ralph Coe, eds. *American Architecture and Other Writings* (Cambridge, MA: Belknap Press, 1961), 174–87. Cited pages refer to the reprint.

BIBLIOGRAPHY

ARCHIVES CONSULTED

New York City
  American Jewish Historical Society
  Avery Library, Columbia University
  Cooper Union Archives
  Cooper-Hewitt, National Design Museum, Library and
    Archives
  Manuscript and Archives Division, New York Public Library
  Municipal Archives of New York
  Museum of the City of New York
  New-York Historical Society
  St. George's Episcopal Church
  St. James's Episcopal Church
  Temple Emanu-El
Albany, New York
  New York State Library
Troy, New York
  Rensselaer County Historical Society
  Troy Public Library
Hinsdale, Masachusetts
  Hinsdale Public Library
Pittsfield, Massachusetts
  First Congregational Church

Springfield, Massachusetts
  Connecticut Valley Historical Museum
Greenwich, Connecticut
  Greenwich Historical Society
  Second Congregational Church
Stratford, Connecticut
  First Congregational Church
  Stratford Historical Society
New London, Connecticut
  First Congregational Church
  New London Historical Society
  New London Public Library
Newport, Rhode Island
  Redwood Library
Rutland, Vermont
  Rutland Historical Society
Washington, D.C.
  American Institute of Architects Archives
  Library of Congress
St. Louis, Missouri
  Missouri Historical Society
Cincinnati, Ohio
  American Jewish Archives

Austin, Texas
    Harry Ransom Humanities Research Center
Vienna
    Jewish Museum
    Universitätsarchiv Technische Universität Wien
Stuttgart
    Universitätsarchiv, Universität Stuttgart
Prague
    Archiv Hlavní Města Prahy (City Archive)
    Jewish Museum
    Státní Ústřední Archiv (Central State Archives)

PUBLISHED WORKS BY LEOPOLD EIDLITZ (CHRONOLOGICAL)
"The Church of All Souls." *Crayon* 5 (1858): 20–22.
"Christian Architecture." *Crayon* 5 (1858): 53–55.
"The Day We Celebrate." *Crayon* 5 (1858): 109–11.
"On Style." *Crayon* 5 (1858): 139–42.
"The T-Squares," nine-part series:
    "No. 1–Philologus Brown." *Crayon* 5 (1858), 48–50.
    "Philologus Brown—Continued." *Crayon* 5 (1858), 77–79.
    "Philologus Brown—Concluded." *Crayon* 5 (1858), 107–8.
    "Mr. Gray, The Gentleman of Taste." *Crayon* 5 (1858), 165–67.
    "Mr. Gray, The Gentleman of Taste (Concluded)." *Crayon* 5 (1858), 196–99.
    "Cute Green—The Building Committee." *Crayon* 5 (1858), 262–64.
    "Cute Green—The Building Committee." *Crayon* 5 (1858), 287–89.
    "Cute Green—The Building Committee." *Crayon* 5 (1858), 318–19.
    "Cute Green—The Building Committee (Concluded)." *Crayon* 5 (1858), 346–51.
"Cast Iron and Architecture." *Crayon* 6 (1859): 20–24.
"The Architect." *Crayon* 6 (1859): 99–100.
"The Plymouth Church." *Crayon* 6 (1859): 150–51.
"The Architect of Other Days." *Architects' and Mechanics' Journal* 1 (1860): 171–72.
"The Architectural Dinner of John Gray, the Gentleman of Taste." *Crayon* 7 (1860), 26–29.

"On Aesthetics in Architecture, Part I." *Crayon* 8 (1861), 89–91.
"On Aesthetics in Architecture, Part II." *Crayon* 8 (1861), 111–13.
A Viaduct Railway for the City of New York; as Designed by John J. Serrell and Leopold Eidlitz. New York, 1870.
"The Qualifying of Architects, Letter to the Editors." *AABN* 3 (1878): 185–86.
"The Vault of the Albany Capitol, Letter to the Editors." *AABN* 10 (1881): 235.
"The Vault of the Albany Capitol, Letter to the Editors." *AABN* 10 (1881): 271.
The Nature and Function of Art, More Especially of Architecture. New York, London: A.C. Armstrong & Son; Sampson Low, Marston, Searle & Rivington, 1881.
Eidlitz, Leopold; H. H. Richardson, and Frederick L. Olmsted. *The New Capitol: An Examination of the Grounds on Which the Security of the Assembly Chamber Is Held to Be in Question,* Submitted to the Governor of New York, November 17, 1882.
"Reply of the Architects of the New Capitol at Albany." *AABN* (1882): 275–78.
"A Word to Sir Edmund Beckett." *AABN* 19 (1886): 311.
Eidlitz, Leopold (A Foreman). *Big Wages and How to Earn Them.* New York: Harper & Bros., 1887.
"The Modern Builder." *Real Estate Record and Builders' Guide* 47 (February 21, 1891): 268–69.
"The Vicissitudes of Architecture." *AR* 1 (1892): 471–84.
"The Architect of Fashion." *AR* 3 (1894): 347–53.
"Competitions: The Vicissitudes of Architecture." *AR* 4 (1894), 471–84.
"Big Wages [brief excerpt from book of same title]." *Manufacturer and Builder* 26 (June 1894): 133.
"The Strength of Pillars—An Analysis." *Transactions of the American Society of Civil Engineers* 35 (July 1896), 371–428.
"The Educational Training of Architects." *Journal of the RIBA* 4 (1897): 213–17.
"The Educational Training of Architects: A Rejoinder." *Journal of the RIBA* 4 (1897): 462–68.
On Light: An Analysis of the Emersions of Jupiter's Satellite I. New York: Knickerbocker Press, 1899.

CREDITS

Avery Architectural and Fine Arts Library, Columbia University in the City of New York. 1.1, 2.23, 5.1, 5.2, 5.7

Harry Ransom Humanities Research Center, University of Texas at Austin. 1.12, 1.18, 1.19, 1.20, 2.17, 3.12, 4.24, 4.35

Prints and Photographs Division, Library of Congress. 2.9, 2.12, 2.25, 2.30, 2.33, 3.8, 3.13, 4.8, 4.21, 4.31, 5.4, 5.5, 5.16

Author photo. 1.3, 2.4, 2.15, 4.25, 4.34, 4.36, 5.15

Rice University Library. 1.6

Historic American Buildings Survey, Prints and Photographs Division, Library of Congress. 1.7, 2.22, 3.3, 4.2, 4.15, 4.33

National Gallery of Canada, Ottawa. 1.8, 1.24

New York Public Library. 1.13, 4.4, 4.17, 4.23, 5.11, 5.12

Author collection. 1.14, 2.20, 3.14, 4.19, 5.3, 5.9

Foto Marburg/Art Resource New York. 1.16

New-York Historical Society. 1.22, 2.28, 3.5

Timothy Cook. 2.1, 2.2, 2.3

First Church of Christ, Pittsfield, Massachusetts. 2.5, 2.6

Greenwich Historical Society, Connecticut. 2.18, 2.19, 2.21

Missouri Historical Society, St. Louis. 2.24

American Jewish Historical Society, Newton Centre, Massachusetts and New York, New York. 2.27

Museum of the City of New York. 2.34, 5.7

Courtesy of the University of Texas Libraries, University of Texas at Austin. 3.4, 3.9, 3.10, 3.16, 4.10, 4.11, 4.12, 4.13, 4.14

New York State Library, Albany, New York. 4.9, 4.20.

The Century Association Archives, New York. 5.13

NOTES

INTRODUCTION

1. Leopold Eidlitz, "Cast Iron and Architecture," *Crayon* (1859): 24.

2. Eidlitz, *The Nature and Function of Art, More Especially of Architecture* (New York and London: A. C. Armstrong & Son and Sampson Low, Marston, Searle & Rivington, 1881).

3. Schuyler, part 3, 187.

4. The Century Association, "Report of the Board of Management," *Reports, Constitution, By-Laws, and List of Members of the Century Association for the Year 1908* (New York: Knickerbocker Press, 1909), 31.

5. Probate records, MANY.

6. The contents of Eidlitz's library have unfortunately been dispersed, and no record exists of what titles comprised it. A 1951 auction catalog indicates that the Eidlitz family library was sold, but no listing of the titles has survived; I was also unable to determine from which side of the Eidlitz family, Leopold's or his brother Marc's, the auctioned materials came. Savoy Art & Auction Galleries, *English, Victorian, French Empire and Other Period Occasional Furniture* [Auction Catalog] (New York: Savoy Art & Auction, 1951). I have been able to determine only three titles that he owned: Pugin's *Floriated Ornament* (now held by the Cooper-Hewitt Library), Decker's *Der Friedhof* (donated by Blesch & Eidlitz to the New York State Library in 1851), and the Viennese periodical *Allgemeine Bauzeitung* (donated by Eidlitz to the AIA Library, which no longer holds the title).

7. A. J. Bloor, "Annual Address to the AIA," *Proceedings of the Tenth Annual Convention of the AIA* [October 1876] (New York: AIA, 1877).

8. See, for example, Richard P. Adams, "Architecture and the Romantic Tradition: Coleridge to Wright," *American Quarterly* 9 (1957); Theodore M. Brown, "Greenough, Paine, Emerson, and the Organic Aesthetic," *Journal of Aesthetics and Art Criticism* 14 (1956); Albert Bush-Brown, " 'Get an Honest Bricklayer!': The Scientist's Answer to Ruskin," *Journal of Aesthetics and Art Criticism* 16, no. 3 (1958); Edward Robert De Zurko, *Origins of Functionalist Theory* (New York: Columbia University Press, 1957). The publication of Greenough's essays as a small paperback in 1947, with an introductory essay proclaiming him as the prophet of American functionalism, is instructive; Horatio Greenough, "American Architecture" (1843) in *Form and Function: Remarks on Art*, ed. Harold Adams Small (Berkeley: University of California Press, 1947).

9. The classic work in this vein is Sigfried Giedion's *Space, Time, and Architecture: The Growth of a New Tradition* (Cam-

bridge, MA: Harvard University Press, 1941); other influential modernist-sympathizing works include Henry-Russell Hitchcock's *Architecture: Nineteenth and Twentieth Centuries*, 4th ed. (New York: Viking Press, 1971). Even Vincent Scully's *The Shingle Style and the Stick Style: Architectural Theory and Design from Richardson to the Origins of Wright* (New Haven, CT: Yale University Press, 1971), though it countered the reductivism of the modernist histories of the American nineteenth century, created a new means of pushing aside independent practitioners in its emphasis on finding an authentic American architecture amid the century's eclecticism. Though more recent works like Dell Upton, ed., *America's Architectural Roots: Ethnic Groups that Built America* (New York: John Wiley, 1995), have tried to embrace the diversity of the century for its own sake, a new survey of the first half of the century, W. Barksdale Maynard, *Architecture in the United States, 1800–1850* (New Haven, CT: Yale University Press, 2002), places a renewed emphasis on style as the determinant factor in American architecture; Eidlitz appears, in the latter, once as a representative of the Orientalist phase with his Iranistan design.

10. In the scheme of nineteenth-century historicist movements, Eidlitz is often presented as a Gothic Revivalist or a proponent of the Romanesque, but the reality of his stylistic views is more complex than simple allegiance to a particular historical model. For the Romanesque label, see Winston Weisman, "Commerical Palaces of New York: 1845–1875," *Art Bulletin* 36 (1954): 295; William H. Pierson, Jr., "Richard Upjohn and the American Rundbogenstil," *Winterthur Portfolio* 21, no. 4 (1986): 228–229. For the Gothic, see Schuyler, part 1; Stephen Garmey, "Leopold Eidlitz," *Macmillan Encyclopedia of Architects*, vol. 2 (New York: Free Press, 1982); Robert A. M. Stern, Thomas Mellins, and David Fishman, *New York 1880: Architecture and Urbanism in the Gilded Age* (hereafter *NY1880*) (New York: Monacelli Press, 1999), 19. As an eclecticist, see H. Allen Brooks, Jr., "Leopold Eidlitz" (M.A. thesis, Yale University, 1955), 1–2.

11. Lewis Mumford, *The Brown Decades: A Study of the Arts in America, 1865–1895*, 2nd rev. ed. (New York: Dover, 1955), 112.

12. Ibid., 111.

CHAPTER 1. BECOMING AMERICAN: FROM THE MOLDAU TO THE HUDSON

1. A Foreman [Leopold Eidlitz], *Big Wages and How to Earn Them* (New York: Harper & Bros., 1887), 1, 3. Montgomery Schuyler attributed this book to Eidlitz; Schuyler part 3, 186.

2. "Those who labor in the earth are the chosen people of God, if ever He had a chosen people, whose breasts He has made His peculiar deposit for substantial and genuine virtue." Thomas Jefferson, *Notes on the State of Virginia* (1782–84),

reprinted in Leland M. Roth, ed., *America Builds* (New York: Harper & Row, 1983), 24.

3. Louis H. Sullivan, *Democracy: A Man-Search* (Detroit: Wayne State University Press, 1961).

4. For a thorough discussion of the relationship between Eidlitz's written theory and the tenets of American transcendentalism, see Erdmann, "Leopold Eidlitz's Architectural Theories and American Transcendentalism."

5. See, for example, Eidlitz's death certificate (MANY), the 1850 U.S. Census for New London, Connecticut, or the 1880 U. S. Census for New York City, all of which list his birthplace simply as Austria.

6. Schuyler, part 1, 137.

7. Rostislav Svacha, *The Architecture of New Prague, 1895–1945*, trans. Alexandra Buchler (Cambridge, MA: MIT Press, 1995); Jiří Rak, Radim Vondráček, and Claudia Terenzi, *Biedermeier: Art and Culture in Central Europe 1815–1848* (Milan and New York: Skira Editore, Rizzoli International, St. Martin's Press, 2001).

8. The question of Eidlitz's religious heritage was long unresolved, with some sources saying he was Jewish and others saying not. The biographical sketches of Eidlitz by Garmey and Erdmann both avoided the difficult issue. Stern et al., *NY1880*, noted that there was no proof he was Jewish and assumed he was not (326). Schuyler's review of Temple Emanu-El also assumed he was not; "Temple Emanu-El," *New York World*, September 12, 1868, 7. Kenneth Jacobs in his Ph.D. thesis similarly concluded Eidlitz was probably not Jewish and that it did not matter one way or the other; Jacobs, "Leopold Eidlitz: Becoming an American Architect" (Ph.D. diss., University of Pennsylvania, 2005, 36–43). The building committee of the Wooster Street Synagogue, however, knew he was Jewish in 1847, referring to him as an "Israelite," in "Consecration of the New Synagogue Shaaray Tefilla, New York," *Occident and American Jewish Advocate* 5, no. 5 (August 1847). The genealogical study by Guido Kisch, *In Search of Freedom: A History of American Jews from Czechoslovakia* (London: Edward Goldston & Son, 1949), 157–58, included entries for Eidlitz and his brother Marc without supporting documentation.

9. Eidlitz's and his brother Markus's birth dates are confirmed in the register of Jewish births and the City of Prague Familianten, Státní Ústřední Archiv. Abraham Eidlitz's occupation is recorded in the Eidlitz family's registration record at the Archiv Hlavní Města Prahy; it is also recorded in Eidlitz's registration record for the Technische Hochschule in Vienna, Prüfungs-Katalog der Komerziellen Abteilung polytechnischen Instituts vom Studienjahre 1839, Archiv Technische Universität Wien (TU-Wien). Curator Dr. Juliane Mikoletzky's extensive research in the TU-Wien archive has

shown that the distinction between the professions *Handels-mann* and *Kaufmann* as listed in fathers' occupation in student records is consistently meaningful; personal communication, June 4, 2002.

10. Hillel J. Kieval, "Autonomy and Independence: The Historical Legacy of Czech Jewry," in David Altshuler, ed., *The Precious Legacy: Judaic Treasures from the Czechoslovak State Collections* (New York: Summit Books, 1983), 84–86. Though it covers a slightly later period, the introductory portions of Kieval, *The Making of Czech Jewry: National Conflict and Jewish Society in Bohemia, 1870–1918* (New York: Oxford University Press, 1988), are also applicable.

11. Kieval, "Autonomy and Independence," 91.

12. Peter Demetz, *Prague in Black and Gold: Scenes from the Life of a European City* (New York: Hill & Wang, 1997), 284–286.

13. The date of Abraham Eidlitz's death and of Markus and Judith Eidlitz's departure for the U.S. is confirmed by the family's registration records at the Archiv Hlavní Města Prahy.

14. Rabbi Eidlitz's book was: *Mel'ekhet mahashevet* (Prague, 1775). *Encyclopedia Judaica*, v. 6 (New York: Macmillan, 1971), 526; for a discussion of Rabbi Eidlitz, see Gutmann Klemperer, "The Rabbis of Prague" (orig. published 1881–84), part 3, trans. Charles Klemperer, ed. Guido Kisch, *Historia Judaica* 13 (1951): 65–66.

15. Demetz, *Prague in Black and Gold*, 282.

16. For the emergence of polytechnic education, see Christopher Long, "East Central Europe: National Identity and International Perspective," *JSAH* 61 (December 2002): 519–29; Gary B. Cohen, *Education and Middle-Class Society in Imperial Austria, 1848–1918* (West Lafayette, IN: Purdue University Press, 1996); and Ulrich Pfammatter, *The Making of the Modern Architect and Engineer: The Origins and Development of a Scientific and Industrially Oriented Education* (Boston: Birkhäuser, 2000).

17. The date of Eidlitz's graduation from the Prague Realschule is recorded in the records of the Technische Hochschule in Vienna, Prüfungs-Katalog der Komerziel-len Abteilung polytechnischen Instituts vom Studienjahre 1839, Archiv TU-Wien. Inquiries at the Prague City Archives indicated no records existed for attendance at the Realschule during this period.

18. Pfammatter, *Making of the Modern Architect and Engineer*, 210–16; Cohen, *Education and Middle-Class Society in Imperial Austria*, 12. Quote from C. Jelinek, *Das ständisch-polytechnische Institut zu Prag. Programm zur fünfzigjährigen Erinnerungs-Feier an Die Eröffnung des Institutes* (Prague, 1856), cited in Pfammatter, 214.

19. Demetz, *Prague in Black and Gold*, 282–83.

20. The police registration records for Vienna that pre-date 1910 have been destroyed, so Eidlitz's registration there can be inferred from notations on his school record at the Technsische Hochschule, Prüfungs-Katalog der Komerziellen Abteilung polytechnischen Instituts vom Studienjahre 1839, TU-Wien.

21. Mitchell Schwarzer, *German Architectural Theory and the Search for Modern Identity* (Cambridge and New York: Cambridge University Press, 1995), 34.

22. Donald G. Daviau, "Biedermeier. The Happy Face of the Vormärz Era"; and Raymond Erickson, "Music in Biedermeier Vienna," papers presented at the Österreichisch-amerikanisches Symposion in New York in 1999, published in Robert Pichl and Clifford A. Bernd, eds., *The Other Vienna: The Culture of Biedermeier Austria*, vol. 5, *Sonderpublikationen der Grillparzer-Gesellschaft* (Vienna: Verlag Lehner, 1999). See also Gerhart Egger et al., *Vienna in the Age of Schubert: The Biedermeier Interior, 1815–1848* (London: Elron Press Ltd. for the Victoria and Albert Museum, 1979).

23. Dr. Juliane Mikoletzky, archivist TU-Wien, personal communication, May 28, 2002.

24. Historians, confronted with an absence of biographical details about Eidlitz, have resultantly overemphasized the role of Eidlitz's studies in Vienna. See, for example, Jordy and Coe, introduction, 21; Curran, *Romanesque Revival*, 266–68.

25. Pfammatter, *Making of the Modern Architect*, 218.

26. The minutes of the American Institute of Architects indicate that Eidlitz donated his copies of the *Allgemeine Bauzeitung* (which he referred to as the *Wiener Bauzeitung* in reference to its place of publication) to the AIA's young library in 1858. The AIA Library now, unfortunately, has no record of these volumes. Minutes of the AIA, meeting date March 2, 1858, AIA Archives.

27. Franz Anton Ritter von Gerstner, quoted in the introduction to Frederick C. Gamst, ed., *Early American Railroads: Franz Anton Ritter von Gerstner's Die innern Communicationen*, trans. David J. Diephouse and John C. Decker (Stanford, CA: Stanford University Press, 1997), 22. Gerstner's original publication is *Innern Communicationen der Vereinigten Staaten von Nordamerica* (Vienna: 1842–43).

28. James Gallier, *Autobiography of James Gallier, Architect* (New York: Da Capo Press, 1973; orig. ed. 1864), 19–21; see also Kathryn Holliday, "The Comfort of the Familiar: The Domestic Architecture of James Gallier in New Orleans, 1830–1850" (M.A. thesis, University of Texas at Austin, 1994).

29. Arthur Scully, *James Dakin, Architect: His Career in New York and in the South* (Baton Rouge: Louisiana State University Press, 1973).

30. Michael J. Lewis, "The Architectural Competition for the Philadelphia Academy of Music, 1854–1855," *Nineteenth Century* 16, no. 2 (1997): 3–10.

31. Gene Waddell, "An Architectural History of Kahal

Kadosh Beth Elohim, Charleston," *South Carolina Historical Magazine* 98, no. 1 (January 1997): 6–55; and Harley J. McKee, "Kahal Kadosh Beth Elohim Synagogue, 90 Hasell St., Charleston, Charleston County, SC (HABS No. SC-81)," National Park Service, Historic American Buildings Survey, 1963.

32. Dennis Steadman Francis, *Architects in Practice, New York City, 1840–1900* (New York: The Committee, 1980); for addresses, see entries under Eidlitz, Warner, and Upjohn.

33. William H. Pierson, Jr., "Richard Upjohn and the American Rundbogenstil," *Winterthur Portfolio* 21, no. 4 (1986): 226.

34. Obituary, Mrs. S. Quackenbush, *NYT*, February 16, 1940.

35. See Eidlitz's death certificate in the Municipal Archives, New York. Other accounts of Eidlitz's life incorrectly report his parents' names as Adolf and Julia Eidlitz.

36. "Weddings in Early June," *NYT*, June 3, 1887, 8.

37. Marc Eidlitz was the builder for several of Leopold's projects, including the Broadway Tabernacle (see appendix for more), as well as for New York landmarks like the Astor Library, J. C. Cady's Metropolitan Opera House, Carl Pfeiffer's German Library and Dispensary and later the St. Regis Hotel, the Harvard Club, the Yale Club, and the New York Yacht Club, among many others. The working relationship seems to have been closer between the brothers' sons, as Marc Eidlitz & Son was the contractor for many of Cyrus Eidlitz's telephone buildings. For Marc Eidlitz, see Marc Eidlitz & Son, *Marc Eidlitz & Son, 1854–1904* (New York: [The Firm], 1904) and Marc Eidlitz & Son, *Marc Eidlitz & Son, 1854–1914* (New York: [The Firm], 1914).

38. The Upjohn Papers contain no specific reference to Eidlitz working in the Upjohn office in the early 1840s; his account books begin recording salaries in 1846. Everard M. Upjohn, *Richard Upjohn, Architect and Churchman* (New York: Columbia University Press, 1939), 104; Judith Hull, "The 'School of Upjohn': Richard Upjohn's Office," *JSAH* 52 (1993): 285. William Pierson argued that Eidlitz was the source for Upjohn's interest. Pierson, "Richard Upjohn and the American Rundbogenstil," 229. Kathleen Curran, on the other hand, ascribes the interest to Upjohn's patron at Bowdoin, Leonard Woods, Jr. Kathleen Curran, "The Romanesque Revival, Mural Painting, and Protestant Patronage in America," *Art Bulletin* 81 (1999): 695.

I conclude that Eidlitz was instrumental in Upjohn's conversion. While, as Curran points out, it was Blesch who was more personally acquainted with the German Rundbogenstil, Eidlitz also knew the primary issues of contemporary German architecture. Furthermore, Eidlitz clearly had a passion for speaking and writing on the subject that Upjohn admired. The two architects held each other in mutual respect in following years, indicating that the relationship was established based

on a history of shared professional and intellectual interests. Upjohn, for example, showing his confidence in Eidlitz as an engineer, asked Eidlitz for his professional opinion about the "strength of stone against crushing weight" (Eidlitz to Upjohn, February 20, 1855); later, showing his confidence in Eidlitz the aesthetician, he asked Eidlitz to give the annual address to the AIA in his stead in 1868; Eidlitz refused the invitation (Eidlitz to Upjohn, September 10, 1868). The Richard Upjohn and Richard Michell Upjohn Papers, Manuscripts and Archives Division, NYPL.

39. For the Rundbogenstil, see Wolfgang Herrmann, ed., *In What Style Should We Build? The German Debate on Architectural Style* (Santa Monica, CA: Getty Center for the History of Art and the Humanities, 1992); and Curran, *The Romanesque Revival*. See also Barry Bergdoll, "Archaeology vs. History: Heinrich Hübsch's Critique of Neoclassicism and the Beginnings of Historicism in German Architectural Theory," *Oxford Art Journal* 5, no. 2 (1983): 3–12.; Winfried Nerdinger, ed., *Friedrich von Gärtner: Ein Architektleben, 1791–1847* (Munich: Klinkhardt & Biermann, 1992); and Oswald Hederer, *Friedrich von Gärtner, 1792–1847: Leben, Werk, Schüler* (Munich: Prestel-Verlag, 1976).

40. See Curran, *Romanesque Revival*, 275–76, for the assertion that Eidlitz may have assisted Upjohn in the 1854 remodeling. Curran cites a letter from Eidlitz to Upjohn telling him that he was willing to inspect the church with him. Eidlitz to Upjohn, November 1, 1854; cited in Curran, *Romanesque Revival*, 327, n. 44.

41. Comparing the text of Upjohn's sample specifications in Richard Upjohn, *Upjohn's Rural Architecture; Designs, Working Drawings, and Specifications for a Wooden Church, and Other Rural Structures* (New York: Putnam, 1852), to Eidlitz's for the Stratford Congregational Church shows that Eidlitz was as exhaustive in his specifications as Upjohn. The specifications are available at Stratford Historical Society, Connecticut.

42. Elizabeth Heywood, "House of the Evangelists," *Christian Advocate* 46 (March 16, 1871): 81. See also Elizabeth Moulton, *St. George's Church, New York* (New York: St. George's Church, 1964), 36; Diana Bass, *Standing Against the Whirlwind: Evangelical Episcopalians in Nineteenth-Century America* (New York: Oxford University Press, 1995).

43. Kathleen Curran, "The Romanesque Revival, Mural Painting, and Protestant Patronage in America," *Art Bulletin* 81 (December 1999): 696. Curran's is the first detailed analysis of the design of St. George's. The discussion here updates a few points and offers a different interpretation of Eidlitz's contributions.

44. Moulton, *St. George's Church*, 39–44.

45. The remaining records of St. George's and of the First Church of Christ in New London, both Blesch & Eidlitz com-

missions, show all communications and contracts signed by Eidlitz alone.

46. For Blesch, see Curran, *Romanesque Revival*, 266–68.

47. Vestry minutes for meeting conducted April 20, 1846, St. George's Episcopal Church, New York, vol. 2, 1821–1848, 342. The names of the other architects who submitted plans is not listed in the minutes, referred to simply as "leading architects in New York and Philadelphia." Thomas U. Walter's rejected design for St. George's is held by the Philadelphia Athenaeum. Charles Rockland Tyng, *Record of the Life and Work of the Rev. Stephen Higginson Tyng, D.D.* (New York: Dutton, 1890), 200.

48. Marriage records, MANY.

49. Total cost reorded in vestry minutes, October 14, 1848, St. George's Episcopal Church, New York, vol. 2, 406.

50. Vestry minutes, October 9, 1856, St. George's Episcopal Church, New York, vol. 3, 1848–76, 146. Robert Bork, "Into Thin Air: France, Germany, and the Invention of the Openwork Spire," *Art Bulletin* 85 (March 2003): 25–53.

51. The rectory cost $20,099.58, including a $900 fee for Blesch & Eidlitz. Vestry minutes, October 14, 1852, St. George's Episcopal Church, New York, vol. 3, 99–100.

52. Schuyler quoted Eidlitz. Schuyler, part 1, 141.

53. As recalled by Eidlitz, quoted in Moulton, *St. George's Church*, 42.

54. Schuyler, part 1, 140, n. 29. Also: ". . . for many years [St. George's] boasted the largest interior space in the city." Stern et al., *NY1880*, 19.

55. The diary of George Templeton Strong indicates that at one point in its design process, St. Patrick's was to use iron extensively; the building as completed, though, does not. See Pierson, *Technology and the Picturesque, the Corporate and the Early Gothic Styles*, 228–233.

56. ". . . St. George's was a hybrid church, lacking the external and internal consistency of its Munich model." Curran, "The German Rundbogenstil," 368.

57. The U. S. Census for 1850 lists Eidlitz and his family living in New London, including his wife Harriet, daughter Elizabeth (age 1), and Mary Eidlitz (age 11, born in Austria); his daughter Harriet Frances was born in New London on April 12, 1851. According to New York City directories, Eidlitz did maintain an office in New York during this period; see the listings in Dennis Steadman Francis, *Architects in Practice, New York City, 1840–1900* (New York: Committee for the Preservation of Architectural Records), 1980. For a history of expansion on the Upper West Side of Manhattan, see Peter Salwen, *Upper West Side Story* (New York: Abbeville Press, 1989).

58. Sarah Landau, "Richard Morris Hunt, the Continental Picturesque, and the 'Stick Style,'" *JSAH* 42 (1983): 273.

59. Leopold Eidlitz, "The Architect of Fashion," *AR* 3 (1894): 349.

60. For Ungewitter, see Michael J. Lewis, *The Politics of the German Gothic Revival: August Reichensperger* (New York and Cambridge, MA: Architectural History Foundation and MIT Press, 1993), esp. 210–11. For a discussion of the influence of German and Continental vernacular architecture on Hunt's later stick-style houses, see Landau, "Richard Morris Hunt," 89.

CHAPTER 2. THE SCIENCE OF THE BEAUTIFUL

1. Emerson, "The Transcendentalist," (1842), reprinted in *Miscellanies: Embracing Nature, Addresses, and Lectures* (Boston: Phillips, Sampson, 1856), 329.

2. Emerson, *Nature* (1836) (Boston: James Munroe, 1849), 21.

3. William Cullen Bryant, "The Ages," in *Poems* (Dessau: Katz Brothers, 1854), 3.

4. Barbara Novak, *Nature and Culture: American Landscape and Painting, 1825–1875*, 3rd ed. (New York: Oxford University Press, 2006); Barbara Novak and Ella M. Foshay, *Intimate Friends: Thomas Cole, Asher B. Durand, and William Cullen Bryant* (Utica, NY: North Country Books, 1991).

5. Emerson, *Nature*, 1.

6. Thomas Cole, "Essay on American Scenery," *American Monthly Magazine* 1 (January 1836): 35.

7. Horatio Greenough, "American Architecture," *United States Magazine and Democratic Review* (1843), reprinted in Greenough, *Form and Function*, 51.

8. David Schuyler, *Apostle of Taste: Andrew Jackson Downing, 1815–1852* (Baltimore: Johns Hopkins University Press, 1996); and Adam Sweeting, *Reading Houses and Building Books: Andrew Jackson Downing and the Architecture of Popular Antebellum Literature, 1835–1855* (Hanover, NH: University Press of New England, 1996).

9. Eidlitz, "On Aesthetics in Architecture, Part I" *Crayon* (1860): 90.

10. Eidlitz, "On Aesthetics, Part I," 89. "Aesthetics is the science of the Beautiful in the (fine) Arts."

11. Eidlitz, "On Aesthetics in Architecture, Part II," *Crayon* (1860): 111.

12. The literature on Ruskin is copious, but a recent volume offers new insight: Brian Hanson, *Architects and the "Building World" from Chambers to Ruskin: Constructing Authority* (Cambridge: Cambridge University Press, 2003); for Pugin, Phoebe Stanton, *Pugin* (London: Thames & Hudson, 1971). Other treatments of the problem of style include J. Mordaunt Crook, *The Dilemma of Style: Architectural Ideas from the Picturesque to the Post-Modern* (London: Murray, 1987) and Mari Hvattum,

Gottfried Semper and the Problem of Historicism (Cambridge: Cambridge University Press, 2004).

13. Neil Levine, "The Book and the Building: Hugo's Theory of Architecture and Labrouste's Bibliothèque Ste-Geneviève" in Robin Middleton, ed., *The Beaux-Arts and Nineteenth-Century French Architecture* (Cambridge, MA: MIT Press, 1982), 138–173.

14. On both Reichensperger and Ungewitter see Lewis, *The Politics of the German Gothic Revival*. For a contrasting view, Karen David-Sirocko, "Anglo-German Interconnexions during the Gothic Revival: A Case Study from the Work of Georg Gottlob Ungewitter (1820–64)," *Architectural History* 41 (1998): 153–78.

15. *Vorlesungen über Ästhetik* (Berlin, 1835, rev. 1842); Eng. trans. by T. M. Knox as *Hegel's Aesthetics: Lectures on Fine Art*, 2 vols. (Oxford: Clarendon Press: 1975).

16. The church committee's minutes indicated that the budget for the building was $21,000 and that Eidlitz, in 1851, wrote a letter to the church advising them that the central tower should be rebuilt because of poor joining work done by the contractor. Eidlitz had consulted Richard Upjohn before advising this course of action. Eidlitz to Andrew Frank, Sydney Minor, and D. S. Perkins, October 12, 1851. See also S. Leroy Blake, *The Later History of the First Church of Christ, New London, Conn.* (New London, CT: Press of the Day, 1900), 316–25.

17. "A House of Worship," *New York Observer and Chronicle*, July 3, 1851, 212. The First Presbyterian Church (Old School) at Clinton and Remsen Streets, built when the congregation split into two competing factions ("Old School" and "New School") is now converted to co-op apartments.

18. Eidlitz, "On Style," *Crayon* 4 (1858): 139.

19. Ibid., 140.

20. Ibid.

21. Ibid., 140–41.

22. Eidlitz, *The Nature and Function of Art*, 118–19.

23. G. W. F. Hegel, *The Philosophy of Fine Art*, 4 vols., trans. by F. P. B. Osmaston (1920), reprint (New York: Hacker Art Books, 1975), v. 1, 101–2.

24. Ibid., 142.

25. Carl Bötticher, "Das Prinzip der hellenischen und germanischen Bauweise hinsichtlich der Übertragung in die Bauweise unserer Tage," *Allgemeine Bauzeitung* 11 (1846), trans. Wolfgang Hermann and reprinted as "Hellenic and Germanic Ways of Building" in *In What Style Should We Build?*, 151.

26. "The New Academy of Music, Brooklyn," *Architects' and Mechanics' Journal* 2 (December 22, 1860): 114; "New Academy of Music, Brooklyn," *Architects' and Mechanics' Journal* 2 (September 20, 1860): 252; "Brooklyn Academy of Music, Its Past, Present, and Future—Description of the Building," *NYT*, January 15, 1861, 2.

27. "The New Academy of Music, Brooklyn," *Architects' and Mechanics' Journal* 2 (December 22, 1860): 114.

28. Eidlitz, "On Aesthetics in Architecture, Part II," 112.

29. Eidlitz, "On Aesthetics in Architecture, Part I," 90.

30. Johann Wolfgang von Goethe, "On German Architecture" (1772), in John Gearey, *Essays on Art and Literature*, trans. Ellen von Nardroff and Ernest H. Von Nardroff (New York: Suhrkamp, 1986), 6.

31. Eidlitz, "On Aesthetics in Architecture, Part II," 113.

32. "Brooklyn Academy of Music," *NYT*, January 15, 1861, 2. Another source describes only six proscenium boxes, but it is more likely that there were six on each side of the stage. Henry R. Stiles, *The Civil, Political, Professional, and Ecclesiastical History, and Commercial and Industrial Record of the County of Kings and the City of Brooklyn* (New York: W. W. Munsell, 1884), v. 2, 1113.

33. Walt Whitman, "Brooklyniana," *Brooklyn Standard* (1862), reprinted in Henry M. Christman, ed., *Walt Whitman's New York: From Manhattan to Montauk* (Freeport, NY: Books for Libraries Press, 1972), 61. Opening night program, Stiles, *City of Brooklyn,* 1113.

34. J. C. Cady to Gordon L. Ford, August 9, 1880, Personal Miscellaneous Collection, Manuscripts and Archives Division, NYPL. My thanks to Brian Clancy for this information.

35. "Brooklyn Academy of Music," *NYT*, December 1, 1903, 8.

36. Ibid.

37. Schuyler, part 2, 160.

38. Description based on "The New Produce Exchange," *Architects' and Mechanics' Journal* 2 (December 8, 1860): 92 and Schuyler, part 2, 166–67.

39. "The New Banking House of the Bank of New-York," *NYT*, March 26, 1858, 4.

40. "New Bank Buildings in New York," *Bankers' Magazine and Statistical Register* 7 (August 1857): 123.

41. "New Bank Buildings in New York," 122. See also Weisman, "Commercial Palaces of New York: 1845–1975," and Sarah Landau and Carl Condit, *Rise of the New York Skyscraper, 1865–1913* (New Haven: Yale University Press, 1996), especially chaps. 1 and 2. Stern et al.'s *NY1880* also provides an excellent overview, focused on the 1870s and later, in chap. 3. For Vaux's Bank of New York, see Francis R. Kowsky, *Country, Park, and City: The Architecture and Life of Calvert Vaux* (New York: Oxford University Press, 1998), 82–85.

42. "An Explosion of Gas," *NYT*, December 26, 1876, 8, reports an explosion due to a gas leak at the American Exchange Bank and in describing the damage also gives a good picture of how the building was constructed.

43. Eidlitz, "On Style," *Crayon* 5 (1858): 140.

44. Eidlitz, "Christian Architecture," *Crayon* 5 (1858): 54.

45. See the comprehensive discussion of the New York Ecclesiological Society in Phoebe Stanton, *The Gothic Revival and American Church Architecture: An Episode in Taste* (Baltimore: Johns Hopkins University Press, 1968), 179–211.

46. Ryan K. Smith, *Gothic Arches, Latin Crosses: Anti-Catholicism and American Church Designs in the Nineteenth Century* (Chapel Hill: University of North Carolina Press, 2006).

47. See Eidlitz, "On Style," 140.

48. "Principles of Gothic Architecture," in *Aesthetic and Miscellaneous Works of Friedrich von Schlegel*, trans. E. J. Millington (London: George Bell & Sons, 1889), 149–99.

49. Sir John Summerson, "Viollet-le-Duc and the Rational Point of View," *Heavenly Mansions and Other Essays on Architecture* (New York: W. W. Norton, 1998), 141.

50. Eidlitz, "The Architect," *Crayon* 6 (1859): 99.

51. Eidlitz, "On Style," 140.

52. Carrol L. V. Meeks, "Romanesque Before Richardson in the United States," *Art Bulletin* 35 (1953): 18.

53. Bruce Kuklick, *Churchmen and Philosphers* (New Haven, CT: Yale University Press, 1985), and Stanton, *The Gothic Revival and American Church Architecture*.

54. Congregational Churches in the United States Central Committee, *A Book of Plans for Churches and Parsonages. Comprising Designs by Upjohn, Downing, Renwick, Wheeler, Wells, Austin, Stone, Cleveland, Backus, and Reeve* (New York: D. Burgess, 1853). For a discussion of the Book of Plans and the Romanesque, see Gwen W. Steege, "The Book of Plans and the Early Romanesque Revival in the United States: A Study in Architectural Patronage," *JSAH* 46 (1987): 215–27.

55. Congregational Churches Committee, *A Book of Plans*, 14.

56. Eidlitz, as recalled by Schuyler, part 1, 147.

57. Eidlitz, "Christian Architecture," 53. This emphasis on verticality is again related to German critical readings of structure and form. See J. Mordaunt Crook, "Coventry Patmore and the Image of Gravity" in *The Architect's Secret: Victorian Critics and the Image of Gravity* (London: John Murray, 2003), esp. 152.

58. Lydia Ferris Lester, "The Second Congregational Church, a History (Ts)," recto in the History files, Second Congregational Church of Greenwich, Connecticut. A transcript of the original building contract, dated June 21, 1856, is also held in the church's history files. See also *A Commemorative Discourse, Delivered on the Occasion of Meeting for the Last Time in the Old House of Worship of the Second Congregational Church in Greenwich* (New York: John A. Gray, 1860), and the recent Rachel Carley, *Building Greenwich: Architecture and Design 1640 to the Present* (Greenwich: Historical Society of the Town of Greenwich, 2005).

59. A copy of the original building contract is in the collections of the Stratford Historical Society.

60. William A. Booth, *Three Score and Ten Years of Active Life in New York, 1821–1892: The Reminiscences of William A. Booth* (New York: n.p. 1896?), 54.

61. Debby Applegate, *The Most Famous Man in America: The Biography of Henry Ward Beecher* (New York: Doubleday, 2006), evokes the cult of Beecher well.

62. As reported by Schuyler, part 1, 151.

63. Eidlitz, "Plymouth Church," *Crayon* 6 (1859): 151.

64. John Durand, "Henry Ward Beecher on Church Architecture," *Crayon* 6 (1859): 154–57.

65. Vestry minutes, Christ Church, meetings held April 19 and May 4, 1859. Collection of the Missouri Historical Society. The society also has photographs showing the construction process and a large plan of the church used in the sale of pews to parishioners.

66. Smaller and rural churches often had a bare quality due to their limited budgets, but large urban churches like Christ Church rarely embraced such severity. See Pierson, *Technology and the Picturesque*, chap. 4, part III, and Stanton on the parish church model, in *The Gothic Revival and American Church Architecture*, xx–xxi.

67. H. H. McFarland, "The Church of the Pilgrims in Brooklyn, New York," *Congregational Quarterly* 13 (1871): 54–70; and "The Church of the Pilgrims in Brooklyn," *New York Evening Post*, June 15, 1870. See also Curran's analysis of the two interiors as important harbingers of the ascendancy of mural painting in America in *Romanesque Revival*, 275–78.

68. Harold Hammer-Schenk, "Die Architektur der Synagoge von 1780 bis 1933," in Hans-Peter Schwarz, ed., *Die Architektur der Synagoge* (Stuttgart: Klett-Cotta, 1988), 157–286; Carol Krinsky, *Synagogues of Europe: Architecture, History, Meaning* (Cambridge, MA: MIT Press, 1985), 81–86; Ivan Kalmar, "Moorish Style: Orientalism, the Jews, and Synagogue Architecture," *Jewish Social Studies: History, Culture, and Society* 7 (2001): 68–100; Olga Bush, "The Architecture of Jewish Identity: The Neo-Islamic Central Synagogue of New York," *JSAH* 63 (2004): 180–201.

69. Shmuel Singer, "Samuel Myer Isaacs: Battler for Orthodox Integrity in Nineteenth Century America," *Jewish Observer* 13, no. 8 (1979): 19–22.

70. "Consecration of the New Synagogue Shaaray Tefila, New York," *Occident and American Jewish Advocate* 5, no. 5 (August 1847): 222.

71. Stern et al., *NY1880*, 328–29.

72. "Descriptive View of the New Synagogue, Now Building at New York, for the Congregation Under the Pastoral Charge of the Rev. S. M. Isaacs," *Occident and American Jewish Advocate* 4, no. 5 (August 1846): 239.

73. *Allgemeine Bauzeitung* (1840): 204–7.

74. "The Corner Stone, a Sermon by the Rev. S. M. Isaacs, Spoken at the Laying of the Corner-Stone of the Synagogue Shaaray Tefila," *Occident and American Jewish Advocate* 4, no. 5 (August 1846): 236.

75. A. Abraham, "Consecration of the New Synagogue Communicated," *Occident and American Jewish Advocate* 5, no. 5 (August 1847): n.p.

76. "Consecration of the New Synagogue Shaaray Tefila, New York," 222.

77. "Descriptive View of the New Synagogue," 239.

78. For the history of the temple, see Ronald B. Sobel, "The Congregation: A Historical Perspective," in Cissy Grossman, *A Temple Treasury: The Judaica Collection of Congregation Emanu-El of the City of New York* (New York: Rizzoli International Publications, 1989), 3–11. See also Rachel Bernstein Wischnitzer, *Synagogue Architecture in the United States: History and Interpretation* (Philadelphia: Jewish Publication Society of America, 1955), 6.

79. For Fernbach, see Stern et al., *NY1880*, 476–77. There is little biographical information on Fernbach available. Joy Kestenbaum of New York is at work on Fernbach; her research will perhaps fill this gap.

80. Bush, "The Architecture of Jewish Identity," 190. The membership rolls of the Temple Emanu-El at the American Jewish Archives do not show Eidlitz as a member.

81. Temple Emanu-El Board of Trustees minutes for May 19, 1867, American Jewish Archives. A list of disbursements included in the minutes indicated that Eidlitz & Fernbach received $4,500 and the other entrants received the following: R. & R. M. Upjohn, $500.00; Renwick & Sands, $400.00; J. Munckwitz, $200.00; A. Saeltzer, $100.00. The elder Upjohn by this time was not as active in designing, so it is my belief that the entry for "R. & R. M. Upjohn" was designed by the son, Richard Michell Upjohn, who would have had more eclectic views about church design than his more orthodox father. See chap. 9 of Upjohn, *Richard Upjohn*, "The Impact of the Victorian," 174–88.

82. Stern et al., *NY1880*, 326.

83. Ibid. Owen Jones publications on the Alhambra include, with Jules Goury, *Plans, Elevations, and Details of the Alhambra* (London: Owen Jones, 1841-45) and Owen Jones, *Details and Ornaments from the Alhambra* (London: Owen Jones, 1845).

84. Alfred J. Bloor, "Annual Address to AIA," *Proceedings of the Tenth Annual Convention of the AIA* [October 1876] (New York: AIA, 1877), 15–34.

85. For Central Synagogue, see Stern et al., *NY1880*, 329–30, and Wischnitzer, *Synagogue Architecture in the United States*, 77–81.

86. A detailed description of the building can be found in an *Evening Post* article reprinted in the *Scientific American*: "The New Temple Emanu-El," *Scientific American* (new series) 19, no. 14 (September 30, 1868): 219.

87. Wischnitzer, *Synagogue Architecture in the United States*, 75–76.

88. Ibid., 74.

89. Grossman, *A Temple Treasury*, 20.

90. "The Hebrew Temple Emanu-El," *Harper's Weekly*, November 14, 1868, 729; "The New Temple Emanu-El," 219; George Templeton Strong, *The Diary of George Templeton Strong*, ed. Allan Nevins and Milton Thomas (New York: Macmillan, 1952), 4: 261–62; Ware to Emerson, May 19, 1897; RIBA Council Minutes for May 31, 1897, RIBA Archives; Bloor, "Annual Address to the AIA," 15–34.

CHAPTER 3. "BY NO MEANS A REPRESENTATIVE MAN": ALLIES AND ENEMIES

1. For a history of the formation of the AIA, see Woods, *From Craft to Profession*, 27–42, and Henry H. Saylor, *The AIA's First Hundred Years* (Washington, D.C.: The Octagon, 1957).

2. Detlef Lienau, toast presented at the Second Annual Convention of the AIA (1859), *Crayon* 6 (1859): 100.

3. Saylor, author of the only history of the AIA, called it a "homogeneous group." Saylor, *The AIA's First Hundred Years*, 7. Phoebe Stanton's account of the AIA's early years emphasizes a perceived general agreement among members about theoretical issues. Stanton, *The Gothic Revival and American Church Architecture*, 324–325. Mary Woods's account glosses over the pre-1870 period in favor of the later nineteenth century, when the organization became more obviously active. Woods writes, "Sheer survival was the AIA's greatest accomplishment in its first twenty years." Woods, *From Craft to Profession*, 38. For account of the AIA's early years emphasizing Lienau's contributions, see *Nineteenth-Century Architects: Building a Profession*, an exhibition catalog produced by the Lockwood-Mathews Mansion Museum in 1990.

4. George B. Post as recorded in Catherine Howland Hunt, "The Richard Morris Hunt Papers," ed. Alan Burnham, 290 pp., TS, p. 55. Drawings and Archives, Avery Architectural and Fine Arts Library, Columbia University.

5. For a detailed account of the Hunt atelier, see Baker, *Richard Morris Hunt*, 100–107.

6. Henry Van Brunt, "Cast Iron in Decorative Architecture" (1858), in *Architecture and Society: Selected Essays of Henry Van Brunt*, ed. William A. Coles (Cambridge, MA: Belknap Press, 1969), 79.

7. Ibid., 84.

8. Ibid., 88.

9. Ibid., 83.

10. For different readings of the debate, see Margot Gayle

and Carol Gayle, *Cast Iron Architecture in America: The Significance of James Bogardus* (New York: W. W. Norton, 1998), 193-95; Mary N. Woods, "Henry van Brunt: The Modern Styles, Historic Architecture," in Craig Zabel and Susan Scott Munshower, eds., *American Public Architecture: European Roots and Native Expressions* (University Park: Pennsylvania State University Press, 1989), 82–113; Baker, *Richard Morris Hunt*, 114–15; Coles, *Architecture and Society*, 54; and Brooks, "Leopold Eidlitz," 20–21.

11. "The Crystal Palace," *Scientific American* 8 (August 6, 1853): 370.

12. Leopold Eidlitz, "Improvement in Burglar-Proof Safes," U.S. Patent No. 18,962, December 29, 1857.

13. Eidlitz, "Cast Iron and Architecture," *Crayon* 6 (1859): 21.

14. Peter B. Wight, "Reminiscences of Russell Sturgis," *AR* 26 (1909): 127; Karin May Elizabeth Alexis, "Russell Sturgis: Critic and Architect," (Ph.D. diss., University of Virginia, 1986), 53; Sarah Landau and Carl Condit, *Rise of the New York Skyscraper*, 54.

15. For a discussion of the history of fireproofing, see Landau and Condit, *Rise of the New York Skyscraper*, 26–30; and Sara E. Wermeil, *The Fireproof Building: Technology and Public Safety in the Nineteenth-Century American City* (Baltimore: Johns Hopkins University Press, 2000).

16. Eidlitz, "Cast Iron and Architecture, " 23.

17. Ibid.

18. Ibid.

19. Ibid., 21.

20. Richard Morris Hunt, reply to Eidlitz in *Crayon* 6 (1859): 24.

21. For a discussion of Hunt's two cast-iron-front stores, see Baker, *Richard Morris Hunt*, 214–17.

22. The series is introduced by: "The T-Squares, no. 1, Philologus Brown," *Crayon* 5 (1858): 49. For the remainder of the series see *Crayon* 5 (1858): 77–79, 107–8; 165–67, 196–99, 262–64, 287–89, 345–51. See Kate Holliday, "The Architecture Profession and the Public: Leopold Eidlitz's 'Discourses Between Two T-Squares'," *Journal of Architectural Education* 61, no. 1 (Sept. 2007): 32–43.

23. Olmsted to James T. Fields, October 21, 1860, reprinted in Charles Capen McLaughlin, ed., *The Papers of Frederick Law Olmsted*, v. 3 (Baltimore: Johns Hopkins University Press, 1977), 269. Later in the article, Olmsted dismissed Hunt as a candidate because of Hunt's desire to design architectural commissions in the park.

24. ". . . 30 or 40 years ago he was perhaps the most conspicuous of the German Architects practising in this city." Ware to William Emerson, May 19, 1897. Recorded in the RIBA Council minutes for the meeting of May 31, 1897. RIBA Archives.

25. Charles Babcock to William Emerson, Hon. Sec. RIBA, March 29, 1897. Recorded in the RIBA Council minutes for the meeting of April 12, 1897. RIBA Archives.

26. Eidlitz, "The Educational Training of Architects," *Journal of the RIBA* 4 (1897): 216.

27. "L. Eidlitz suggested the propriety of appointing a committee of 3 who should have power to associate with themselves 5 gentlemen not members of the Institute with the object of establishing a Library and a College for the education of Architects." The committee was approved and included Eidlitz, James Renwick, Jr., Frederick Diaper, J. W. Ritch, and Richard Upjohn. Minutes of the AIA for January 17, 1860, AIA Archives.

28. Eidlitz, "Report of the Committee on Education," *Proceedings of the Annual Convention of the American Institute of Architects 1867* (New York: Raymond & Caulon, 1867): 13–16. For a more detailed discussion of the proposed school, see Kate Holliday, " 'Build More and Draw Less': The AIA and Leopold Eidlitz's Grand Central School of Architecture," *JSAH* 65, no. 3 (September 2006): 378–401.

29. Eidlitz's departure was probably due to a conflict over the administration of the newly implemented chapter system. Eidlitz appears to have objected to the means by which the New York Chapter of the AIA was formally established; he wished it to have higher dues and a library, at least, in order to justify its position as "head" of the new national system. His motion to delay the formation of the New York Chapter (not the chapters of other cities) was tabled by an unidentified member of the AIA (identified only as Mr ____ in the minutes—this lack of identification is extremely unusual in the minutes and I saw no other instances of it during my research). Calvert Vaux and Frederick Clarke Withers sided with Eidlitz in the vote and also resigned at the same time. See Minutes of the AIA for December 8, 1868, AIA Archives.

Though the cause may never be known, its dramatic nature is definite. When a member resigned, the AIA sent a representative to convince him to return. Eidlitz himself had performed this service in the past. In Eidlitz's case, the service was not performed: "The President presented letters of Resignation from the Institute of Messrs. Calvert Vaux and Leopold Eidlitz and reported that another letter of similar import had been received from Mr. F. C. Withers, but had been lost in the confusion in his (The President's) office resulting from the fire in Trinity Building. Mr. Wight moved that the resignations be accepted. Mr. Post in seconding the motion remarked that usually, in such a case, he should move a committee to confer with the gentlemen offering resignations, but that, much as it was to be regretted, such action would clearly be useless in this instance. The resignations were accepted; and the Treasurer was instructed to collect the dues of the three gentlemen only up to Oct 1st 1868." Minutes of the AIA Board of Trustees, January 11, 1869, AIA Archives.

30. See comments by Ware and Richard Morris Hunt in *Proceedings of the Third Annual Convention of the American Institute of Architects 1869* (New York: American Institute of Architects, 1870), 170–172. Jeffrey A. Cohen, "Building a Discipline: Early Institutional Settings for Architectural Education in Philadelphia, 1804–1890," *JSAH* 53 (1994): 139–83.

31. For discussion of the various models of education in central Europe, see Long, "East Central Europe: National Identity and International Perspective"; Cohen, *Education and Middle-Class Society in Imperial Austria, 1848–1918*; and Pfammatter, *The Making of the Modern Architect and Engineer*.

32. William Ware to Waldstein, 1904. Ware Papers, MIT Archives. Quoted in J. A. Chewning, "William Robert Ware at MIT and Columbia," *Journal of Architectural Education* 33 (November 1979): 25.

33. On Peter Cooper and the Cooper Institute, later Cooper Union, see C. Edwards Lester, *Life and Character of Peter Cooper* (New York: J. B. Alden, 1883); Miriam Gurko, *The Lives and Times of Peter Cooper* (New York: Crowell, 1959); and Phyllis D. Kransick, "Peter Cooper and the Cooper Union for the Advancement of Science and Art" (Ph.D. diss., New York University, 1985).

34. Eidlitz greatly admired Cooper, and in his socioeconomic analysis of architecture and building, *Big Wages and How to Earn Them*, he dedicated a passage to discussing the good example Cooper and his family set both by being successful in business and by generously using their earned wealth to promote the interests of the less fortunate. Eidlitz, *Big Wages*, 123–25.

35. Steven M. Bedford and Susan M. Strauss, "History II: 1881–1912," in Richard Oliver, ed., *The Making of an Architect, 1881–1981* (New York: Rizzoli, 1981), 33.

36. Emlen T. Littell, "Annual Report of the Committee on Examinations," *Proceedings of the AIA, 1869*, 15.

37. *Proceedings of the AIA, 1869*, 172. On Sturgis see, "The Writings of Russell Sturgis and Peter B. Wight: The Victorian Architect as Critic and Historian" (Ph.D. diss. City University of New York, 1999).

38. See Roula Geraniotis, "The University of Illinois and German Architectural Education," *Journal of Architectural Education* 38, no. 4 (1985): 15–21; and Anthony Alofsin, "Tempering the École: Nathan Ricker at the University of Illinois, Langford Warren at Harvard," in Gwendolyn Wright and Janet Parks, eds., *The History of History in American Schools of Architecture 1865–1975* (New York: Princeton Architectural Press, 1990).

39. Alofsin, *The Struggle for Modernism*, see chap. 2; and Alofsin, "Towards a History of Teaching Architectural History: Herbert Langford Warren," *Journal of Architectural Education* 33 (1983): 2–7.

40. Catherine Howland Hunt wrote that "he was a keen and fierce Republican, believing that the prosperity of the country and its safety lay in the principles of that party." Catherine Howland Hunt, "The Richard Morris Hunt Papers," ed. Alan Burnham, 290 pp. TS, p. 80. Drawings and Archives Collection, Avery Architectural Library, Columbia University. Later Beaux-Arts practitioners put Hunt's lessons to different uses. See, for example, Daniel M. Bluestone, *Constructing Chicago* (New Haven, CT: Yale University Press, 1991); and Richard Longstreth, *On the Edge of the World: Four Architects in San Francisco at the Turn of the Century* (Cambridge, MA: MIT Press, 1983).

41. Leopold Eidlitz, "The Architect," *Crayon* 6 (1859): 99–100.

42. On Hunt, see Paul R. Baker, *Richard Morris Hunt* (Cambridge, MA: MIT Press, 1980). On Post, see Sarah Landau, *George B. Post, Architect, Picturesque Designer, and Determined Realist* (New York: Monacelli Press, 1998). On Mould, personal communication with Lucille Gordon, April 15, 2003. Gordon is at work on a biography of Jacob Wrey Mould that updates Van Zanten's "Jacob Wrey Mould: Echoes of Owen Jones and the High Victorian Styles in New York, 1853–1865," *JSAH* 28 (March 1969): 41–57. On Withers, see Francis R. Kowsky, *The Architecture of Frederick Clarke Withers and the Progress of the Gothic Revival in America After 1850* (Middletown, CT: Wesleyan University Press, 1980).

43. Eidlitz called attention to the investment at the December 4, 1866 AIA meeting: "As Mr Eidlitz had referred in complimentary terms to the frugality of our prudent Treasurer in laying up a reserve from the very moderate dues and fees, and had so wisely and profitably invested the same—Mr Hatfield rose to state that Mr Eidlitz had therein only been 'glorifying' himself, as the project for investing in 7.30 [U.S. bonds issued by the Union to pay for the Civil War] had originated with him." AIA minutes, AIA Archives.

44. "The New Academy of Music, Brooklyn: Report of the Building Committee," *Architects' and Mechanics' Journal* 2 (December 22, 1860): 115. Eidlitz's fee was reported at $5,000, with part paid in stock.

45. Schuyler, part 1, 143.

46. Joel Benton, *Life of Hon. Phineas T. Barnum* (Philadelphia: Edgewood, 1891), 256–57.

47. Schuyler, part 1, 143.

48. On Iranistan, see W. Barksdale Maynard, *Architecture in the United States 1800–1850* (New Haven, CT: Yale University Press, 2002), 173–75; Phineas T. Barnum, *Struggles and Triumphs; or, The Life of P. T. Barnum* (New York: Knopf, 1927; orig. ed., 1869); Irving Wallace, *The Fabulous Showman: The Life*

and Times of P. T. Barnum ([New York]: The New American Library, 1962). The Barnum papers at the New York Public Library do not shed light on the Eidlitz-Barnum relationship; interviews with the archivist at the Bridgeport Public Library and the curators at the Barnum Museum in Bridgeport similarly indicated that no documentation supported the connection between Eidlitz and Barnum despite the extensive research that went into an attempt to re-create the library of Iranistan for an exhibit at the museum.

49. Materials, dimensions, and costs taken from L. Nelson Nichols, *History of the Broadway Tabernacle of New York City* (New Haven, CT: Tuttle, Morehouse & Taylor, 1940), 110–11; and *Sermons Preached at the Dedication of the Broadway Tabernacle, New York, Sunday, April 24, 1859* (New York: N. A. Calkins, 1859), 8–14.

50. *Sermons Preached at the Dedication of the Broadway Tabernacle,* 14, 8.

51. Edward K. Spann, *The New Metropolis: New York City, 1840–1857* (New York: Columbia University Press, 1981), ix.

52. Peter George Buckley, "To the Opera House: Culture and Society in New York City, 1820–1860" (Ph.D. diss., State University of New York at Stony Brook, 1984).

53. The literature on Barnum's and Olmsted's achievements is copious, but for accounts that emphasize the social history of their endeavors, see, respectively, Janet M. Davis, *The Circus Age: Culture and Society Under the American Big Top* (Chapel Hill: University of North Carolina Press, 2002); and Stephen Germic, *American Green: Class, Crisis, and the Deployment of Nature in Central Park, Yosemite, and Yellowstone* (Lanham, MD: Lexington Books, 2001).

54. Leopold Eidlitz, "The Day We Celebrate," *Crayon* 5 (1858): 110.

55. Eidlitz, *Big Wages*, 202.

56. The patent numbers are 18,962; 27,116; and 36,821, respectively. The first two were published in *Scientific American* (new series) 2, no. 9 (February 25, 1860): 140, and v. 7, no. 20 (November 15, 1862): 317. Poitevin was a major figure in the creation of photolithography. See his *Traité de l'Impression Photographique sans Sels d'Argent; Contenant: l'Histoire, la Theorie et la Pratique des Methodes et Procèdes de l'Impression au Charbon, de l'Helioplastie, de la Photolithographie, de la Gravure Photochimique* (Paris: Leiber, 1862).

57. The constitution of the American Photographical Society is reproduced in William Welling, *Photography in America: The Formative Years 1839–1900* (New York: Thomas Y. Crowell, 1978), 137. My thanks to John S. Craig, who maintains http://www.daguerreotype.com, for the citation.

58. Eidlitz, *On Light: An Analysis of the Emersions of Jupiter's Satellite I* (New York: Knickerbocker Press, 1899), in the collections of the Science and Business Library, NYPL. In my analysis, Eidlitz based his astronomical observations on James Bradley's 1728 use of stellar aberration to measure the speed of light. He had two goals: To show that Ole Rømer's 1676 calculation of the speed of light based on his observations of Jupiter's Satellite I were incorrect because they did not account for the stellar aberration that Bradley had observed. Second, he wished to reconcile the aberration method with the more recent measurements of Louis Fizeau (1849) and Léon Foucault (1850) using light reflected between rotating wheels (Fizeau) and mirrors (Foucault). Eidlitz hoped to show that both Fizeau and Foucault, to obtain the most accurate estimate of the speed of light, also needed to account for aberration, even though they were not observing light emitted by astronomical bodies.

59. Erdmann, "Leopold Eidlitz's Architectural Theories," 146, n. 26. John J. Serrell was on the Brooklyn Bridge Design Review Committee, 1869. "The East River Bridge," *Scientific American* (New Series) 20, no. 13 (March 27, 1869): 201. See also D. B. Steinman, *The Builders of the Bridge: The Story of John Roebling and His Son* (New York: Harcourt, Brace, 1942), 189, 316.

60. Stern et al., *NY1880*, 69–81, contains an excellent overview of the various mass transit schemes proposed from the 1850s to the 1870s, although it does not discuss the Eidlitz-Serrell scheme in depth.

61. Jordy and Coe assume incorrectly that Eidlitz was in on the fraudulence of the scheme; see their annotation of Schuyler in *American Architecture*, 172–73, n. 86. Stern et al., *NY1880*, stops short of suggesting that Eidlitz and Serrell were part of the scheme.

62. Schuyler part 2, 163.

63. Eidlitz, "The Day We Celebrate," 110.

64. Biographical information about William Ague Booth (1805–1895) taken from the Biography Files at the Stratford Historical Society, Stratford, Connecticut, which includes three obituaries from unidentified newspapers. Additional information can be found in William A. Booth, *The Reminiscences of William A. Booth* (n.p.: n.p., 1892). Booth never specifically mentions Eidlitz at any point in his *Reminiscences*; my reconstruction of their relationship is based on the timing of Booth's appointments at institutions for which Eidlitz designed buildings.

65. *Exercises at the Dedication of the New City Hall, Springfield, Mass.,* 18.

66. No drawings or plans of the Springfield City Hall have survived. The city's records of construction perished along with the building in the 1905 fire. All references to specifics of scale, dimensions, and proportion come from the detailed description contained in *Exercises at the Dedication of the New City Hall, Springfield, Mass., January 1, 1856* (Springfield, MA:

Samuel Bowles & Co., 1856). Eidlitz's City Hall surprisingly escapes discussion in Michael Frisch's *Town into City: Springfield, Massachusetts, and the Meaning of Community, 1840–1880* (Cambridge, MA: Harvard University Press, 1982), which otherwise contains an interesting account of the importation of New York architects (like Upjohn and Richardson) to design important Springfield buildings and residences in the 1850s and 1860s.

67. *Exercises at the Dedication of the New City Hall*, quotes from 6–7, 15–16, 18.

68. Ibid., 34–35. All quotes this paragraph, p. 34. Thackeray's sentiments are recorded in "Editorial Melange," *Ballou's Pictorial Drawing Room Companion* 10, n. 8 (February 23, 1856), 127.

69. The corporate members of the "Viaduct Railway Company" are listed in "The Viaduct Railway," *NYT*, March 10, 1871, 5, and in an untitled piece, *Brooklyn Daily Eagle*, March 11, 1871, 2.

70. "The Mayoralty," *NYT*, October 8, 1876, 12.

71. Inscribed copy of *The Nature and Function of Art* held by the New York Public Library: "To my friend Simon Sterne, Leopold Eidlitz." Sterne was the commissioner of the Commission of Seventy, which was set up to catalog the offenses of "Boss" Tweed and his cronies.

72. Edward Cooper's copy of Eidlitz's book is in the personal collection of John Ferguson.

73. Erdmann, "Leopold Eidlitz's Architectural Theories," 124. Erdmann notes that Eidlitz and Serrell presented a report to the New York state legislature on March 3, 1859, entitled: "Report of the Majority of the Committee on Cities and Villages, in Relation to the Bill Authorizing the Construction of a Railroad in New York City."

74. Jerome Mushkat, *Fernando Wood: A Political Biography* (Kent, OH: Kent State University Press, 1990), vii–vii, 245.

75. Schuyler, part 2, 173.

76. For the Tribune Building, see Landau and Condit, *Rise of the New York Skyscraper, 1865–1913*, 83–90; Baker, *Richard Morris Hunt*, 219–223; Stern et al., *NY1880*, 401–5, Lee E. Gray, "Type and Building Type: Newspaper/Office Buildings in Nineteenth Century New York," in Roberta Moudry, ed., *The American Skyscraper: Cultural Histories* (Cambridge: Cambridge University Press, 2005), 85–97.

CHAPTER 4. ARCHITECTURE AS CRITIQUE: THE NEW YORK STATE CAPITOL COMMISSION

1. "The Jefferson Market Monument," *NYT*, May 9, 1877, 4, as quoted in Stern et al., *NY1880*, 132. For the market, see also Kowsky, *Frederick Clarke Withers*, 109.

2. "Gothic Architecture," *Real Estate Record and Builders' Guide* 6 (December 3, 1870): 1.

3. Schuyler, part 2, 289.

4. "Dr. Tyng's New Church," *NYT*, April 18, 1874, 4. See also "New Churches in New York," *NYT*, October 8, 1872, 2; "Holy Trinity Church," *NYT*, June 9, 1873, 8; "The Churches Yesterday," *NYT*, April 20, 1874; and Schuyler, part 1, 149-54.

5. Heywood, "House of the Evangelicals," 81. See also James Elliott Lindsley, *A History of St. James' Church in the City of New York, 1810–1960* (New York: St. James Church, 1960), 47–58.

6. "The Holy Trinity Charities," *NYT*, January 5, 1878, 2; "Mr. Kimball's Work in New-York," *NYT*, December 22, 1877, 2.

7. "The Church of All Souls," *Crayon* 5 (1858), 20–22.

8. Henry Philpotts, quoted in *Ecclesiologist* 12 (1852): 219, as cited in George L. Hersey, *High Victorian Gothic: A Study in Associationism* (Baltimore: Johns Hopkins University Press, 1972), 96.

9. Hunt's role in the controversy over the capitol design indeed appears quite different when presented from his point of view. Compare my treatment to Baker's in *Richard Morris Hunt*, 258–61, which portrays Hunt as a rather passive participant in the attacks; and in Francis R. Kowsky, "The Central Park Gateways: Harbingers of French Urbanism Confront the American Landscape Tradition," in Stein, ed., *The Architecture of Richard Morris Hunt*, 86, in which Hunt appears as the victim.

10. Richardson scholars have not attempted to assess the working relationship between Eidlitz and Richardson. Little evidence outside of Schuyler's articles on Eidlitz remains to document their relationship. For Richardson's involvement in the project, see Jeffrey Karl Ochsner, *H. H. Richardson, Complete Architectural Works* (Cambridge, MA: MIT Press, 1982), 157–67; James F. O'Gorman, *H. H. Richardson: Architectural Forms for an American Society* (Chicago: University of Chicago Press, 1987), 40. For Olmsted, Laura Wood Roper, *FLO: A Biography of Frederick Law Olmsted* (Baltimore: Johns Hopkins University Press, 1973), chap. 3. For a comprehensive history of the capitol's design, see Cecil R. Roseberry, *Capitol Story* (Albany: State of New York, 1964); New York State Temporary Commission on the Restoration of the Capitol, *The Master Plan for the New York State Capitol* ([Albany]: The Commission, 1982); and the magisterial historic structure report done by the Ehrenkrantz Group, "New York State Capitol Historic Structure Report" (New York: Ehrenkrantz Group, 1983), 18 vols.

11. For various contrasting discussions of the World's Fair and the Transportation Building, see Schuyler, "Last Words About the World's Fair," *AR* 3 (1894), reprinted in Schuyler, *American Architecture*, 564–65; Thomas Hines, *Burnham of Chicago: Architect and Planner* (Chicago: University of Chicago Press, 1979), 98–101; Robert Twombly, *Louis Sullivan: His*

Life and Work (Chicago: University of Chicago Press, 1986), 259–69; Lauren S. Weingarden, "A Transcendentalist Discourse in the Poetics of Technology: Louis Sullivan's Transportation Building and Walt Whitman's 'Passage to India,'" Word and Image 3 (1987): 202–19; and, Van Zanten, Sullivan's City: The Meaning of Ornament for Louis Sullivan (New York: W. W. Norton, 2000), 47–55.

12. Kowsky, "The Central Park Gateways," 79–89; Catherine Howland Hunt, "The Richard Morris Hunt Papers," 79–80, Avery Architectural and Fine Arts Library, Columbia University.

13. In 1860, for example, Eidlitz, J. W. Ritch, and James Renwick formed a committee to present the AIA's newly drafted "Responsibility" law to the New York state legislature. The law was designed to encourage architects to fireproof their buildings or be held liable for the consequences. Mintues of the AIA, February 20, 1860, AIA Archives.

14. Schuyler, part 3, 366 (pagination refers to the original AR article here, as Jordy and Coe deleted this portion of Schuyler's article in their reprinting).

15. Schuyler, part 3, 187.

16. The Builder (1875): xxxiii, 774, 820; Building News (1875): xxix, 166, 196, 224 cited in Priscilla Metcalf, "Mother of Parliaments? Architectural Influences from the New Palace," in M. H. Port, ed., The Houses of Parliament (New Haven, CT: Yale University Press, 1976), 302–5. For Scott's design and the Reichstag competition in general, see also Lewis, Politics of the German Gothic Revival, 251–55.

17. Richard Morris Hunt to the Senate of the State of New York, March 29, 1876, as published in AABN 1 (April 8, 1876): 118.

18. Letter signed by George B. Post, Richard Morris Hunt, Napoleon LeBrun, Henry Dudley, and Detlef Lienau, sent to "the leading New York newspapers" and published as "The Experts and the New York Capitol," AABN 2 (March 17, 1877): 85.

19. Detlef Lienau, toast presented at the second annual dinner of the AIA, Crayon 6 (1859): 100.

20. James K. Wilson had founded the Cincinnati Chapter of the AIA in 1870, which joined in the denunciation of the capitol design. Wilson had formerly been a friend to Eidlitz, as he had copied Eidlitz's American Exchange Bank in his home city, apparently with his blessings. Eidlitz nominated him as a fellow of the AIA in 1865. Minutes of the AIA for December 19, 1865, AIA Archives; Schuyler, "A Great American Architect" (part 2), AR 24 (1908).

21. Resolution of the Rhode Island Chapter of the AIA, as published in AABN 1 (April 15, 1876): 127.

22. See, among many others, Ronald Takaki, Race and Culture in 19th-Century America, rev. ed. (New York: Oxford University Press, 2000).

23. "After further discussion the following resolution was passed: Resolved, That the New York Chapter of the American Institute of Architects re-affirms the views expressed in the Fifth Annual Convention of the Institute held in Boston in 1871: viz., 'that the architect and author of the design of any proposed work should retain the supreme control and general supervision of the execution of the work.'" AABN 1 (April 8, 1876): 117.

24. Lewis, Frank Furness: Architecture and the Violent Mind, 88–91, 91 quoted.

25. As reported in "Remonstrance of Certain Citizens of the State of New York Against the Changes Which Have Been, and are Being Made, on the New Capitol Building," December 1876. Letter printed in New York State Assembly Report No. 28, January 17, 1877.

26. At the 1876 annual meeting held in September, Longfellow was called to testify before the officers of the AIA. At the request of the AIA's Committee on Publications, Longfellow was questioned about "how far the serial is to be considered its mouthpiece." In his position as secretary of the AIA, A. J. Bloor reminded the general assembly and Longfellow that during the previous year, 1875, it had been voted that the AABN would be "the organ of the Institute." In the wake of the Albany controversy and the resulting public confusion about the relationship between the journal and the AIA, the board decided to define the relationship between the two more explicitly. The AABN would be the organ of the AIA for "publication purposes"—and would ostensibly stay out of editorial matters. AIA, Proceedings of the Tenth Annual Convention, October 11 and 12, 1876 (n.p.: Committee on Publications, American Institute of Architects, 1877), 3.

27. Unsigned, "The Design for the Albany Capitol," AABN 1 (March 18, 1876): 94.

28. "The Albany Capitol," unsigned, AABN 1 (April 4, 1876): 115.

29. Van Rensselaer, Henry Hobson Richardson and His Works, 75. Van Rensselaer also mentions that a draft of a reply, never sent, existed in Richardson's papers, but this letter has not survived.

30. "I did not learn until this week and through the newspapers that your Chapter last Wednesday addressed a communication to the Senate of New York. . . . I think that I am entitled to be informed of the question raised and to know why I have not been invited to respond to it. . . . It [the Chapter] nonetheless saw fit to take a performance of public duty into formal consideration . . . and without consideration to address our employer in harsh terms apparently in a continuing attempt to

destroy all confidence in our taste and professional knowledge." Olmsted to Hunt, April 4, 1876, FLOLC.

31. Charles Eliot Norton to Olmsted, April 4, 1876, FLOLC.

32. Norton to Olmsted, March 25, 1877, FLOLC.

33. Ibid.

34. *Annual Report of the New Capitol Commissioners*, New York State Assembly Report No. 6; January 9, 1877. In the monthly expenditures, Eidlitz & Richardson's monthly salary was reported at $1,666.66.

35. A sensitive rendering of Richardson can be found in James F. O'Gorman, *Living Architecture: A Biography of H. H. Richardson* (New York: Simon & Schuster Editions, 1997).

36. Schuyler, part 3, 177.

37. Ochsner, *H. H. Richardson*, 158; Schuyler, part 3, 368 (pagination refers to the original *AR* article here, as Jordy and Coe deleted this portion of Schuyler's article in their reprinting).

38. *AABN* 3 (March 24, 1877): 89.

39. Henry Van Brunt, "The New Architecture at Albany," *AABN* 5 (January 8, 1879), reprinted in Coles, ed., *Architecture and Society*, 129.

40. Eidlitz to Olmsted, May 9, 1887, FLOLC.

41. "The New Capitol. Remarks of Hon. Benj. C. Butler," January 20, 1881, 2. Copy in the Roseberry Papers, NYSL.

42. Ibid., 8.

43. W. P. Trowbridge, Charles Babcock, George B. Post, "Report of the Commissioners to Examine and Report on the New Capitol Building," September 26, 1882. FLOLC.

44. H. W. Fabian, "The Large Groined Vault in the Assembly Chamber of the New Capitol at Albany, N.Y.," *AABN* 6 (1881): 207.

45. Eidlitz, "The Vault of the Albany Capitol," letter to the editor, *AABN* 7 (1881): 235.

46. Eidlitz, "The New Capitol, An Examination of the Grounds on Which the Security of the Assembly Chamber Is Held to be in Question," November 17, 1882. FLOLC.

47. Eidlitz to Governor Hill, quoted in Roseberry, *Capitol Story*, 84, date not cited.

48. Commission Concerning the Assembly Chamber of the New Capitol, *Final Report* (Albany: Troy Press, April 26, 1888). Also published as J. Bogart, T. C. Clarke, and R. J. Upjohn, "Report to the Governor on the Condition of the Assembly Chamber Vaulting at Albany," *AABN*, June 9, 1888.

49. See the complete account of the ceiling investigations in Ehrenkrantz Group's historic structure report, vol. 1, chap. 8, "The Fall and Rise of the Assembly Chamber Ceiling."

50. "The Albany Capitol Investigation," *AABN* 12 (October 14, 1882): 177.

51. Van Brunt, "The New Architecture at Albany," 129.

52. "Chronological History of a Great Work of Architecture," [1879], 16. Copy in Roseberry Papers, NYSL.

53. Eidlitz, "The Strength of Pillars—An Analysis," *Transacations, American Society of Civil Engineers* 35 (July 1896): 371–428.

54. Pierson, *Technology and the Picturesque: the Corporate and the Early Gothic Styles*, 242.

55. Eidlitz, *The Nature and Function of Art*, 409. See also chap. 19, "Form and Construction," in particular pages 270–72), and Erdmann, "Leopold Eidlitz's Architectural Theories," 84.

56. Karl Marx, *Capital: A Critical Analysis of Capitalist Production* (1867), trans. Samuel Moore and Edward Aveling and ed. Frederick Engels (New York: Modern Library, 1906), 198.

57. Friedrich Vischer, *Aesthetik oder Wissenschaft des Schönen* vol. 3 (Reutlingen und Leipzig: Verlag Carl Mäden, 1851), 331–38. Narciso Menocal first elaborated a potential connection between Eidlitz and Vischer. See Twombly and Menocal, *Louis Sullivan: The Poetry of Architecture*, 428, n. 93. Menocal's suggestion is certainly correct, as Eidlitz sent his son Cyrus to study at the polytechnic institute in Stuttgart while Vischer taught there (see chap. 5). Eidlitz's conception of the organic connection between use and ornamentation is clearly linked to Vischer's discussion of the same subject in this passage. On Vischer, see the introduction to Harry Francis Mallgrave and Eleftherios Ikonomou, eds., *Empathy, Form, and Space: Problems in German Aesthetics, 1873–1893*, trans. Harry Francis Mallgrave and Eleftherios Ikonomou (Santa Monica, CA: Getty Center for the History of Art and the Humanities), 1994, 18ff.

58. Eidlitz, *The Nature and Function of Art*, 226.

59. Ibid., 409, 410.

60. For a thorough account of the experiments with electric lighting in the Assembly Chamber, see Ehrenkrantz Group, "New York State Capitol Historic Structure Report," vol. 1, 116–18. The desire for electric lighting seems to have been spearheaded by Eidlitz and investigated by Olmsted and his son John.

61. Eidlitz, *The Nature and Function of Art*, 320.

62. One is tempted also to toy with the notion that Eidlitz was thinking of Gottfried Semper's explanation of the origin of ornament as the merging of textile and construction. The ornament of the Chamber did, in some places, appear as tapestry hangings on the wall. But while Eidlitz had clearly read Semper, he appears not to have assimilated the implications of his writing. Semper's development of the Rundbogenstil into classical architecture would not have appealed to Eidlitz; and his cultural evaluation of architecture, seemingly without the guide of science, would not have been sufficiently rigorous to his thinking. Because Semper was nearly unknown to Eidlitz's

peers and audience, this perhaps further justified the lack of a concerted effort to grapple with him. Eidlitz tended to deal publicly, meaning by name, with architects and writers that were common currency in the United States.

63. My reading of the importance of Goethe's theory of color to Eidlitz is based on Eidlitz's statements about color in *The Nature and Function of Art* and the resultant designs. Johann Wolfgang von Goethe, *Theory of Colors*, trans. Charles Lock Eastlake (London: John Murray, 1840 (orig. published in German 1810); reprint, Cambridge, MA: MIT Press, 1970), esp. Part VI, "Effect of Colour with Reference to Moral Associations."

64. Eidlitz, *The Nature and Function of Art*, 322.

65. Goethe, *Theory of Colors*, 314–17.

66. Ibid., 311.

67. Owen Jones, *The Grammar of Ornament* (1856), reprint (New York: Portland House, 1986), 6.

68. Eidlitz, *The Nature and Function of Art*, 327–28.

69. William Morris Hunt, "The New Capitol," *Albany Argus*, November 27, 1878, clipping in William Morris Hunt scrapbook, The Octagon.

70. Schuyler, part 3, 178.

71. On the murals, see Sara B. Webster, "The Albany Murals of William Morris Hunt," (Ph.D. diss., City University of New York, 1985); and Henry Adams, "The Development of William Morris Hunt's the Flight of Night," *American Art Journal* 15, no. 2 (Spring 1983): 43–52.

72. Clarence Cook, "A Description of the Building," *New York Tribune* (December 24, 1878), 4.

73. Eidlitz, *Nature and Function of Art*, vii.

74. Cook, "A Description of the Building," 4.

75. Holland, "From an Albany Correspondent," *Independent* 3, no. 114 (February 6, 1851), 1. Arnold Guyot, *The Earth and Man: Lectures on Comparative Physical Geography in its Relation to the History of Mankind* (Boston : Gould & Lincoln, 1849).

76. Eidlitz was obviously interested in evolution, but his writing does not specifically mention any particular evolutionary theorist. Instead, he treats evolution as a general concept, noting that the hostility of the church toward new scientific theories was deplorable: "The priesthood of the Christian Church is sensitive to every theory advanced in science, for fear that it may contradict some innocent simile in the Bible." *Nature and Function of Art*, 242. C. L. [Charles Loring] Brace, "Darwinism in Germany," *North American Review* 110, no. 227 (1870): 284–99; Martin Kemp, "Haeckel's Hierarchies," *Nature* 395 (October 1, 1998): 447. Brace was the founder of the Childrens' Aid Society, a friend of Frederick Law Olmsted's, and in the late 1870s and 1880s hired Calvert Vaux to design numerous schools and shelters for the Society.

77. Otto von Simson, *The Gothic Cathedral: Origins of Gothic*

Architecture and the Medieval Concept of Order, 3rd ed. (Princeton, NJ: Princeton University Press, 1988), 220.

78. In my iconographic interpretation of the Senate Staircase, I am treading on ground that others have traversed before without coming to firm conclusions. In conversations with Andrea Lazarski, she expressed reservations about the iconographic meanings of the sculptural program of the staircase for which I have the utmost respect: she was uncomfortable with the staircase's lack of link between various species and the fact that it ends with a camel as well as the possibility that the stonemasons had more to do with the animals chosen than Eidlitz. The lack of a link between animals is, I feel, explained by Eidlitz's use of Haeckel's hierarchies rather than a pure Darwinian evolution; on the ending with a camel, I can offer no firm interpretation. As for the programmatic content, I cannot imagine Eidlitz, who personally attended to much of the construction process, not prescribing the sculptural program. The stonemasons may, of course, have taken some liberties, but the overarching concept must have been Eidlitz's. He staunchly believed that it was the architect's role to design all ornamental details.

79. NYLPC, "Tweed Courthouse," LP-1122, October 16, 1984, 23, n. 32.

80. "The Committee of Fifty," NYT October 24, 1877, 8; the committee also included Simon Sterne, Cornelius Vanderbilt, and Theodore Roosevelt. In 1872 and 1873, Calvert Vaux and his assistant Edward C. Miller (also a drawing instructor at the Cooper Union) were paid for "preparing estimates" for the completion of the new courthouse "exclusive of the dome." Vaux's estimate was that an additional $168,869.87 was needed to complete the building without the dome. Tweed Papers, Box 8, MCNY.

81. The restoration is documented in John G. Waite, *Tweed Courthouse: A Model Restoration* (New York: W. W. Norton, 2006).

82. W. J. Linton, *The House That Tweed Built* (Cambridge, MA: The author, 1871), 4.

83. *AABN* 3 (March 16, 1878): 94.

84. Schuyler, part 1, 143.

CHAPTER 5. THE NATURE AND FUNCTION OF ART

1. Sir George Gilbert Scott, *Personal and Professional Recollections by the Late Sir George Gilbert Scott* (London: Sampson Low, Marston, Searle & Rivington, 1879).

2. See, for example, Jordy and Coe's introduction to Schuyler, *American Architecture*, which considers Eidlitz as a theorist and doubted that his architectural career could be evaluated at all (22); Erdmann's dissertation, "Leopold Eidlitz's Architectural Theories" concurred: "Jordy and Coe did not exaggerate when they said that it would be impossible to review Eidlitz's

career as an architect" (4). Though Eidlitz rarely appears in histories of American architecture, when he does appear, it is generally as a theorist: James Early's *Romanticism and American Architecture* (New York: A. S. Barnes, 1965) included Eidlitz as a theorist; Vincent Scully's survey *American Architecture and Urbanism* (New York: Praeger, 1969) briefly mentions Eidlitz as a theorist as well (97). Donald Hoffmann's anthology *The Meanings of Architecture: Buildings and Writings by John Wellborn Root* (New York: Horizon Press, 1967), describes Eidlitz as "a nearly forgotten thinker in the organic tradition" (22); Menocal's *Architecture as Nature* and *Louis Sullivan: The Poetry of Architecture* consider Eidlitz's theory in relation to Sullivan; Neil Levine's "The Idea of Frank Furness' Buildings" (Master's thesis, Yale University, 1967), considered it in relation to Frank Furness. Excerpts from *The Nature and Function of Art* have been anthologized more often than Eidlitz's buildings have been included in general architectural histories: for example, in Leland Roth's *America Builds: Source Documents in American Architecture and Planning* (New York: Harper & Row, 1983); and in Don Gifford, ed., *The Literature of Architecture: The Evolution of Architectural Theory and Practice in Nineteenth-Century America* (New York: Dutton, 1966). Eidlitz's theory is also discussed in Peter Kohane, "Architecture, Labor, and the Human Body: Fergusson, Cockerell and Ruskin" (Ph.D. diss., University of Pennsylvania, 1993). Notably absent (except in Early) is consideration of Eidlitz's earlier papers to the AIA published in the *Crayon*, which, coupled with the general neglect of his architecture, has resulted in his reputation standing on a single book.

3. Wight and Sturgis founded the short-lived journal (1863–65) with a group of six other men at the behest of English painter Thomas Farrar as an adjunct to their group the "Association for the Advancement of Truth in Art." The journal's editor was Clarence Cook. Marjorie Pearson, "The Writings of Russell Sturgis and Peter B. Wight: The Victorian Architect as Critic and Historian" (Ph.D. diss., City University of New York, 1999), 41–62; Sarah Landau, *P. B. Wight: Architect, Contractor, and Critic, 1838-1925* (Chicago: Art Institute, 1981), 19. See also David Dickason, *The Daring Young Men: The Story of the American Pre-Raphaelites* (Bloomington: Indiana University Press, 1953), and William H. Gerdts and Linda Ferber, *The New Path: Ruskin and the American Pre-Raphaelites* (New York: Schocken Books, 1985).

4. Eidlitz, *Nature and Function of Art*, 375–76.

5. Ibid., xx.

6. Though Ruskin and Fergusson both produced numerous publications, those most relevant to Eidlitz's critiques are John Ruskin, *The Seven Lamps of Architecture* (London: Smith, Elder & Co., 1849), and his *Stones of Venice*, 3 vols. (London: Smith, Elder & Co., 1851–53); James Fergusson, *The Illustrated Handbook of Architecture: Being a Concise and Popular Account of the Different Styles of Architecture Prevailing in All Ages and All Countries*, 2 vols. (London: J. Murray, 1855), and his *History of the Modern Styles of Architecture: Being a Sequel to the Handbook of Architecture* (London: J. Murray, 1862).

7. Eidlitz, *Nature and Function of Art*, ix–xx.

8. Eidlitz specifically grappled with the tenets of socialism; there is a chapter in his *Big Wages* entitled "Socialism." Karl Marx's *Communist Manifesto* was published in 1848; the first volume of *Das Kapital* appeared in 1867.

9. Eidlitz, *Nature and Function of Art*, 117–20.

10. Ibid., 191.

11. Ibid., 385–86.

12. Ibid., 207.

13. Ibid., 208. For Hegel on architecture, see Richard Dien Winfield, "The Challenge of Architecture to Hegel's Aesthetics," and David Kolb, "The Spirit of Gravity: Architecture and Externality," in William Maker, ed., *Hegel and Aesthetics* (Albany, NY: State University of New York Press, 2000).

14. Ibid., 310, 211.

15. Eidlitz served as a major source for an article on fireproofing in the *New York Times*, "New-York's Great Peril: The Worst Built City in the World," January 20, 1879, 5; and, "A Card from Mr. Eidlitz," *NYT*, January 21, 1879, 8. The 1876 Brooklyn Theatre fire generated much discussion in the *AABN*; see for example, "The Brooklyn Disaster," *AABN* 1 (December 30, 1876): 423; in the same issue, inquiries about the "Fall of a Flouring-Mill" and the "Weight of Snow" on a roof appeared (423). "Does It Pay to Employ Experts?" discussed the design of sewers, *AABN* 2 (February 10, 1877): 45.

16. See, for example, "Journey of an Architect in the North-West of Europe," *AABN* 2 (February 24, 1877): 63. This was part of a serialization of a translation from French of a book with the same title, by Felix Narjoux, to be published by James R. Osgood (also the publisher of the *AABN*).

17. Joanna Merwood, "The Mechanization of Cladding: The Chicago Skyscraper and the Constructions of Architectural Modernity" (Ph.D. diss., Princeton University, 2003).

18. Eugène-Emmanuel Viollet-le-Duc, *Discourses on Architecture*, trans. Henry Van Brunt (Boston: James R. Osgood & Co., 1875); translated from *Entretiens sur l'Architecture* (Paris: A. Morel, 1863).

19. See the compilation of American architectural publications by Henry-Russell Hitchcock, Jr., *American Architectural Books: A List of Books, Portfolios, and Pamphlets on Architecture and Related Subjects Published in America Before 1895*, 3rd rev. ed. (Minneapolis and London: University of Minnesota Press, G. Cumberlege, Oxford University Press, 1946). For a discussion of American architectural books before 1870, see Elizabeth Blair MacDougall, "Before 1870: Founding Fathers and Ama-

teur Historians," in MacDougall, ed., *The Architectural Historian in America; Studies in the History of Art*, vol. 35 (Hanover, NH, and London: University Press of New England, 1990).

20. Eidlitz, *Nature and Function of Art*, 314.

21. Erdmann made this juxtaposition as well as several others that are quite revealing of the overlap between Eidlitz and Emerson in chap. 2 of "Leopold Eidlitz's Architectural Theories." Ralph Waldo Emerson, *Nature* (1836), reprinted in *Essays of Ralph Waldo Emerson Including Essays, First and Second Series, English Traits, Nature and Conduct of Life* (New York: Book League of America, 1941), 343; Eidlitz, *Nature and Function of Art*, 161.

22. Lewis, *Politics of the German Gothic Revival*; see for example the discussion of the Hamburg Nikolaikirche, 101–6, and the later Berlin Rathaus, 231–33.

23. Eidlitz, *Nature and Function of Art*, 379.

24. Eugène Emmanuel Viollet-le-Duc, *The Foundations of Architecture: Selections from the Dictionnaire Raisonné*, trans. by Kenneth D. Whitehead (New York: George Braziller, 1990), 233.

25. Eidlitz mentioned Viollet-le-Duc specifically only once, in support of his fight against classical style: "The students of the Ecole des Beaux Arts felt that Renaissance architecture was true art, and they mobbed Viollet le Duc because he doubted it." Eidlitz, *Nature and Function of Art*, 79. For the influence of Viollet-le-Duc in America, see Daniel D. Reiff, "Viollet-le-Duc and American 19th Century Architecture," *Journal of Architectural Education* 42 (1988): 32–47; for a contrasting view, see Kristin Otteson Garrigan, *Ruskin on Architecture: His Thought and Influence* (Madison: University of Wisconsin Press, 1973). See also Robin D. Middleton, "Viollet-le-Duc's Influence in Nineteenth-Century England," *Art History* 4 (1981): 203–19; and W. Sauerländer, "Viollet-le-Duc über die Münchener Ludwigstrasse," in Werner Hager and Norbert Knopp, eds., *Beitrage zum Problem des Stilpluralismus, Studien zur Kunst des neunzehnten Jahrhunderts*, vol. 38 (Munich: Prestel, 1977).

26. John Ruskin, *The Seven Lamps of Architecture*, 2nd ed. (1880), reprint (New York: Dover, 1989), 8–9.

27. Ibid., 37.

28. Ibid., 66–67, 67 quoted.

29. Eidlitz, *Nature and Function of Art*, 56.

30. On the Cologne campaign, see Lewis, *Politics of the German Gothic Revival*, ch. 2. On Milan, see Maria Luisa Gatti Perer, ed., *Il Duomo di Milano*, 2 vols. (Milano: La Rete, 1969).

31. Jacob Burckhardt as translated and quoted by Eidlitz in ch. XXVI, "Criticism," *Nature and Function of Art*, 454.

32. Ibid., 67. Eidlitz nominated Scott for membership in the AIA on October 4, 1859; the nomination was seconded by Richard Upjohn. Scott later accepted the nomination, as noted at the meeting held February 7, 1860. Minutes of the AIA, AIA Archives.

33. Ibid., 67–68. Sir Gilbert Scott, *Remarks on Secular and Domestic Architecture: Present and Future*, 2nd ed. (London: J. Murray, 1858). For Scott, see David Cole, *The Work of Sir Gilbert Scott* (London: Architectural Press, 1980).

34. "Principles of Gothic Architecture. Notes of a Journey Through the Netherlands, the Rhine Country, Switzerland, and a Part of France, in the Years 1804, 1805," in *The Aesthetic and Miscellaneous Works of Friedrich von Schlegel*, trans. E. J. Millington (London: George Bell & Sons, 1889), 150.

35. Friedrich Vischer, *Aesthetik oder Wissenschaft des Schönen*, vol. 3 (Reutlingen und Leipzig: Verlag Carl Mäden, 1851), 331–38. Narciso Menocal first elaborated a potential connection between Eidlitz and Vischer. See Twombly and Menocal, *Louis Sullivan: The Poetry of Architecture*, 428, n. 93. On Vischer, see the introduction to Harry Francis Mallgrave and Eleftherios Ikonomou, eds., *Empathy, Form, and Space: Problems in German Aesthetics, 1873–1893*, trans. Harry Francis Mallgrave and Eleftherios Ikonomou (Santa Monica, CA: Getty Center for the History of Art and the Humanities), 1994, 18ff.

36. In a passage that surely refers to Richardson, Eidlitz praised architects who worked in the way he proposed: "[The architect] must . . . study the conditions, analyze the environment, yield to it everywhere, respond to it always, until the functions resulting from all this are fully expressed in the organism; and while he is thinking of all this, forms will grow under his hands, forms which will often surprise him by their novelty, by their force of expression (beauty) and then again perhaps by their simplicity, which in connection with other structural parts of a more complicated and a more expressive nature serves as a foil to enhance the value of the whole. Many an earnest architectural mind has no doubt of late pursued architecture in this sense, if not precisely in this manner. There are unmistakable indications of it in modern work." Eidlitz, *Nature and Function of Art*, 358.

37. Ibid., 215–17.

38. This story is related by Schuyler, part 1, 154–55. See also Schuyler, "The Brooklyn Bridge as a Monument," *Harper's Weekly* 27 (May 26, 1883): 326.

39. Eidlitz, *Nature and Function of Art*, 380–81.

40. Ibid., 317.

41. Eidlitz was clearly familiar with Alberti and objected strenuously to Renaissance architecture and theory: ". . . this failure is to be found in the fact that the architecture of the time was not in the hands of architects, but in those of gentlemen of liberal literary and artistic education indeed, who, however, knew nothing of the relations of architecture to construction, and but little of construction itself, either as

a science (for in that form it did not then fairly exist) or as a trade, because their apprenticeship was served with sculptors, painters or goldsmiths." Ibid., 81. He found classical and Renaissance architects' preoccupation with using accepted rules of proportion to arrange masses, spaces, and ornament misguided, instead believing in his more subjective criteria: expression. See Eidlitz, *Nature and Function of Art*, chap. 20, "Proportion," for an extended and at times mathematical comparison of the Renaissance and medieval conceptions of proportion (292–306); compare with the proscriptions enumerated in book 7, section 9, for example, in Leon Battista Alberti, *On the Art of Building in Ten Books*, trans. Joseph Rykwert, Neil Leach, and Robert Tavernor (Cambridge, MA: MIT Press, 1988), 210–18.

42. Eidlitz, *Nature and Function of Art*, 122–134; Frank Lloyd Wright, "In the Cause of Architecture," *AR* 23 (1908): 155–221.

43. "Art and Architecture," *NYT*, December 12, 1881, 3.

44. William Ware to William Emerson, May 19, 1897, recorded in the minutes of the RIBA Council meeting of May 31, 1897. RIBA Council minutes, 1896–1897, RIBA Archives.

45. Henry Van Brunt, "Eidlitz's Nature of Art," *Nation* 33 (December 29, 1881): 515–516, reprinted in Coles, ed., *Architecture and Society*, 149.

46. Ibid., 145.

47. See for example Withers, "A Few Notes on Church Building," which clearly derived from his reading of Pugin. Discussed in Kowsky, *The Architecture of Frederick Clarke Withers*, 40–41, 56.

48. I did investigate whether or not Eidlitz had been lecturing in New York and simply collected those lectures into a single volume. My perusals of the archives of the Cooper Union indicate that Eidlitz did not lecture there; he certainly did not lecture at Ware's Columbia University; and there is also no record of his being associated with the City College of New York.

49. Charles Henry Hart, "Art in Architecture; Review of the Nature and Function of Art," *AABN* 11 (1882): 172–73.

50. Eidlitz, *Nature and Function of Art*, viii.

51. Woods, *From Craft to Profession*, 38–42, and Baker, *Richard Morris Hunt*, 327–28. Thomas S. Hines, *Burnham of Chicago: Architect and Planner* (Chicago: University of Chicago Press, 1979).

52. For the Chicago School, Carl Condit, *The Chicago School of Architecture: A History of Commercial and Public Building in the Chicago Area, 1875–1925* (Chicago: University of Chicago Press, 1964). For a reassessment of the meaning of the Chicago School and the concept of functionalism, see Robert Brueggman, *The Architects and the City: Holabird & Roche of Chicago, 1880–1918* (Chicago: University of Chicago Press, 1997). On

Root, see Harriet Monroe, *John Wellborn Root: A Study of His Life and Work* (Boston: Houghton, Mifflin & Co., 1896); and Donald Hoffmann's *Meanings of Architecture* and his *Architecture of John Wellborn Root* (Baltimore: Johns Hopkins University Press, 1973).

53. For Wight and Root, see Landau, *P. B. Wight*, 30.

54. John Wellborn Root, "Broad Art Criticism," *Inland Architect and News Record* 11, no. 1 (February 1888): 3–5, reprinted in Hoffman, *Meanings of Architecture*, 31.

55. Ibid., 26–27.

56. Ibid., 28.

57. Root, "Expression in Form," *Inland Architect and News Record* 16, no. 3 (October 1890): 30–31, reprinted in Hoffman, *Meanings of Architecture*, 31.

58. Narciso Menocal has done the most thorough evaluation of the overlap between Sullivan's and Eidlitz's theory. Narciso G. Menocal, "The Iconography of Architecture: Sullivan's View," in Twombly and Menocal, *Louis Sullivan: The Poetry of Architecture*, 113–15.

59. Ibid., 113.

60. See Van Zanten's evocative interpretation of Sullivan's ornament in *Sullivan's City*.

61. See Hugh Morrison, *Louis Sullivan: Prophet of Modern Architecture* (New York: W. W. Norton, 1935), for an interpretation that focuses on the functionalist aspects of Sullivan's designs to the detriment of his ornamental schemes. See also van Zanten's discussion of nineteenth-century conceptions of architectural ornament in ibid., 9, and also his discussion of interpretation of Sullivan that ignored his ornament, ibid., 12–13.

62. "Autumn in Washington," *NYT*, October 30, 1886, 3.

63. The building's foundations had been altered in 1881 to make space for additional classrooms in the basement. "Building Intelligence," *Manufacturer and Builder* 13, no. 10 (October 1881): 224. These alterations, in addition to the stories added in a previous alteration in 1880, may have been the source of the problem Eidlitz was called in to deal with. For Eidlitz's contributions, see "Repairing the Cooper Institute," *Scientific American, Architects and Builders Edition* 1, no. 3 (December 1885): 39.

64. Alan Lessoff, Christof Mauch, eds., *Adolf Cluss: From Germany to America* (Berghahn Books: 2005).

65. For the broader context of labor disputes and political economy in nineteenth-century America, two works offer different perspectives: Bruce Laurie, *Artisans into Workers: Labor in Nineteenth-Century America* (Urbana and Chicago: University of Illinois Press, 1997); and Amy Schrager Lang, *The Syntax of Class: Writing Inequality in Nineteenth-Century America* (Princeton, NJ: Princeton University Press, 2003).

66. The archives of the Broadway Tabernacle Church contain numerous receipts and contracts signed by Eidlitz and various contractors, including his brother, that form a complete picture of the building process. Archives of the Broadway United Church of Christ, NYHS.

67. Correspondence and copies of legislation regarding labor issues can be found in the Marc Eidlitz & Son Papers, Manuscripts and Archives Division, NYPL. Marc Eidlitz was often quoted in the press about labor problems; see for example, "The Builder's Combination; The Subject of Protection Against Labor's Demands," *NYT*, March 19, 1884, 5; and "Strikes in Progess; No Work on the Gallatin Building, Coopers and Shoemakers," *NYT*, February 20, 1887, 3.

68. *Big Wages*, 128; see chap. 11, "A Model Labor Union," for Eidlitz's discussion of cooperative societies.

69. "Our Book Table," *New York Evangelist* (December 8, 1887), 1. "Recent Publications on Economics," *Quarterly Journal of Economics* (January 1888): 247.

70. "Recent Works on Economics," *Literary World* 19 (March 3, 1888): 71.

71. Peter Kropotkin, "The Industrial Village of the Future," *Eclectic Magazine of Foreign Literature* 48 (December 1888): 756; reprinted from *Nineteenth Century*.

72. Eidlitz, "The Architect of Fashion," *AR* 3 (April–June 1894): 347.

73. Robert A. M. Stern, Gregory Gilmartin, and John Massengale, *New York 1900* (New York: Rizzoli, 1995), 113–115.

74. "Last Service Held in Temple Emanu-El, " *NYT*, July 24, 1927, 18.

75. "Wreckers Start Work on Temple Emanu-el," *NYT*, September 2, 1927), 14.

76. Little scholarly attention has been devoted to Cyrus L. W. Eidlitz. On him, see Schuyler, "The Works of Cyrus L. W. Eidlitz," *AR* 5 (1896): 411–435, and "The Evolution of a Skyscraper," *AR* 14 (1903): 329–43. His design for the Buffalo Public Library is also in an article on Richardson's rejected proposal: Francis R. Kowsky, "H. H. Richardson's Project for the Young Men's Association Library in Buffalo," *Niagara Frontier* 25, no. 2 (1978): 29–35.

77. My thanks to Dr. Norbert Becker, director of the Universitätsarchiv Stuttgart, for confirming the dates that Cyrus Eidlitz studied in Stuttgart. Detailed student records were destroyed during World War II, so Eidlitz's attendance is confirmed from a reconstructed roster.

78. Lübke's comprehensive history of art was translated into English and published in the United States as Wilhelm Lübke, *Outlines of the History of Art*, trans. Clarence Cook, 2 vols. (New York: Dodd, Mead, & Co., 1877). For Lübke, see Jürgen Joedicke, *Architekturlehre in Stuttgart: Von Der Real— Und Gewerbeschule Zur Universität*, ed. Jürgen Hering, vol. 46, *Reden Un Aufsätze* (Stuttgart: Universitätsbibliothek Stuttgart, 1994); and Herwarth Röttgen, "Nachvollziehende Gedanken Zur Geschichte Des Instituts Für Kunstgeschichte," in *125 Jahre Institut Für Kunstgeschichte Universität Stuttgart*, ed. Johannes Zahlten, *Reden Und Aufsätze* (Stuttgart: Universitätsbibliothek Stuttgart, 1991).

79. On the Times Building , see "City's Tallest Building from Base to Top," *NYT*, January 1, 1905, suppl., and Landau and Condit, *Rise of the New York Skyscraper*, 309–13. On Cyrus see Montgomery Schuyler, "Cyrus L. W. Eidlitz," *AR* (April 1896): 411-35 and Robert B. Mackay, Anthony K. Baker, and Carol A. Traynor, eds., *Long Island Country Houses and Their Architects* (New York: W. W. Norton, 1997).

80. Membership application records, AIA Archives.

81. For the subsequent history of Cyrus Eidlitz's firm, which later became McKenzie, Vorhees & Gmelin and then Vorhees, Gmelin & Walker, eventually morphing into today's HLW, see *Haines, Lundberg, and Waehler, Architects* (New York: Haines, Lundberg & Waehler, 1969) and a rev. ed. from 1976.

82. About Leopold Eidlitz, Jr., I have been able to discover very little. He was born in 1855, and his occupation is listed as "Engineer" on a ship's manifest for the S. S. *Treut*, sailing from Bermuda to New York, February 21, 1901. He is listed in the New York City directories at the same business address as his father and brother from 1897 to 1901 and became a partner in the engineering firm Eidlitz & Ross. He appears not to have married but lived with his sisters Elizabeth and Julia at 309 W. 89th St. in 1900, according to the census for that year. He is buried in the same Green-Wood Cemetery plot in Brooklyn as his parents, grandparents, sisters, and brother-in-law.

83. Eidlitz, "The Architect of Fashion," 348.

84. Augustine E. Costello, *Our Firemen: A History of the New York Fire Departments, Volunteer and Paid* (New York: A. E. Costello, 1887), chap. 50, part 5. D'Oench also worked on Hunt's Tribune Building.

85. Peter B. Wight, "How Best Now to Study the Medieval Architecture of France with Some Confessions of a Retired Architect," *Western Architect* 31 (1922): 51–55.

86. Russell Sturgis, *Dictionary of Architecture and Building: Biographical, Historical, and Descriptive*, 3 vols. (New York: Macmillan, 1901-2), and his "Correspondence: The State Capitol at Albany," *AABN* 4 (December 14, 1878): 196–98.

87. Karin May Elizabeth Alexis, "Russell Sturgis: Critic and Architect" (Ph.D. diss., University of Virginia, 1986); Landau, *P.B. Wight*; Pearson, "The Writings of Russell Sturgis and Peter B. Wight;" Peter B. Wight, "Reminiscences of Russell Sturgis," *AR* 26 (1909): 123–31.

88. Jordy and Coe, editors' introduction, *American Architecture*, 15.

89. Schuyler, "The Bridge as a Monument," *Harper's Weekly* (26 May 1883): 326.

90. Schuyler, "A Long-Felt Want," *AR* 7 (1897): 118–20; reprinted in Schuyler, *American Architecture*, 580.

91. Schuyler, "The Works of the Late Richard M. Hunt," *AR* 5 (1895): 97–180. Compare with his earlier, more scathing comments on Hunt and his "fitful and eccentric" Tribune Building in Schuyler, "The New Tribune Building," *New York World*, May 2, 1875, 4–5.

His 1895 obituary for Hunt in *Harper's Weekly* was less enthusiastic than the *AR* piece. Schuyler, "Richard Morris Hunt," *Harper's Weekly* 39 (August 10, 1895): 749.

92. Jordy and Coe come to a similar conclusion about Schuyler, although for slightly different reasons. See their Editors' Introduction to Schuyler, *American Architecture*, 3, 87ff.

93. For Schuyler, see Jordy and Coe, editors' introduction to *American Architecture*, and William John Thorn, "Montgomery Schuyler: The Newspaper Architectural Articles of a Protomodern Critic, 1868–1907" (Ph.D. diss., University of Minnesota, 1976).

94. Schuyler, "An Architectural Pioneer: Review of the Portfolios Containing the Works of Frank Lloyd Wright," *AR* 31 (1912), reprinted in Jordy and Coe, *American Architecture*, 640.

95. Schuyler, "The People's Savings Bank of Cedar Rapids, Iowa—Louis H. Sullivan, Architect," *AR* 31 (1912), reprinted in Jordy and Coe, *American Architecture*, 627–28. Jordy and Coe also saw this passage as a reference to Eidlitz, 628, n. 6.

96. For Sullivan's bank, ibid., 629; and for Eidlitz's, Schuyler, part 2, 162–63.

97. Schuyler, part 3, 186.

98. "The Need of Unity," *AABN* 1 (January 1, 1876): 2–3.

99. Eidlitz to Olmsted, May 9, 1887, FLOLC.

100. Anthony Alofsin, *The Struggle for Modernism* (New York: W. W. Norton, 2002), see chap. 4 and 5.

101. Eidlitz, *Nature and Function of Art*, 489.

102. Mumford, *The Brown Decades*, 119. One imagines that Mumford's disdain for "weird combinations of architectural souvenirs" (110) would certainly have extended to Eidlitz's designs.

INDEX